ANALYSES OF CONCEPT LEARNING

CONTRIBUTORS TO THIS VOLUME

E. James Archer

David P. Ausubel

Nancy Bayley

Cynthia P. Deutsch

Howard F. Fehr

Robert M. Gagné

Rom Harré

James J. Jenkins

Arthur R. Jensen

Jerome Kagan

Stanley Kegler

Kenneth Lovell

Philip R. Merrifield

Joseph D. Novak

J. Richard Suchman

Benton J. Underwood

Conference on ANALYSES OF
CONCEPT LEARNING

EDITED BY

HERBERT J. KLAUSMEIER   *and*   CHESTER W. HARRIS

*Research and Development Center
for Learning and Re-education,
University of Wisconsin,
Madison, Wisconsin*

*Department of
Educational Psychology,
University of Wisconsin,
Madison, Wisconsin*

1966

ACADEMIC PRESS   New York and London

ACADEMIC PRESS INC.
111 Fifth Avenue, New York, New York 10003

United Kingdom Edition published by
ACADEMIC PRESS INC. (LONDON) LTD.
Berkeley Square House, London W.1

LIBRARY OF CONGRESS CATALOG CARD NUMBER: 66-26255

PRINTED IN THE UNITED STATES OF AMERICA

LIST OF CONTRIBUTORS

Numbers in parentheses refer to the pages on which the contributors' articles begin.

E. JAMES ARCHER (37), *University of Colorado*, Boulder, Colorado

DAVID P. AUSUBEL (157), *University of Illinois*, Urbana, Illinois

NANCY BAYLEY (117), *University of California*, Berkeley, California

CYNTHIA P. DEUTSCH (189), *New York Medical College*, New York, New York

HOWARD F. FEHR (223), *Teachers College, Columbia University*, New York, New York

ROBERT M. GAGNÉ (81), *University of California*, Berkeley, California

ROM HARRÉ (3), *University of Oxford*, Oxford, England

JAMES J. JENKINS (65), *University of Minnesota*, Minneapolis, Minnesota

ARTHUR R. JENSEN (139), *University of California*, Berkeley, California

JEROME KAGAN (97), *Harvard University*, Cambridge, Massachusetts

STANLEY KEGLER (255), *University of Minnesota*, Minneapolis, Minnesota

KENNETH LOVELL (207), *University of Leeds*, Leeds, England

PHILIP R. MERRIFIELD (19), *Kent State University*, Kent, Ohio

JOSEPH D. NOVAK (239), *Purdue University*, Lafayette, Indiana

J. RICHARD SUCHMAN (177), *University of Illinois*, Urbana, Illinois

BENTON J. UNDERWOOD (51), *Northwestern University*, Evanston, Illinois

PREFACE

This volume contains papers presented at a Conference on Analyses of Concept Learning, sponsored by the Research and Development Center for Learning and Re-education of the University of Wisconsin, held in October, 1965. The goal of the R & D Center is to secure more efficient learning for children, youth, and adults, particularly related to concept learning, problem solving, and the nurturance of related cognitive abilities. To achieve this goal, knowledge must be brought to bear upon concept learning. At this Conference, sixteen eminent scholars—psychologists, philosophers, subject-matter and curriculum specialists—from the United States and England dealt with four main topics: schemes for classifying and relating concepts, the learning of concepts, learning-teaching processes, and concepts in various subject fields.

In the first chapter, Professor Rom Harré, a philosopher whose specialty is the theory of knowledge, presents a formal analysis of concepts. He outlines two major views of the nature of concepts and the logical characteristics of these views. Related to this analysis he discusses some methods for classifying concepts. In the second chapter, Professor Philip Merrifield provides an analysis of concepts from the point of view of the structure of intellect. After describing the origin and current status of the structure of intellect, he relates it to the nature of concepts and concept learning.

Seven psychologists present views about the learning of concepts in Part II. In Chapter 3, E. James Archer delineates the psychological characteristics of concepts. Especially noteworthy is his treatment of the utility of concepts in human behavior. Next, Benton J. Underwood discusses some relationships between concept learning and verbal learning. Many similarities in methods of study and principles of learning are indicated. With his usual incisiveness, Underwood points to the need for greater familiarity with verbal learning on the part of those studying concept formation. James J. Jenkins argues that stimuli achieve meaningfulness through their relationship to a conceptual system and describes as an example a systematic linguistic approach to the meaningfulness of verbal stimuli. From this point of view, it is reasoned that it is the possession of complex conceptual schemes by the subject that bestows meaning on the stimuli encountered rather than the meaningfulness being given to concepts by the number of stimuli being associated with them. Jenkins makes a strong case for increased study of conceptual systems. In Chapter 6, Robert M. Gagné differentiates between concepts and principles and proposes that the conditions for learning principles differ in certain respects from those for concepts. He describes a number of research questions pertaining to the conditions of principle learning. Jerome Kagan presents a developmental approach to conceptual learning in Chapter 7. He clarifies two problems: (1) How and why do conceptual structures change with experience? (2) What is the organization of conceptual units at different developmental stages? These questions properly indicate that prior proposed solutions, including those by Piaget, are incomplete. Next, Nancy Bayley draws from her extensive longitudinal data, including that gathered in 1965, to describe the growth of intellectual abilities from infancy into adulthood. Implications for learning in adulthood are given. In the last chapter of Part II, Arthur R. Jensen discusses the problems and current status of knowledge regarding individual differences in concept learning. Our current knowledge about individual difference in the *processes* of learning is meager as compared with our knowledge of individual differences in status or the *products* of learning. Jensen's chief contribution is the definition of the problem of individual differences in learning in terms that permit an experimental analysis of the basic dimensions or sources of individual variation.

The papers in Part III deal with learning-teaching processes. David P. Ausubel discusses the nature of meaningful reception learning and its relative role and importance in the total enterprise of classroom learning. He differentiates between concept formation and concept assimilation in terms of meaningful learning and their application to the usual subject matter of the schools. Based on seven years of research with elementary school children, J. Richard Suchman presents a model for the analysis of the behavior of inquirers. His model relates the functions of storage, retrieval, perception, overt action, and motivation through a central mediating function. In Chapter 12, Cynthia P. Deutsch presents a discussion of the verbal, perceptual, and attentional characteristics of the disadvantaged child with respect to some of the skills underlying concept learning. Using data collected from studies of pre-school and elementary school children, Dr. Deutsch evolves a cultural relativism hypothesis to explain the intellectual retardation of the lower class child and suggests compensatory instructional approaches.

The last four chapters deal with concepts in various subject matter fields. In the first of these, Kenneth Lovell answers the following questions. What is the nature of mathematical concepts? What are the major points of view regarding the learning of mathematical concepts? To what extent is Piaget's developmental psychology useful in determining the nature of and the learning of mathematical concepts? Howard F. Fehr defines the mathematical concept as a complex entity and delineates fourteen basic concepts to be taught in the elementary school. He clarifies the problem of categorization of such concepts and suggests learning outcomes, other than concepts, which are major objectives of mathematical instruction. In his chapter on concepts in science, Joseph D. Novak describes the major problems which arise in attempts to define and categorize scientific concepts. He deals with implications of this for curriculum development and classroom instruction. In the final chapter, Stanley Kegler answers the question, "What is English?" and identifies some concepts in the study of language.

The editors' convictions about the importance of concept learning resulted in outlining certain questions that must be considered and eventually answered if understanding and control of concept learning are to be advanced. The contributors clarified some of these questions and also raised others. All of us are indeed fortunate that so many able contributors gave generously of their knowledge and time. Each contributor not only prepared, presented, and then discussed his paper at the Conference, but he also revised it after the Conference. Thus, the final content of each paper is the sole responsibility of the contributor. The editors merely developed the framework for the Conference, planned the details, and did minor editing, mainly to insure consistency of form and style.

HERBERT J. KLAUSMEIER AND CHESTER W. HARRIS

Madison, Wisconsin
August, 1966

CONTENTS

PART I / SCHEMES FOR CLASSIFYING AND RELATING CONCEPTS

PART II / LEARNING OF CONCEPTS

PART III / LEARNING–TEACHING PROCESSES

PART IV / CONCEPTS IN VARIOUS SUBJECT MATTER FIELDS

PART I

SCHEMES FOR CLASSIFYING AND RELATING CONCEPTS

CHAPTER 1

THE FORMAL ANALYSIS OF CONCEPTS

ROM HARRÉ

LINACRE COLLEGE

OXFORD, ENGLAND

The first question I asked myself when thinking about this paper was how it was that a philosopher has anything to contribute to a conference that is attended mainly by psychologists. The reason lies in our common interest in concepts. Not so long ago philosophers were saying that what they were doing when they were "doing" philosophy was really conceptual analysis. I shall not try to say why they have recently stopped saying this because I suspect the reason is a matter of change in fashion rather than sudden enlightenment. I shall say something of the history of this conception of philosophy and in so doing try to bring out the important points about the ultimate products of that history, the various methods for the more or less formal analysis of concepts. And I shall try, too, though briefly, to indicate why linguistic philosophy is now being abandoned, at least in its place of origin, and the tie-up between concepts and language loosened, since postlinguistic philosophy has much to offer any scientific investigation of concept formation by providing some new conceptual tools without which no scientific investigation could be carried out.

What is our common field of interest? What *are* concepts? *Concepts are the vehicles of thought.* When we talk about "employing concepts," "acquiring concepts," "analyzing concepts," we are talking of using, learning, and anatomizing the entities by means of which thinking is carried on. But to have said this is not yet to have said much. Until one knows what concepts are in a more specific way, that is, is able to identify a concept, one can hardly be said to be in a position to analyze anything. On the other hand, no answer to any question as to the nature of concepts is required before one can employ or acquire concepts. One does not need to understand economics in the sense of being able to state explicitly the principles of that science to be able to make money; flair is enough. It is a well-known fact that paying attention to the way one brings the racquet into contact with the ball spoils one's game, at least to begin with, though no doubt one plays better later on. But in order to analyze some entity, a specimen must be identifiable. You must catch your worm before you begin a lesson in vermiform anatomy. Furthermore, the method of analysis, the analytical tool chosen, will depend on the nature of the entity in question. It may be that difficulties arise because the wrong tool is chosen from the right box, as when one chooses a screwdriver to analyze a machine that has been bolted together. It may be that one has not come equipped with the right kind of tool. One must have a firm idea of what a concept is before one can begin to analyze. By calling concepts "vehicles for thought" I have roughly indicated where I think we all believe these entities are to be found, but so far I have said no more than I might have said to an explorer when I tell him "The Okapi will be found among the fauna of Central Africa." Concepts, we all agree, are involved with the means of thinking.

Philosophers have had two answers to the question "What exactly is a concept?" From these, two main kinds of conceptual analysis have proceeded. The first answer is arrived at by connecting concepts with images, the second by connecting concepts with language. Philosophers have a habit of going whole hog for some view or other which they favor at any one time. While connecting concepts with images they were not much bothered about language, and, similarly, while connecting concepts with language they were not much bothered by former connections with images. In the imagist period the meanings of words were identified as images; in the linguistic period the image and its objective counterpart, the picture and model, were eliminated in favor of sentences describing the picture and the model. What postlinguistic philosophy is doing is seeking to restore the image and its counterparts to their rightful independence without losing the insights obtained from the attempts to analyze concepts as linguistically connected entities.

But why analyze concepts? What is to be gained by this activity if, indeed, there is really any such activity that is legitimate? I suppose the short answer is the pursuit of clarity and the elimination of muddle, so that certain ways in which we can be misled are eliminated. Something of which the delineation is vague can be mistaken for something else, and so on. It is a very old philosophical doctrine that some ideas are muddled, confused, unclear, and misleading, and other ideas are ordered, clear, and veridical. And it is a very old philosophical aim to replace the former by structures of the latter. Of course, the question of which ideas are the clear ones and which the muddled has always been a matter of dispute, and one of the things that philosophers do is to try to show that some ideas which some other philosopher thinks are clear are actually muddled and indistinct. The simplest analysis of this kind would be what is called these days "disambiguation." Suppose someone says, (A) "The cat is on the mat." This is disambiguated by producing, (B) "The feline animal is on the mat," and (C) "The nine-thonged whip is on the mat." The game now is to show that one or both of these is ambiguous by producing, for instance, as disambiguators of (B), (B1) "The feline animal is on the small floor covering," and (B2) "The feline animal is in disgrace." One can go one step further at least by disambiguating (B1) with (B1a) "The feline animal is on the covering of the small floor" and (B1b) "The feline animal is on the small covering of the floor."

The aim of analyzing concepts is clarity, and so one would, after analysis, be able to replace the muddled or terse concept by other concepts not muddled, not terse. For this to be possible there must be at least less muddled and less internally complex concepts. Indeed, there must be a recognizable ordering or hierarchy of concepts from the less to the more clear. What makes a concept less clear? Is it perhaps a psychological question? It seems that conceptual analysis roughly amounts to the breaking down of complex concepts into structures of simpler concepts. And if clarity is achieved in this way it might be because the simpler concept is easier to understand, and the more complex is more difficult. But how can one tell if a concept is easier to understand? Is it not possible that, as a matter of fact, a simpler concept may be more difficult to grasp than a complex one? This is true of certain sorts of understanding, for instance, the way some children find the word "elephant" easier to remember how to spell than the word "pet." Any criterion of simplicity must be extrapsychological, it seems, so if there really is to be proper conceptual analysis there must be some objective way of ordering concepts in a hierarchy so that we can know what needs analysis and into what elements. The difficulty of meeting this requirement in an agreed way has been one of the chief stumbling blocks to conceptual analysis.

The subject of this paper is the formal analysis of concepts, and formal analysis, that is, analysis using the techniques and technicalities of logic, can only be appropriate when concepts and language have been connected. I believe, however, that a more just appreciation of logical and linguistic analysis is obtained when a passing glance has been given to their predecessors—the analysis of concepts as images, or ideas, as they were then called. Analyses of this sort were performed in the age when concepts and mental images were connected. They were connected in the simplest possible way, for it was assumed that concepts *were* mental images, that images were the prime vehicles of thought, and that speech and language were generally secondary. "The general use of speech," wrote Hobbes, "is to transform our mental discourse" by which he meant a train of images, "into verbal." As he said, it ". . . transfers a train of thoughts into a train of words." Its utility is then solely that of communicating ideas, as they used to say.

Descartes expressed the "Faith of the Analyst" in the "Fifth Rule for the Direction of the Mind." He said, "Method consists entirely in the order and disposition of the objects towards which our mental vision must be directed if we would find out any truth. We shall comply with it exactly if we reduce involved and obscure propositions step by step to those that are simpler, and then starting with the intuitive apprehension of all those that are absolutely simple, attempt to ascend to the knowledge of all others by precisely similar steps."

Analysis has usually been practiced in order to show that some concept is worthless, obscure, or muddled. An analyst feels that some concept is unsatisfactory somehow, but in the first instance he is unsure just what is wrong with it. By breaking it down into its simpler elements he hopes to show its internal structure. If his intuition was right he will find something wrong in the internal structure of the concept which his analysis has brought to light. In this way his suspicions will be confirmed. Berkeley was suspicious of the concept of *reality,* as used by philosophers. In his analysis of this conception he tries to show into what more primitive ideas the concept can be analyzed. For some entities to be more real than others, ". . . it is meant," he said, and now follows the analysis, "that they are affecting, orderly and distinct, and that they are not fictions of the mind perceiving them." And what does Berkeley think is the test for the correctness of this conceptual analysis? He stated, "Whether others mean anything by the term *reality* different from what I do, I entreat them to look into their own thoughts and see." Ultimately, analysis, in the older conception, is a subjective examination of one's own images. What are the characteristics of our images when they denominate reality? And in answer to this, Berkeley gave his three characteristics. Then we have analyzed the concept of reality. In the old imagist theory of concepts the technique was introspective. The objective counterparts for images had not then been identified.

Formal analysis of concepts is ushered in with the connecting of language and concepts by the principle that words are the vehicles of thought. But are *words* concepts? One could hardly say that. Are the *meanings of words* concepts? This seems a bit more like it, but what then are the meanings of words? Concepts are certainly not meanings in the sense of things signified, since concepts are the vehicles of thought and things signified are among the objects of thought. One reaction to this kind of difficulty is to say that whatever concepts may be we can be sure of words and statements, so let linguistic analysis stand in for conceptual analysis. By and large it is this attitude that informs the formal analysis of concepts. It was widely, if tacitly, held that whatever concepts may be, their formal analysis is achieved through analyzing words and statements. This is clearly shown in Carnap's account of formal analysis. He said, ". . . it consists in the clarification of the statements of empirical science; more specifically in the decomposition of statements into their parts (concepts), the step by step reduction of concepts to more fundamental concepts and of statements to more fundamental statements."

More specifically, the substitution of word and statement questions for concept questions has been proposed by P. T. Geach, in his book *Mental Acts* (1956), in the formula, "N has acquired concept *P*" is to be read as "N has learned how to use the word *P*." A concept and the *use* of a word are thus connected, so instead of trying to describe and analyze concepts, we try to do something more within our reach, we try to describe and analyze the uses of words.

From this common point the two great modern movements of analysis diverge. It is agreed that words (in particular the uses of words) and statements (structured groups of words in use) should be the *analysandum*, but it is not agreed what the *analysans* should be. Is the result of the analysis to be expressed in the commonest words of everyday language or is it to be expressed in an artificial language, based upon a logical calculus? Perhaps we should specially create artificial languages for the job of analysis. Before I attempt to weigh these views let me give you some characteristic and famous examples of each.

For a first example, consider Bertrand Russell's analysis of statements using the definite article in the subject phrase. Long ago G. Frege had provided a schema for the analysis of sentences, which he hoped would supersede that of Aristotle. Frege's scheme depended on the idea that a sentence, when used to make a statement, performed two distinct semantic functions: it referred us to some object (its subject), and it described it—that is, asserted some predicate of it. These elements of sentence function he called "having a reference" and "having a sense."

Every meaningful sentence had to be capable of being used to refer to something and to predicate something of that entity to which reference was made. Frege devised a schema not unlike an algebraic function which reflected this idea. For those sentences that used proper names of persons and things for the referring function, no serious problem arose, because, presumably, reference for the proper name was more or less guaranteed by the fact that a proper name is introduced into a community's linguistic apparatus by some ceremony in which the object of which it is the name plays some part. Therefore, for every genuine proper name there has to be a referent. But what about other referring expressions, especially those where reference is achieved by unique description? Some noun phrases with the definite article will have referents, such as "The Second President of the University of Wisconsin"; some will not, such as "The Second President of the Republic of Wisconsin." As far as verbal form goes, the two sentences, "The Second President of the University of Wisconsin was a native son," and "The Second President of the Republic of Wisconsin was a native son," are exactly alike—so if the subject of the first has a referent, why not the subject of the second? What is the difference between the two nominative concepts? There has never been anyone to which the subject of the second sentence refers, and, unless something very unexpected occurs, there never will be. Does it then refer to possible people? What could they be? Do not sentences of this form require us to postulate a realm of entities, the possibles, to provide referents for such expressions, so that all nominative concepts should have meaning? Russell's answer to these questions is to analyze and to analyze formally, that is, to use the symbolic apparatus of logic to make the structure of the sentence clear, and, in so doing, one might say that he analyzes, *inter alia,* the nominative concepts. In words, his analysis goes like this: "There is an *x*, who was the Second President, and no one else was the Second President, and *x* was a native son." Now for the first sentence, clause (1) of this analysis is true; for the second sentence, clause (1) is false. All is now clear—the nominative concept turns out to be a complex of existence and exclusiveness, and looked at in that way we are not committed to including in our universe only real past presidents of real universities, but also possible future presidents of as yet undeclared republics. If, as Carnap says, analysis is the decomposition of statements into their parts, Russell has done some analysis—since a statement which did not seem to have parts, that is to be made up of simpler statements, has been analyzed into a conjunction of three such allegedly simpler statements, its parts. The result of the analysis is supposed to be a much clearer expression of the statement we were trying to make all along and of which the unanalyzed sentence was a muddled and misleading expression.

For a second example of formal analysis using logic, I shall choose the analysis of a word, as an example of what Carnap calls the step by step reduction of concepts to more fundamental concepts. I should, perhaps, point out that at this stage of the history of conceptual analysis it was generally agreed that the simplest and hence most fundamental concepts were those which were expressed in words definable simply by an act of pointing to a sample. Any words which had to be defined by verbal definition, with several words in the *definiens*, had to be complex. Ultimately, analysis would reveal only ostensively defined words in the *definiens*, and then the analysis would be complete. There are all sorts of difficulties with this. For instance, in giving the meaning of words by ostension or pointing, do we "point" to elementary sensations as the most fundamental parts of experience (but then to each person there would be a private world of meanings) or do we point to public objects? But objects are complex. Can we then really have simple concepts expressed in words ostensively definable? Let us ignore this difficulty and see how a concept was supposed to be analyzed. The example from Carnap concerns the analysis of the psychological concept "excited," which for purposes of exposition I shall change to "annoyed." We are asked to analyze the concept of someone else's being annoyed. Since only expressions, postures, gestures, and the like can be pointed to in acts of ostensive definition, our analysis must finally terminate on this view in logical concatenations of words so ostensively defined. Someone else's annoyance must, then, be analyzed into dispositions to have certain expressions, to adopt certain postures, and to make certain gestures. Thus, for "He is annoyed," we put "He is likely to snarl, become red in the face, to make menacing gestures, and to make hurtful and cutting remarks." It is not said that his is making such gestures or adopting such postures, but that if he is annoyed he is disposed to do so. But one might be inclined to say that being disposed to do some action is to be in a certain state. And it was the ascription of states of mind to other people that Carnap wanted to avoid. A second step of analysis is required. Any reference to inner states of other persons must be eliminated by showing that when analyzed the *analysans* contains no expressions referring to such states. Are dispositions inner states? No. Carnap's suggestion is that statements about other people's states of mind are to be analyzed by turning the sentences in which they appear into conditionals, so the fact that someone is disposed to act in a certain way can be expressed by saying that he will probably act in that way *if* he is stimulated in a certain way. This is the crucial step, and if it is accepted that dispositional statements can be analyzed into statements that contain words referring only to stimuli and reactions, then analysis would have shown that mental states are an unnecessary fiction. Therefore, finally, we analyze "A is annoyed" as "If A is stimulated in such and such a way he will probably react in such a way, i.e., by adopting certain postures, making certain gestures, and exhibiting certain expressions."

Therefore, with logic as the arbiter of syntax and ostension as the arbiter of meaning, we arrive at the analytical program of logical positivism. It was magnificent, extravagant, and absurd. It was bound to produce a reaction in favor of a more realistic and more temperate analytical method. Linguistic philosophy was that reaction. Though sharing the views of the logical positivists on the priority of language as the vehicle of thought, linguistic philosophers did not try to produce definitions in terms of allegedly more primitive words expressing allegedly more primitive concepts, nor did they have much faith in any particular logical system as the arbiter of propriety of logical form. Instead they operate on the principle "The analysis of the concept *P*" is "A description of how the word '*P*' and related words are used." This principle presupposes neither the priority of any particular kind of logical structure nor the ultimacy of any particular concepts, that is, the unanalyzability of any particular words, since the use of any word can be described and therefore the concept it expresses analyzed. Here is an example of linguistic analysis of a concept, again the concept of reality, analyzed by Berkeley by introspecting our images when we imagine something to be real.

J. L. Austin (1962) wanted to analyze the "concept of reality," we might say. What he actually did was to describe how the word "real" and cognate expressions are used. In effect this amounted to the analysis of the role of the words in various linguistic enterprises. In short, it was a description of the jobs for which we use the word "real" and cognate expressions. Here, in selective quotation, is Austin's "analysis of the concept of reality."

"1. First, 'real' is a word that we may call *substantive-hungry*. . . . That is, we must have an answer to the question 'A real *what*?', if the question 'Real or not?' is to have a definite sense. . . .

"2. Next, 'real' is what we call a *trouser-word* . . . with 'real' . . . it is the *negative* use that wears the trousers. That is, a definite sense attaches to the assertion that something is real . . . only in the light of a specific way in which it might be . . . *not* real.

"3. Thirdly, 'real' is (like 'good') a *dimension-word*. I mean by this that it is the most general and comprehensive term in a whole group of terms of the same kind. . . . Other members of this group . . . are . . . 'proper,' 'genuine,' . . . 'fake,' 'makeshift,'. . . .

"4. Lastly, 'real' also belongs to a large and important family of words that we may call *adjuster-words*—words, that is, by the use of which other words are adjusted to meet the innumerable and unforeseeable demands of the world upon language . . . if I can say, 'Not a real pig, but like a pig,' I don't have to tamper with the meaning of 'pig' itself" (Austin, 1962, pp. 68-75).

In this sort of conceptual "analysis" we do not provide either a formula or a verbal *analysans* to replace locutions in which the word appears. We attempt to understand the locutions by trying to identify the linguistic job we use a word to do (have a concept for). "Do the Urbangi have the concept of *number*?" becomes according to this view, "Can the Urbangi do sums?"

I think it will be instructive now to look a little more closely at how the two great modern schools of conceptual analysts differ. I think it is fair to say that they differ with regard to what they take the meaning of a word to be; and that is to differ about what they think a concept is. For the school of Russell and Carnap, the meaning of a word is intimately bound with the method and means by which statements containing the word are checked for truth and falsity. This was sometimes put, rather crudely, in the slogan, "The meaning of statement is its method of verification." A psychological word is applied to another person on the basis of his behavior, and we check the truth of assertions that other people are in certain psychological states by how they behave (including verbal behavior), it is alleged. According to the Carnap school this must exhaust the meaning of psychological concepts, and so the analysis of a psychological concept must terminate in behavioral concepts. Thus, in the 1930's, Carnap would have held that behavioral psychology not only had the sort of rightness that derives from being the *dernier cri*, but also was supported by the irresistible force of the formal analysis of concepts. For the linguistic philosophers the meaning of a word was shown by the way it was used and by its role in the language *and life* of people. One of the great achievements of linguistic philosophy was to make a beginning, at least, on the study of the ceremonial uses of language. In this study, their method of analysis was at its most fruitful. They analyzed the concept of promising by analyzing statements such as "I promise to answer any of your questions" by describing the way expressions such as "I promise" and "I will" were used in the life of people. Although some practitioners were fond of calling this art *"logical* geography," it is clear that formal methods would not have been much use, since the areas of language which were studied were not those in which syntax was exhausted by formal logic. The statements made in a ceremony, for instance, are not statements in which truth or falsity is our primary interest: the sincerity of the speaker may be our greatest concern. The concepts being analyzed in these studies were not exclusive to the natural sciences.

Recently, however, a revival of a much older kind of formal analysis than any I have discussed has occurred. This is the attempt by J. A. Fodor and J. J. Katz (1964) to develop an analytical technique by which quite unambiguous readings of sentences can be expressed. It is strikingly like the eighteenth century idea of the Universal Character. This was to be a system of symbols representing concepts, not sounds, which the written languages of mankind now represent. A Chinese author would write in the Universal Character, and, since what he wrote would not be a representation of the verbal language but rather of the conceptual structure of his thought, what he wrote could be read, in English, by an Englishman who knew the Universal Character, or, in his own verbal language, by anyone else. It was felt that the representation of concepts, first by verbal sounds with each language having its own system and then by representing these idiosyncratic *sound* sequences in inscriptions, interposed between author and reader an unnecessary and pointless middle term. Concepts should be represented directly. The project was enthusiastically supported by scientific academies all over Europe, and several systems of concept signs and modifiers were developed. Roughly, the idea was to build a vocabulary of signs. The main signs distinguished grand categories such as human and animal and matter and spirit. A particular concept sign is then built by adding modifiers to the main sign. Therefore, the concept, "the left hand of a good man," would be built by first putting down the grand category sign MAN, and then by modifying that by G or B, getting MAN^G. This would itself be attached as a modifier to the sign for "left hand" and so, since all mankind has the concepts and could, in principle, learn the Universal Character, everyone, whatever their verbal language, could read this sign. An Englishman would read it as "the left hand of a good man"; a Frenchman as "le main gauche d'un bon homme."

Although Fodor and Katz are not trying to build a Universal Character, but rather are tackling different problems, the analysis they propose has much in common with the analyses developed by the promoters of the Universal Character. Fodor and Katz employed three main classes of analyzers in the analyses. These are grammatical markers, semantic markers, and semantic distinguishers. The principle of analysis is the separation of the concepts under a word, as we might put it, by using markers and distinguishers to note all alternative readings of the word. For instance, a dictionary entry for the word "bed" would have the following form:

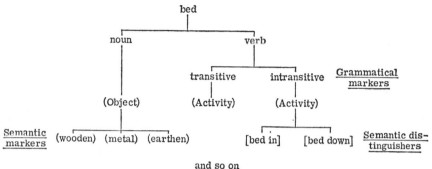

and so on

Taking any line through the "tree" yields a clear, fully analyzed concept, because it yields a fully defined (that is, completely disambiguated) word, at least in theory. Thus, we might get "bed" = noun → (physical object) → (wooden) → (four legged) → [feather].

In all these analyses, concepts and language are connected. If we are to regard the work of Fodor and Katz as providing us with a method of conceptual analysis as a by-product, we have to believe that the process of defining a word, providing a reading as they say, gives us the analysis of a concept. One might say, following this line of thought, that ordinary dictionaries rather imperfectly express lists of conceptual analyses, particularly where they list the several senses of a word. The senses of a word, one might say, are the concepts which that word, in its different employments, is used to express. Linking words and concepts was, as I have already pointed out, a step taken after the abandonment of the identification of concepts with images. Now there seems to be a possibility that the old connection may be to some extent reestablished.

Postlinguistic philosophy is characterized by the insight that *language is not the only vehicle of thought.* There may be concepts which are not connected, at least in the first instance, with the uses of words. The additional vehicle is the image which linguistic philosophy expelled from paradise. The restoration of the image has come about through the realization that the study of images need not be entirely subjective or without strict canons. Image thinking does have an objective counterpart. Just as propositions have their objective counterpart in sentences, which can be serious objects of study, carrying propositions independent of individual thinkers, so models and pictures can perform the same task of objectivization for image thinking. Thus, a new analytical discipline has appeared in the last year or two—the formal analysis of models. The study has been slow in emancipating itself from its linguistic predecessor, for, until recently, analysis of models was carried out by analyzing the description of models, a task for linguistic analysis. It is easy to see that such an attempt at analysis will not do because of the immense richness of models and pictures compared with their description in words. I turn now to an example of how image thinking can be studied in terms of its objective counterpart—model-building.

The essential tool in the study of models is the distinction and identification of the source and subject of the model. "What is M a model of?" is one question; "What is M modeled on?" is another. The great classes of models, *homoeomorphs* and *paramorphs,* are distinguished by whether the answers to these questions for any particular model are different or the same. If they are the same, if a model Duesenberg is both a model *of* the Duesenberg and modeled *on* the Duesenberg, then the model is one of the many kinds of homoeomorph. If the answers to the questions are different, e.g., Bohr's model of the atom is a model *of* an unknown mechanism producing line-series spectra, but modeled on known mechanical and electromagnetic devices, though admittedly combined in a novel way, then the model is one of the many kinds of paramorph. Working with models is the objective counterpart of thinking with images. We can study how scientists, engineers, architects, and artists work with models. We can even study how they work with imaginary models, for many scientific theories are built around a model. The passage from the known to the unknown in thought is not only by logical inference, an essentially linguistic move, but also by the construction of a picture, of a model of the unknown; and this, though it may be greatly aided by logical inference, is not essentially a linguistic move. It is the building of an image. I sincerely hope that the deliberations of this conference will be based upon a broader idea of concept formation than the narrowly linguistic.

Formal analysis of concepts has given us many profound insights into our conceptual apparatus. I would not wish to suggest otherwise. But, since it is predicated on the connection between words and concepts, the standards of rationality which it imports into conceptual analysis are those of word structures, and these quickly become assimilated to the standards of rationality enshrined in formal logic. The identity or nonidentity of meanings, the principle of noncontradiction, the relation of entailment, become the main building strands of the network of understanding we throw over our systems of thought. But our system of thought also requires the vitally important relations of relative likeness and unlikeness. Most reasoning is carried on with concepts which are not naturally related by strict identity or entailment. And in the formal analysis of concepts such relations simply disappear because they cannot be represented in a formal system. Are they then irrational, as some of the proponents of formal analysis seem to imply (e.g., Popper, 1962)? They are, only if, by fiat, standards of rationality are forever linked to the principles of formal logic. Rational principles of likeness and unlikeness are to be found in the study of models and pictures. It is to the analysis of concepts as images, as they would have called it in the nineteenth century, that philosophy is now beginning to turn.

The final section of this chapter will deal with the classification of concepts. Once again two great systems seem to dominate the history of concept taxonomy. I shall call the systems the *categorial* and the *hierarchical*. The categorial taxonomy stems from Aristotle and, indeed to this day, is essentially in its original form. Aristotle's categories are perhaps most easily understood as the major divisions of concepts. He distinguished such familiar categories of concepts as Substance, Accident, Relation, Quantity, Quality, and so on. His categories were derived from the kinds of questions that he thought it was possible to ask about anything. He wrote, "Each simple expression signifies either of what substance or how much, or of what sort, or related to what, or where, or when, or in what attitude, or how appearing, or to be acting or to be acted upon." The conceptual system of categories deals with what can properly be asked about anything. It is a system of concepts adjusted to what we think of the world. It is also flexible, since it seems evident that we might find ourselves asking a new and different sort of question about any subject matter, and this would provide us immediately with a new taxon of concepts. Aristotle provided us with taxa derived from the questions he held to be askable about things, and he took pains to show how particular questions, such as "How large is it?", presuppose concepts fitting into his categories. For instance, "large" and "small" are, he argued, to be classified as relational concepts since they assume standards of comparison for size and are not absolute designations. It is not contradictory to say in the same breath, "The box is too small," and, "The box is too large," since in the first instance we might be considering it as a cage for an elephant, and in the second as a cage for a flea. Therefore, "How large is it?" is actually a relational question, not a quantitative one, and the concept of *largeness* must be classified under the category of relation and not under the category of quantity. We still use Aristotle's method to distinguish between quantitative and qualitative concepts, between substance concepts and attribute concepts. Furthermore, one should note, too, that this old system has the merit of closely linking the concept taxonomy with linguistic analysis. It is not only a way of classifying concepts but also a way of classifying statements by the kind of question to which they would properly be given in answer. A different version of more or less the same style of concept classification is found in I. Kant's *Critique of Pure Reason*, "Transcendental Analytic," Book I, Chapter 1. In that work it is not the form of questions upon which the taxonomy of concepts is based, but rather the kinds of propositional forms or judgments that Kant thinks are possible. It is still a categorial system though its basis is different.

The hierarchical classification of concepts depends on the idea that some concepts have more explanatory power than others. The introduction of a new concept sometimes illuminates and brings order and structure to a previously inchoate field of fragmentary knowledge. The concept of *Universal Gravity* was such a concept. It could be used in the explanation of a very wide range of previously unconnected phenomena. The apple and the moon, despite their seeming to move in quite different modes, were both subject to it. The concept of Universal Gravity was more powerful than the concept of Natural Motion, since it explained different kinds of motion *in the same way*, whereas the concept of Natural Motion explained different kinds of motion in different ways. This suggests a classification of concepts with respect to their power to explain and order subject matter. One such taxonomy might run as follows. Concepts of the first level, or phenomenological concepts, would explain nothing but would be the concepts used for describing the observations we make. Then would come concepts of the second level, or physicalist concepts, which would relate to a system of physical things of which the observations would be the effects or appearances. And level after level of concepts would be disclosed as a hierarchy of explanations is constructed. At length, a termination is reached, *for any era,* in the general conceptual system of the era. The concepts that make it up are *the explainers* and do not themselves call for explanation, while they have that role. What I have in mind here is illustrated by the concepts of Natural Motion from the medieval system and from the modern system. In the Aristotelian cosmology there were two kinds of natural motion—downward for terrestrial bodies and in circles, around the earth, for celestial ones. These two kinds of natural motion were enshrined in the general conceptual system of the

Middle Ages and, as such, did not call for explanation. There was just no sense to the question, "Why does a body fall toward the center of the Earth?", and no sense to the question, "Why does a celestial body move in a circle around the Earth?", since it was in terms of these motions as natural that all else was explained. In the modern system both of these questions can be answered, but they are answerable only because we have adopted a different concept of natural motion, the geodesic, and enshrined it in our system. The senseless question for us is, "Why does a body, if unimpeded, continue in its state of motion or rest?" All we can explain are changes in such states. The hierarchical taxonomy then works as follows. Order concepts by the relation of *explanans* to *explanandum*. The lowest level concept will be an *explanandum* only, and will not itself explain anything. The highest level concept will be an *explanans* only and will explain everything below it but not itself be explicable. It is becoming customary to call the set of concepts of the highest level the general conceptual system. This taxonomy is still more flexible than that of Aristotle. It will reflect within it, by the place it assigns to given concepts, the current state of science, and it will therefore always be in a state of flux somewhere. Usually, however, the general conceptual system remains fairly stable for considerable lengths of time, and its identification is then both important and fairly easy. It determines, one might say, the conceptual style of an epoch.

REFERENCES

Austin, J. L. *Sense and sensibilia*. London & New York: Oxford Univer. Press (Clarendon), 1962.

Fodor, J. A., & Katz, J. J. (Eds.), The structure of a semantic theory. In *The structure of language*. Englewood Cliffs, New Jersey: Prentice-Hall, 1964.

Geach, P. T. *Mental acts: Their content and their objects*. London: Routledge & Kegan Paul, 1956.

Kant, I. *Critique of Pure Reason*. Book I, Chapter I.

Popper, K. R. *Conjectures and refutations*. New York: Basic Books, 1962.

CHAPTER 2

AN ANALYSIS OF CONCEPTS FROM THE POINT OF VIEW OF THE STRUCTURE OF INTELLECT

PHILIP R. MERRIFIELD

KENT STATE UNIVERSITY
KENT, OHIO

"A model is a sometime thing." Typically, a model is a relatively formal description of abstractions from ideas or phenomena in which we are interested. Models can be used as theoretical bases for deductions; when these deductions are tested, we usually call them hypotheses. As good logicians, we stand ready to modify the model if a deduction from it leads to a hypothesis that is rejected. The rules for rejection are many because they tend to be situation-specific, but they share the common premise that the observation of an event that has a low probability of occurrence, given that the hypothesis is true, is a necessary ground for rejection of the hypothesis.

EDUCING THE MODEL

The model under discussion—the structure-of-intellect—was evolved from observations of consistencies in mental behavior in the domain of "thinking." These consistencies were based on intercorrelations of samples of thinking, i.e., tests, and the apparent similarities among groups of tests, where the groups were obtained by factor analysis. Consider these well-known factors and typical tasks: verbal comprehension—know the meanings of words; general reasoning—understand the meaningful and complex interrelations in a problem preparatory to solving it, as in a word problem; word fluency—list words containing the letter E; eduction of figural relations—comprehend the relations among given space forms, diagrams, etc.; spatial orientation—recognition of figures in which elements have the same interrelationships; and associational fluency—writing synonyms (loosely defined) for given words, or producing a variety of words having similar meanings.

COMMON REQUIREMENTS

Now consider what the three tests, verbal comprehension, general reasoning, and spatial orientation have in common. The diagram in Fig. 1 represents the areas of overlap of these factors. All involve recognition or awareness or what is called, traditionally, cognition. Thus, the intersects of the factors verbal comprehension (1) and general reasoning (2) contain the operation of cognition; further, both factors involve meaningful

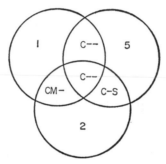

FIG. 1.   Early emergent factors. Common requirements of (1) verbal comprehension—CMU, (2) general reasoning—CMS, and (5) spatial orientation—CFS.

material. The two-factor portion of the intersection has been labeled CM-, for reasons that shortly will become apparent. Similarly, the two-factor intersection of verbal comprehension (1) and spatial orientation (5) is labeled C--, because they have only cognition in common. A comparison of general reasoning (2) and spatial orientation (5) discloses that both involve knowing (cognition) and interrelationships of a sufficiently complex kind to be called systems. Thus the two-factor intersection of these abilities is labeled C-S, indicating that they share cognition and systems. Finally, the three factors represented in Fig. 1 share the requirement of cognition, and that central intersection is labeled C--. One may question whether a distinction should be made between the C-- from (1) and (5) and the C-- from (1), (2), and (5), but I should prefer to put that discussion aside for the present and move on to Fig. 2.

Consider the common requirements among verbal comprehension (1), word fluency (3), and associational fluency (6). Verbal comprehension and word fluency both involve single elements, meanings of words in

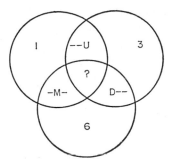

Fɪɢ. 2.   Common requirements of (1) verbal comprehension—CMU, (3) word fluency—DSU, and (6) associational fluency—DMR.

the first and spelling of words in the second. The intersection is labeled - -U, for units of thought. The cognition in verbal comprehension differs from the productive thinking required in word fluency, but the latter shares the requirement of productive thinking with associational fluency (6); thus their intersection, (3) and (6), is labeled D- -, where D specifies the divergent type of productive thinking. Similarly, associational fluency and verbal comprehension share the requirements of thought about meaningful material; their intersection is labeled -M-, where the M denotes the requirement that verbal comprehension and general reasoning shared in Fig. 1. The three-factor intersection presents an interesting logical problem, one that might be avoided by drawing ellipses rather than circles. It may be a null set, by definition; or an empty set, in this particular model; or a part of Spearman's g. I prefer the second alternative.

In continuing the comparisons, consider the three factors eduction of figural relations (4), spatial orientation (5), and associational fluency (6). As depicted in Fig. 3, the first two named have in common the

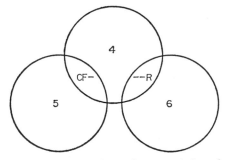

Fɪɢ. 3.   Common requirements of (4) eduction of figural relations—CFR, (5) spatial orientation—CFS, and (6) associational fluency—DMR.

requirements of cognition and thinking about figural materials; their intersection is labeled CF-. The systemic emphasis in spatial orientation is not shared by the other two factors. They do, however, share the requirement of thinking about relations and their intersection is labeled - -R. One could draw the circles for (5) and (6) overlapping, which would generate two intersections like the central one in Fig. 2, but that would complicate the discussion unnecessarily. Finally, in Fig. 4, all six factors and their common requirements are shown.

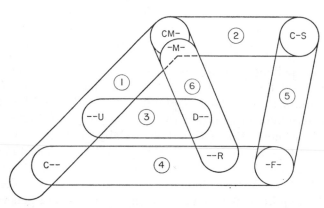

Fig. 4. Common requirements of six factors. Key: (1) verbal comprehension—CMU, (2) general reasoning—CMS; (3) word fluency—DSU; (4) education of figural relations—CFR; (5) spatial orientation—CFS; (6) associational fluency—DMR.

OTHER CONSIDERATIONS

Manipulations analogous to those displayed above were followed by Guilford and his staff in evolving what now constitute the major parameters of the structure-of-intellect model. One may question the choice of the three-category scheme—why not a two-category description, or one with four categories? Two categories seemed too few to account for the observed differences among factors, and four categories seemed more than necessary. Without straining too hard to find historical referents, one may recall the distinction between sensation, percept, and concept as compared to content in the model; the variety of tasks in the complication experiments at Leipzig and, later, the emphasis on totality of phenomena at Berlin as possible precursors of the different products; and Brentano's division of psychic acts into sensing, imagining, acknowledging, perceiving, and recalling, among others, as foreshadowing the five operations.

THE PRESENT MODEL

One does not, in terms of the structure-of-intellect model, merely "think"; rather, one thinks about some content. The "things thought about" may be described in a two-category scheme: kind of material and kind of outcome of the thinking. I should now like to turn to a rather formal presentation of the three categories—thinking operation (process); content (material); and outcome (product)—and the 15 primitive notions involved within these categories in the model.

OPERATIONS

This category concerns the kind of thinking performed. As implied in the preceding comments, thinking always involves an object of thought. The objects are described in detail in later sections. The code letter for the operation is given in parentheses in the following discussion.

Cognitive (C)
> To be aware of, to "know," to sense, to realize, to comprehend, to perceive (in the classic meaning).

Memorative (M)
> To recall, to reminisce, to reproduce exactly from specified cues, to recognize from previous experience, to retain, to produce a facsimile of.

Productive
> To generate, to discover what was not evident before, to educe, to make anew, to think differently from the general.

Divergent (D)
>> Producing a variety of solutions in some quantity, the amount depending in part on the kind of product; producing many alternatives fitting criteria which are relatively vague or broad, e.g., producing the names of a number of objects that have one or a few specified attributes.

Convergent (N)
>> Producing a single solution or small class of solutions to a fairly well-structured problem, for which the acceptability criteria are well defined, e.g., producing the name of an object having a rather large number of specified attributes.

In some of the recent literature, divergent and convergent thinking have been discussed as though they were opposites. Such is not the case—both are kinds of productive thinking, divergent more related to "creativity," convergent more related to "problem solving." Each is distinct from the other, and from the other three operations.

Evaluative (E)

To judge, to compare correctly elements with reference to a given standard, to assign consistent values to elements in a group, to rate in terms of a consensus, to leap over uncertainty and land "on target."

CONTENTS

These descriptions are similar to those in Guilford and Merrifield (1960) and in Guilford and Hoepfner (1963). The code letter appears in parentheses.

Figural (F)

Obtained through the sensorium, e.g., space, color, loudness, smoothness, sweetness, saltiness, proportion. The emphasis here is on the elemental sensations, not the concepts frequently associated with them.

Symbolic (S)

Signs in a scheme of notation, deriving their information content from their function and definition in the scheme. Examples of such signs are letters and numbers, musical symbols, and other "codes." These are not to be confused with the symbols of "symbolism" reflecting the intangible invariants of a culture.

Semantic (M)

The information content most obviously involved in language used for the communication of ideas. Some notational schemes other than words are so generally comprehended as to qualify as languages, in this semantic sense, e.g., familiar formulas in mathematics and science. Sufficiently detailed pictorial representations have a great deal of semantic content, especially when the picture is interpreted as a meaning, not as a space-form. Critiques of painting or sculpture that consider primarily the intellectual intent of the artist, or the proper interpretation in terms of social constructs, or the like, are primarily semantic. Those dealing with balance or composition or choice of hue or medium, for example, are more figural in emphasis, even though words are used to communicate the critics' ideas.

Behavioral (B)

Information dealing with human feelings, intentions, reactions, and interactions with objects and other humans (and animals); the mode of communication is often nonverbal, e.g., by gesture, inflection of words, sounds, or stance.

PRODUCTS

Products must be considered in the context of a problem—a class in one context may be a unit in another, or a system in a third. Part of the problem, for the psychologist, is the problem-solver; one child's unit may be another's system, if they are at differing levels of what used to be called analytic ability. The classic "intelligence" seems to be a measure of the child's ability to operate on the systemic properties of a problem, hence the definition of general reasoning as the intersection CMS, cognition of semantic systems. It is convenient to begin with a discussion of system as a product.

System (S)

An aggregate of interrelated components—the "whole" of Gestalt psychology that is "greater than the sum of its parts." To operate on a system as a system, the thinker must be able to consider the components as they are related to each other. If he cannot consider the systemic properties of a thing, he must think about it as though it were a class of elements. If he cannot differentiate it at all, he must treat it as a unit. It is tempting, but perhaps not necessary, to require a system to contain at least three elements and at least two relations.

Class (C)

An aggregate of components essentially unrelated, but having at least one attribute or characteristic in common.

Unit (U)

A thing which, in the context, is undifferentiated; note that in another context it may not be undifferentiable. A unit is a whole that can be considered intact without loss of information. Consider three aspects of a football team. To the crowd and the cheering section, "the team" is a unit that they occasionally differentiate a bit to reward by acclaim an outstanding player; to the acute sports writer, to the coaches and opponents, to themselves, the team playing the game on the field is a system; to the dietitian who prepares the training table, or the conductor of transportation, they are a class. To the coeds, they are individual units, or perhaps systems, depending on the level of interest.

Relation (R)

Stumpf called the study of relations, logology; Spearman emphasized its importance (eduction of correlates), but we still have some trouble defining it. It is a functional linkage of some sort, more than having attributes in common (which is the class property). In quantitative context, relations are expressed by such phrases as more than, equal to, and half of. In semantic discourse, we say means the same as, or analogous to. In spatial context the terms are above, to the right of, inside, and the like. And in the sensory context, some familiar relations are those described by more acrid than, softer, louder, and redder.

Transformation (T)

A change, a redefinition, a realignment. One could almost consider "transforming" as an operation; as a counter to this possibility is the feeling that a transformation can be operated on like other products—cognized, produced, remembered, evaluated. A transformation seems to be the kind of product that is characterized by the "closure" that leads from a class to a system; or the "insight" that leads to a reinterpretation of a unit in terms of its newly considered relations to other units or classes or systems; or the substitution of some relations for others that leads from a given system to a different system. Its essence is change—its occurrence is necessary in what is called creativity.

Implication (I)

That which can be made explicit in the absence of new information, in contrast to that which is already explicit; the result of operating to complete, explicitly, a relation inherent in the context, e.g.— solutions to an algebraic equation; the size of an angle in a triangle for which the sides are specified; prior and future conditions; and other kinds of extrapolations based on information inherent in that explicitly given.

Within each category, the primitive notions are considered as mutually exclusive. Each specific mental function includes one notion from each of the three categories: operation, content, and product. Thus, a mental function may be defined as shown in Fig. 5(a). The intersection of cognition (operation C), semantic material (content M) and system (product S) is the mental function CMS, earlier referred to as general reasoning. Other combinations are shown in Fig. 5 for the mental functions DMU ideational fluency [Fig. 5(b)], for NFT figural redefinition [Fig. 5(c)], and for ESC evaluation of symbolic classes [Fig. 5(d)].

USING THE MODEL

In the model, as it is currently used, the parameters serve to define not only the existing mental functions, as in the earlier eduction phase, but also to predict mental functions not now having empirical referents. The mental functions diagrammed in Fig. 5(a–c) were fairly well known prior to the formulation of the structure-of-intellect model, but have been refined, we think, in recent research. The mental function ESC

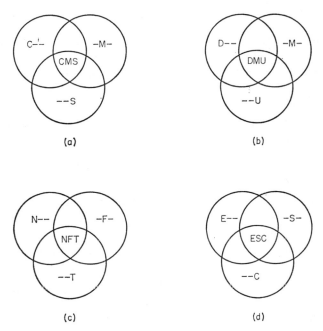

FIG. 5. Mental functions as intersections of parameters. (a) General reasoning; (b) ideational fluency; (c) figural redefinition; (d) evaluation of symbolic classes.

was not empirically evidenced until last year (Hoepfner, Guilford, & Merrifield, 1964). Its name indicates the current tendency to explicate the code letters rather than to invent a new name. I have, perhaps, described the model in too much detail, but I hoped to reach a common understanding prior to recommending the model as a framework for analyzing concepts in learning.

Thus, I have come full circle to my initial observations regarding models and testability. Deductions now available from the model are testable within a factor-analytic framework. The empirical referents for mental functions described in the structure of intellect are factors based on intercorrelations of tests which are designed especially to elicit performances judged to be operationally descriptive of the functions. In the typical exploratory study, factors (mental functions) substantiated in previous research are represented by at least two tests, in order to identify the framework within which the new factors will, hopefully, be defined. These reference factors are chosen to measure factors that are possibly related to the new tests. The mental functions that have not been previously identified are represented by three or more specially designed tests. If the deductions from the model are correct and the tests are appropriate operational definitions, then the tests designed to measure the same mental function may intercorrelate sufficiently to support a factor. This factor serves as evidence for the existence of the new mental function. The possibility of logical circularity is plain; external criteria for the existence of a factor must be applied. We have adopted the criteria of simple structure with the additional stipulation that the factors be mutually orthogonal. The degree to which we have, in our published results, met these criteria has been challenged. The more significant challenges (e.g., Harris & Liba, 1965) question whether the factors are as separate as claimed. If they are not, the degree to which the primitive notions discussed previously are mutually exclusive within their respective categories is debatable. Though I share some of these doubts, I should like to believe that a large part of the apparent confounding of factors is owing to our present deficiencies in attempting to construct univocal tests. Furthermore, the circumstance that the factors are not equally represented in the battery is a possible source of apparent confounding.

MODEL PARAMETERS AND CONCEPTS IN LEARNING

Assuming that the primitive notions in the structure of intellect provide, at the least, an interesting way of talking about mental functions, consider the degree to which concepts in learning may be described. We should first understand the limits of the model in this context. Aspects of learning situations such as motivation, drive, fatigue, psychomotor speed, dexterity, and sensory acuity, are outside the model. Similarly, prior intellectual achievements are, strictly speaking, outside the model. These aspects of performance I consider as facilitating, whereas the concern of the structure-of-intellect model is with differentiating components of thought (Merrifield, 1964)—the way in which the information received is processed by the thinker. Thus in mapping concepts from the study of learning into the model, we are restricted to consideration of individual differences in learning. However, precisely because individual differences are involved in the group differences on which judgments of learning conditions are based, we may increase the sensitivity of our experiments by using measures of relevant mental functions as controls.

We are fortunate in having available a naturalistic description of eight types of learning in terms of their conditions (Gagné, 1965). Some speculations relating Gagné's types of learning to the parameters of the structure-of-intellect model are summarized in Table I. Professor Gagné was not consulted regarding the comparisons, and, therefore, bears no responsibility for them; it seems likely that he would not agree entirely with the approach taken here. Pointing out some of the more plausible relations, however, may serve to suggest ways in which learning studies may be made more sensitive to components of the experimental outcomes that are attributable to individual differences among the subjects. The mapping is discussed in greater detail in the following paragraphs.

Type 1: Signal learning is typified by the classic conditioning paradigm. It is perhaps discouraging to suggest, this early, that individual differences in acquisition of a conditioned response seem to involve the primitive notions, implication and memory. Further, since experience with the signal and its concurrents may change the organism's expectancies, some evaluation of the most recent signal seems likely. These notions, especially evaluation and implication, are frequently reserved by theorists to describe higher levels of thought. Perhaps the change in level is a function of the content of the signal. Signals used in classic conditioning are mostly figural, whereas those objects of "higher thought processes" are more generally semantic or symbolic. Recent work by Stott and Ball (1965) indicate that factors derived from intercorrelations of items from infant and preschool mental tests can be interpreted in structure-of-intellect terms. Perhaps we have been so impressed with interspecie differences and intraspecie developmental changes that we have missed the differentiation present within specie and within developmental level.

Type 2: Stimulus-response learning seems to require more evaluation than does Type 1, because of its greater emphasis of discrimination. The phenomenon called shaping is related to convergent productive thinking. The response is produced, whether to the stimulus to which the experimenter is attending or to some other, and the focusing behavior is one aspect of convergent thinking. Implicitly, in the development of the learner's preference for one response over others, evaluation is involved.

TABLE I

HYPOTHESIZED RELATIONS AMONG TYPES OF LEARNING AND PARAMETERS OF ABILITY

Structure-of-intellect parameters	Gagné's types of learning							
	Signal (1)	S-R (2)	Chain (3)	Verbal association (4)	Multiple discrimination (5)	Concept (6)	Principle (7)	Problem solving (8)
Operations								
Cognitive (C)	X		X			X	X	X
Memorative (M)	X			X	X	X	X	
Productive								
Divergent (D)		X	X	X				X
Convergent (N)		X		X	X	X		X
Evaluative (E)	X			X	X	X		X
Contents								
Figural (F)	X	X	X	X	X			X
Symbolic (S)			X	X	X			X
Semantic (M)		X	X	X	X	X	X	X
Behavioral (B)					X	X	X	
Products								
System (S)	X		X		X	X	X	X
Class (C)					X	X		
Unit (U)	X			X		X	X	X
Relation (R)		X		X	X	X	X	
Transformation (T)	X	X		X				X
Implication (I)	X	X					X	X
Selected Abilities								
Potential covariants in learning studies	MFR EFI MFU EFU	NFR NFI NMR NMI EFR EFI EMR EMI	CFS CSS CMS NFS NSS NMS	MMR MSR DMR DMT NFU EFR EMR	MSR EFC EFR EMR EMR EMS EBC	CMC CMR CMS NMC NMR NMS EMS	CSI CMS CMU CMI CMR	CMT DMT NMT CMI EMI NMI DFT

One might surmise that those who learn slowly are treating stimulus (external plus internal)–response (Ss-R) as an if-then type of implication, while those who learn more rapidly are able sooner to regard Ss as a unit and Ss-R as a relation. Again, differences in the content of the stimulus, and of the response, lead to individual differences in learning. Those who learn quickly to deal with figural stimuli may, or may not, learn as quickly to deal with semantic material.

Type 3: Chaining, the learning of sequences of previously learned links, may be interpreted as the acquisition of a system. Probably the dominant operation (process) is cognition; convergent productive thinking is also highly involved.

Type 4: Verbal association may be classified as a subtype of chaining, as Gagné suggests. The rapid learner seems to generate links not provided explicitly in the material. This mental function resembles a transformation in that a part of the stimulus is isolated and reinterpreted in terms of the rest of the stimulus and of the response. Learning foreign languages by cognates is another example of using transformations. Although memory is involved in providing the generated link, divergent productive thinking may be more important in providing a variety of possible links; from these, the learner selects the one most efficient as a mediator for the particular association task. Those who learn by this procedure use divergent productive thinking of transformations—an essential component of "creativity"—and evaluation of relations, both probably in semantic content. Some learners, I am sure, do well at nonsense syllables because they can recall the configuration of letters that "look right" when they are presented with the first of the pair. The latter mental function involves a convergent production of units and evaluations of relations, probably in figural content.

Type 5: Multiple discrimination involves thinking about class properties, mostly figural in Gagné's example of naming cars, probably symbolic in learning the meanings to be attached to words (e.g., learning to read), semantic in differentiating concepts, and behavioral in telling a friendly wave from a threatening gesture. Rote learning has been classified in the model as memory for symbolic relations. Multiple discrimination of complex stimuli may well involve thinking about systems. The dominant operation seems to be evaluative thinking.

Type 6: Concept learning, as traditionally viewed, draws heavily on thought about semantic material. It is the naming of a class of objects, not the objects themselves, that is crucial, although awareness and evaluation of the properties of the objects is at least facilitating. Probably most situations involving concept learning require the learners to think in a cognitive, or perhaps convergently productive, way about semantic aspects of classes and relations. Marked ambiguity among the objects to be conceptualized (interference) requires the learner to do evaluative thinking, perhaps about systems, as well as about classes and relations.

Type 7: Principle learning seems to be a "higher process" in much of the literature. Yet, in structure-of-intellect terms, it seems to involve the unitization of what were previously classes or relations or systems. The controversy between S-R and Gestalt interpretations becomes a little clearer in this context. Certainly having rather involved ideas available as units makes their recall more efficient. To the extent that application is overlearned, it becomes a facilitator for the response, not a differentiator of learning. Principles may be learned in all types of material; those involved in semantic material have been investigated more frequently. The dominant operation in principle learning seems to be cognition.

Type 8: Problem solving, as investigated by Merrifield, Guilford, Christensen, and Frick (1962), draws on evaluative, cognitive, and divergently productive thinking, where the objects of thought are units, implications, and transformations. It is reasonable that convergent productive thinking as an operation, and system as a product should be included; tests for these factors were not available at the time that study was initiated. The study was confined to semantic content; parallel studies in other content areas should be done.

CONCLUSIONS

The possibility of describing learning in terms of the structure-of-intellect model is properly restricted to the description of individual differences among learners. "Laws of Learning" may be, at present, partially obscured by individual differences in the learners. Even the simplest forms of learning may be, in terms of the mental functions discussed, rather complex. It seems unlikely that random assignment to groups, or even simple covariance designs, will provide the greater control and sensitivity required for further exploration of learning. Utilization of measures from the structure-of-intellect model should help to clarify and delimit the generality of laws of learning appropriate to the complex human organism.

REFERENCES

Gagné, R. M. *The conditions of learning.* New York: Holt, Rinehart, & Winston, 1965.

Guilford, J. P., & Hoepfner, R. Current summary of structure-of-intellect factors and suggested tests. *Rep. psychol. Lab.*, 1963, No. 30. Los Angeles: Univer. Southern Calif.

Guilford, J. P., & Merrifield, P. R. The structure-of-intellect model: Its uses and implications. *Rep. psychol. Lab.*, 1960, No. 24. Los Angeles: Univer. Southern Calif.

Harris, C. W., & Liba, Marie R. *Component, image, and factor analysis of tests of intellect and of motor performance.* U.S. Office of Education Cooperative Research Project No. S-192-64. Madison: Univer. of Wisconsin, 1965.

Hoepfner, R., Guilford, J. P., & Merrifield, P. R. A factor analysis of the symbolic-evaluation abilities. *Rep. psychol. Lab.*, 1964, No. 33. Los Angeles: Univer. Southern Calif.

Merrifield, P. R. Facilitating vs. differentiating components of creativity. *J. educ. Measml.*, 1964, 1, 103-107.

Merrifield, P. R., Guilford, J. P., Christensen, P. R., & Frick, J. W. The role of intellectual factors in problem solving. *Psychol. Monogr.*, 1962, 76, No. 10 (Whole No. 529).

Stott, L. H., & Ball, Rachel S. Infant and preschool mental tests. *Society for Research in Child Development Monographs,* 1965, 30 (3), 1-151 (Serial No. 101).

PART II

LEARNING OF CONCEPTS

CHAPTER 3

THE PSYCHOLOGICAL NATURE OF CONCEPTS

E. JAMES ARCHER
UNIVERSITY OF COLORADO
BOULDER, COLORADO

In order to provide some structure to this problem, I think it might be well to start with a definition of a concept. In a sense, when one seeks to identify the psychological nature of a concept, one is identifying the attributes that serve to distinguish *concepts* from other psychological phenomena. Curiously, therefore, I find myself in the position of defining the concept of a concept, and this just naturally leads back to the paper by that title which Howard Kendler gave at the ONR symposium at the University of Michigan in 1962. I had the privilege of responding to Kendler's paper, and I now have had the added motivation to go back and reread his paper (Kendler, 1964) as well as my reply (Archer, 1964). The task of defining a concept is not an easy one, and Howard Kendler suggested that his paper might be a "first approximation." What follows is at best a second approximation, or at least a different first approximation.

To start with, let me suggest the simple definition of a concept as the *label* of a set of things that have something in common. I am proposing essentially the kind of definition which Earl Hunt used in his book (1962, p. 6) in which he wrote, ". . . concept learning is defined as a term which applies to any situation in which a subject learns to make an identifying response to members of a set of not completely identical stimuli. . . ." Hunt also added the following restrictions, although the first seems excessively constraining:

"1. The subject must, conceivably, be able to instruct a human to apply the classification rule. The subject is not allowed to use examples during the course of this instruction.

"2. The rule to be learned must be one that can be applied to any appropriate stimulus regardless of the context in which the stimulus appears.

"3. The rule must be deterministic; once a given stimulus is completely described it must be uniquely classifiable" (Hunt, 1962, p. 7).

This definition of a concept is essentially what Bruner, Goodnow, and Austin described as a conjunctive concept. However, they also identified several other types of concepts (Bruner, Goodnow, & Austin, 1956). How shall we handle these under the simple description that I have advocated for all concepts? I propose that we might locate the variety of concepts along certain dimensions. Rather than have distinctly and apparently unrelated categories of concepts, I suggest that we think in terms of an n-dimensional space in which the various dimensions are different ways of manipulating the complexity of concepts. If there is any one distinctive feature about concepts in general, it is that they vary very widely in terms of complexity.

The simplest concept would require but one bit of relevant information and nothing more; for example, a sense impression, such as the one for "cold." To play on this theme for a bit, I would suggest a complex concept might be illustrated by the two words "cold war." On the one hand, the simple concept has but one bit of relevant information and no irrelevant information, whereas, on the other hand, the complex concept involves a set of many relevant attributes and is embedded in many irrelevant attributes.

The center of the n-dimensional space locates the simplest concept with but one dimension and nothing else, and radiating out from this origin we can identify one dimension of increasing complexity, which is defined by increasing amount of *irrelevant* information. In a sense this way of manipulating complexity is one in which the concept is simply found in a wider and wider variety of contexts. This need to filter out the many different contexts obviously proves to be a difficult task for a subject. This effect has been demonstrated repeatedly during the past 10 years (e.g., Archer, Bourne, & Brown, 1955).

Another dimension that radiates out from this origin of our n-dimensional space is the variation in complexity due to increasing amounts of *relevant* information. This, of course, just identifies the information that a subject must take into account in order to identify the concept. Although there were some methodological issues unresolved, Walker (1958) seems to have demonstrated the degrading effect of increasing the amounts of relevant information. More recently it has been demonstrated (Bulgarella & Archer, 1962) that not only was the amount of relevant information effective, but the phenomenon could also be generalized to auditory stimuli, as well as to visual stimuli.

So far this ordering of complexity is obvious and has been dealt with previously. Going back to the origin of the n-dimensional space, however, I suggest that there is still another dimension which corresponds to increasing the number of *alternatives* to the positive instance at the origin. Basically, I am suggesting that one could arrange disjunctive and conjunctive concepts along a single dimension. The simplest case of a concept would be when there was but one alternative, the original instance at the origin of my imaginary space. The further out I go on this dimension of alternatives, the more disjunctive possibilities can be entertained. To use the example suggested by Bruner *et al.* (1956, p. 158), ". . . to be a member of the class admissible to the Altavista civic association, one must *either* reside legally in Altavista, *or* own property there, *or* be engaged in business within the town's limits." In short, all the members of the Altavista civic association *do* have something in common; they are members of the association, but they achieve this membership by meeting any of several requirements. I think one could describe the dimension of complexity here in terms of the number of alternatives that are possible. It would be easier to identify the concept of what members of the Altavista civic association have in common if only *two* alternatives were allowed, *either* legally residing in Altavista *or* owning property there. When, however, one allows this to be expanded to include engaged in business within the town's limits, then the heterogeneity of the set becomes greater and the concept becomes less clearly defined. It would become *even* less clearly defined if one admitted still further alternatives, such as, having the written recommendations of five present members of the Altavista civic association. And, of course, identifying the communality of membership would be even more difficult if one only needed to be a friend of someone who had five recommendations of other members to become a member. Basically, I am suggesting that conjunctive and disjunctive concepts are not qualitatively different, but may be considered as lying along a dimension of complexity defined by increasing heterogeneity of rules for class membership.

To round out the picture and include probabilistic concepts, we could assume that we have a dimension of decreasing probability of occurrence of the relevant attribute(s) necessary and sufficient to identify the concept. With 100% probability we are at the origin of the n-dimensional space and the concept becomes more complex as we move away from this origin and the previously necessary and sufficient attributes for defining the concept are only *sometimes* appropriate.

Undoubtedly there are other dimensions which might be added to this *n*-dimensional space, but for the time being I think this model will serve the purpose of permitting the definition of the concept as the label of a set of things which have something in common.

PSYCHOLOGICAL CHARACTERISTICS OF CONCEPTS

IDENTIFIABILITY

The first, and probably most obvious characteristic of a concept is that it is *identifiable*. If, in fact, the concept could not be identified, then I suspect as far as we would be concerned, it does not really exist. As Kendler (1964) indicated, considerable research has been directed at the problem of identifying the variables that alter the speed and accuracy with which a concept can be identified.

Many studies (e.g., Archer *et al*, 1955; Bourne, Guy, Dodd, & Justesen, 1965; Bulgarella & Archer, 1962; Lordahl, 1961) make it abundantly clear that increasing the amount of irrelevant information degrades the speed with which a concept can be identified.

It also appears that it is possible to offset the effectiveness of large amounts of irrelevant information by including redundant relevant information (Bourne & Haygood, 1959; Bourne & Haygood, 1961).

The effectiveness of varying the amount of relevant information has also been fairly well documented at this time (Bulgarella & Archer, 1962; Walker, 1958) to permit the conclusion that increasing the amount of relevant information required also degrades the speed with which a concept might be identified.

The results have been interesting in the effect of secondary variables which might affect the obviousness of the relevant and irrelevant information (Archer, 1962) to support the predicted conclusion that the identifiability of a concept will be facilitated if the relevant information is obvious and the concept will become more difficult to disentangle from its context if the irrelevant is obvious.

Recently Dominowski (1965) reviewed the literature on the role of memory in concept learning. Obviously, before the learning could take place, the concept had to be identified. Much of the literature reviewed by Dominowski in the interest of concept learning would also be relevant to concept identification. Although Dominowski concluded, "The question of memory effects during acquisition has no simple answer," he was able to provide two generalizations: "Performance is generally improved by increasing the availability of previous stimulus information. The degree to which instances of the same concept occur contiguously directly affects acquisition of the concept" (Dominowski, 1965, p. 271).

LEARNABILITY

After a concept has been *identified,* it might be *learned* by a subject. As Kendler (1964) pointed out, these two phases of identification and acquisition might even go on simultaneously and, perhaps, the acquisition could even precede the identification. This latter would occur when the subject was acquiring information about the relevant dimensions and had not yet identified the total concept. There is, however, a clearly defined phenomenon of acquiring a concept or learning it which can be separated out from the process of identification. Because of the orientation of research workers in this area and because of the nature of the concepts that have been studied to date, many of the same variables that have been used in verbal learning have been applied to concept learning. Again, Dominowski's review supports the generalization that some of the variables which apply in verbal learning might be applied in concept learning, but by no means is the relationship between the two fields identical. For example, distribution of practice is a relatively weak variable in verbal learning and it is almost without effect in concept learning.

The effectiveness of instance–contiguity is considerable. The clustering of positive instances obviously places a smaller memory requirement on the subject and seems, thereby, to facilitate the identification and learning of concepts. There have been many examples of this facilitation by contiguity, and this generalization seems to apply to a wide class of material. Newman (1956) used simple geometric forms as stimuli and letters of the alphabet as responses. Hovland and Weiss (1953) used more complex geometric forms as stimuli and words as responses. Underwood and Richardson (1956) used words (nouns) as stimuli and words (sense impressions) as responses. In short, the generalization that instance–contiguity has a desirable effect upon identification and the acquisition of concepts seems to stand the test over a wide range of experimental conditions.

Again, probably because of the learning orientation of researchers in concept identification and acquisition, the role of delay of feedback was a "natural" variable to explore. This has been particularly well examined by Bourne and his students (Bourne, 1957; Bourne & Bunderson, 1963). Whereas at first it appeared that the effect of information feedback was the same or at least similar to that which occurred in other forms of learning, it later proved of less importance. The most effective variable was the postinformation feedback interval.

Needless to say, concepts are not only learnable, but this characteristic has been demonstrated in very young children (Kendler, Kendler, & Wells, 1960; Sanders, Ross, & Heal, 1965) as well as in the average college sophomore (e.g., Pishkin & Wolfgang, 1965). Furthermore, the possibility of the acquisition of a concept is not limited only to subjects of normal intelligence (Sanders *et al.*, 1965).

Furthermore, the acquisition of a concept seems to be dependent upon the same reward mechanisms as in other fields of learning. For adults, it may be sufficient to say, "Uh huh," whereas with young children an M & M or even a Cocoa Puff will serve as the necessary reinforcement.

Labelability

Another obvious psychological characteristic of concepts is that they can be *labeled* or *named*. In many studies, the subject is specifically asked to supply the name of the concept as evidence of his having acquired it. In most experiments, however, we have tended to avoid such "introspection" and have, instead, relied upon more objective evidence of the subject's acquisition of a concept, such as requiring a criterion of so many consecutively correct responses before the subject's service is terminated. Even if the subject is not required to provide the label for the concept, it is evident that he is using such labels and names from the conversations he has with himself. The use of labeling or naming is especially evident when the subject is searching through a large number of instances. When, for example, the subject serves in a subset selection experiment and is confronted with a large display of stimuli, we can expect that he will repeat the names of the combination of attributes he is searching for over and over as he continues his search. Some of the less inhibited subjects will even say these aloud so that their use of labeling is quite obvious. Sometimes it is apparent that the subjects have even made up short code names to abbreviate some of the descriptions of the dimensions. Undoubtedly what a subject says to himself while he performs a search for a concept is one of the major variables in concept learning. Regrettably, it is not easy to listen in on the subject's inner speech; so we do the next best thing and try to alter that speech. And one of the less successful experiments designed to alter the probability of concept identification through the use of verbal pretraining was performed by Rasmussen and Archer (1961). Clearly the interest in labelability of concepts derives from the interest in mediational processes which we assume exist. Perhaps this psychological characteristic of concepts, the quality of being labeled or named, is one of the most important characteristics. It seems obvious that if a concept can be named or labeled, we will more easily achieve the first requirement that Hunt (1962) had stated for concepts, namely, the ability to instruct another human as to the nature of the concept. Surely, I can communicate the nature of a concept I have in mind if I give the name of it rather if I use an involved circumlocution and play a "twenty questions" type of game in order to describe the concept. Undoubtedly, the fields of concept identification and concept learning intersect the field of verbal learning on this particular characteristic.

I suspect that as some experimenters discover what subjects say to themselves while trying to solve concept identification problems, and other researchers in the field of verbal learning explore the roles of *representational responses* (Bousfield, Whitmarsh, & Danick, 1958) and *implicit associative responses* (Underwood, 1965), we will discover that we are working on the same problems. Since, as Underwood (1965) indicated, it is possible for a subject to confuse what he has said to himself (the *implicit associative response*) with specific words which were really presented to him, then we can assume that the subject will form concepts by combinations of either or both the representational responses and implicit associative responses made to attributes of stimuli in his world. Accordingly, I suspect that experiments using the Underwood and Richardson materials (1956) the Connecticut word association norms (Bousfield, Cohen, Whitmarsh, & Kincaid, 1961) and the Minnesota norms (Russell & Jenkins, 1954) will become much more common.

In the early years of research in concept formation there was an inclination on the part of experimenters to require subjects to learn nonsense words as labels for the concepts (Heidbreder, 1949; Hull, 1920; Reed, 1946). This use of an artificial label that was meaningless to the subject inevitably delayed the efforts of researchers to examine "what a subject says to himself." Perhaps only the more schizophrenic would talk to themselves in the nonsense languages demanded by Hull, Heidbreder, and Reed. As the subject is permitted to use his own conventional language and, in fact, communicates with that language back to the experimenter, then the possibilities of meaningful manipulations of the subject's inner speech become possible. One illustration of this is suggested in an experiment (Archer, 1962) in which a performance difference between the sexes appeared to depend upon the differential ability of the two sexes to name geometric shapes.

It seems obvious that as the subjects are permitted to use meaningful language in their inner speech and as researchers discover ways of enhancing or diminishing certain elements of that speech, we will thereby be able to control the speech of identification and acquisition of concepts.

TRANSFERABILITY

Another obvious psychological characteristic of concepts is that of transferability. The acquisition of one concept can have a positive or negative effect upon the acquisition of a second concept. There is a considerable history of research in the positive transfer of concepts in the field of animal learning, where this phenomenon of positive transfer has been referred to as learning set (Harlow, 1949) and in humans it has been referred to as learning-to-learn (e.g., Archer *et al.*, 1955). The general characteristic of transferability is easily and simply summarized by saying that subjects apparently learn not only the specific concept at hand but they also learn something about *how* to form concepts. If the concepts are of the same general type, there will be a considerable improvement in performance over successive concepts apparently because of transfer of certain nonspecific skills from one problem to another. A more specific consideration of the transferability of specific skills related to concept learning is found in the literature on reversal and nonreversal shifts (e.g., Kendler & D'Amato, 1955).

In the first of these cases, the interest is in the transfer of fairly nonspecific skills from one concept-learning problem to another. In the second, the interest is in the transfer from one specific task to another and in which the relevance of attributes has been systematically manipulated. Again, this phenomenon of transferability seems to apply to human subjects of all ages, and under certain circumstances mentally retarded children are even superior to normal children (Sanders *et al.*, 1965).

Perhaps a more interesting area of transfer in concept learning is in terms of generalization, and in particular mediated generalization (e.g., Mednick & Freedman, 1960). Once again we come back to the role of implicit verbalizations, or "what the subject says to himself" in the study of concept learning. Another variant of this approach which will surely receive greater attention in the future is the matter of alteration of the meaningfulness of words as defined by a semantic profile (Osgood, 1961) and the subsequent alteration of the mediated generalization which will ensue. Although at first glance it looks like everything is related to everything else, it also seems probable that through a careful analysis of the changes in meaningfulness of words, as measured by a semantic differential profile, it will be possible to predict which concepts are likely to be formed and identified and which will not.

FORGETTABILITY

It seems safe to assume that concepts that are identified, learned, named and generalized, or transferred, can also be forgotten. There really has not been enough research in this area truly to test for the retention of concepts. I suspect that all of us have at some time or another learned some basic concepts in physics or chemistry or mathematics and have since forgotten at least certain parts of these concepts. Over years of nonuse a concept appears to become fuzzy and nonspecific. Although concepts seem to be fairly resistant to forgetting, as compared to isolated words, or even the words used to describe the concept, it would appear that long-term retention studies are needed in this area.

On the positive side, it appears that the concepts can be relearned to a high level with only occasional practice.

Up to this point I have enumerated some of the more obvious psychological aspects of concepts. Moreover, I have also enumerated these in something of a chronological sequence that would be involved when a subject progressed from an initial identification of a concept through its acquisition and through to its forgetting.

There are, however, other interesting psychological aspects of concepts that have received relatively little experimental attention. The reason for the limited attention, I suspect, is because we lack ready experimental paradigms to apply to the study of these aspects.

I would classify these psychological aspects of concepts under the rubric of the *utility* of concepts. In short, what good are they? In a sense I am raising the issue of motivation as to why a subject would be interested in forming a concept.

I think the most eloquent and succinct listing of utility of concepts is found in *A Study of Thinking* by Bruner and associates (1956). They asked and answered their question, "What does the act of rendering things equivalent achieve for the organism?" (p. 11).

They enumerated five achievements:

"... the organism *reduces the complexity of its environment.*

"... categorizing is the *means by which the objects of the world about us are identified.*

"... a category based on a set of defining attributes *reduces the necessity of constant learning.*

"... the *direction it provides for instrumental activity.*

"... the opportunity it permits for *ordering and relating classes of events*" (Bruner *et al.*, 1956, pp. 12-13).

Underlying these five achievements seems to be a basic assumption that an organism is striving to minimize the complexity of its environment, either through reducing "cognitive load" in the immediate world as perceived; or the organism is striving to assure a minimal cognitive load by avoiding surprises just around the corner.

The list of achievements also makes some assumptions, it seems, about the basic inquisitiveness of the organism which may, in fact, be characteristic of the more intelligent members of our society, but I think some of the achievements would be regarded as having little utility for many people. I have in mind in particular the fifth achievement of "the opportunity it permits for ordering and relating classes of events." I suspect the Bruner *et al.* example of "consider the possibility of a nuclear particle whose orbit is a spiral" would *add* to the cognitive strain of some people more than it would reduce it. Nonetheless, Bruner *et al.* have provided an intriguing list of aspects of concepts which deserves closer experimental study than it has received to date. The area of research of *motivation* to formulate concepts includes much of what interests Piaget, but it is broader than just his work.

It seems that a promising area of research would be to identify the variables, both environmental and organismic, which would alter the probability with which an organism would be inclined to reduce the complexity of its environment. I suspect an organism *may* strive to reduce the complexity of its environment if, in fact, it is chaotic, but, on the other hand, that very same organism may seek to search out peculiarities and differences in the elements in its environment in order to optimize its environmental complexity.

Speculating still further on this first achievement, I suspect that the motivation to reduce complexity in the environment may, in fact, be closely related to chronological age and to intelligence. For example, the child who has just learned that the household pet belongs to the species called "dog" seems impelled to assign almost all four-footed animals, whether they be cats, horses, or cows, to this category of "dog." There seems to be, in short, the strong motivation to reduce the complexity of the environment. As the child grows older, however, the need seems either to reduce or the child becomes more sensitive to stimulus differences, which accounts for why dogs are dogs and cats are cats. It seems that the highest levels of intellectual sophistication are achieved when the organism can with ease "reduce the complexity of its environment," and yet at the same time appreciate the subtle differences among the elements within its environment. I think this intellectual and esthetic sophistication is most eloquently described in a sentence in Fitzgibbon's recent *Atlantic* article on the young Dylan Thomas in which he stated, "One of the functions, perhaps the most important and fruitful function, of the artist is to make a pattern out of chaos, to find an imaginative synthesis for the antitheses about him" (1965, p. 63). Now it is quite true, of course, that one can overdo the stimulation of these antitheses, and you end up with Antoine's bizarre world in Sartre's *La Nausée*.

The second achievement of categorizing described by Bruner *et al.*, i.e., "the means by which the objects of the world about us are identified," is, of course, closely related to the first achievement of reducing complexity of the environment. This second achievement, however, points up an interesting motivational property of a concept. "To what extent does the organism's knowledge of a concept motivate him to try out his concept on stimulus objects in his environment to see if they will fit?" I think this is what the child who has just discovered the meaning of the word "dog" does. As this imaginary child goes through his imaginary day, looking at imaginary dogs, his behavior is being controlled by his drive to reduce the complexity of his environment by identifying objects in his world. However, I think this model of behavior has some disturbing implications for the educative process. A logical extension of the model I have described would argue that the concepts which a child first learns will, in fact, affect the nature and the extent of the concepts he will subsequently learn. Until the child is able to specify his concept of "dog" he will probably have considerable difficulty distinguishing between dogs and cats. However, until he has successfully differentiated the two concepts of "dog" and "cat" he will probably have considerable difficulty distinguishing foxes, wolves, hyenas, and domesticated dogs. And, of course, the real world will not leave well enough alone; after our imaginary child has finally figured out all of these beasts, it will be his misfortune to encounter a Tasmanian tiger.

Through all of this exposition and description of the psychological nature of concepts, I have rather carefully avoided much of an involvement with the role of language. At some point we obviously must *do* something about the relationship between words and concepts. In replying to Kendler's paper, I blithely identified words and concepts as essentially the same things. I think, however, a better way of describing the relationship is to think in terms of the meaning of the representational response as equivalent to the concept. This, however, puts the final complicating touch to a description of the psychological nature of concepts. An experimenter cannot present or manipulate a concept directly.

At best he can present stimuli, which, in turn, induce representational responses which may have meaning for the subject and which, in turn, might be identified as the concept. Essentially, therefore, we have a remote control system with a great deal of slack in the geartrain. The complexity of the problem is magnified still further when one thinks back to Ben Underwood's recent paper on the false recognition produced by implicit verbal responses and comes to realize that the last gear in the train might not even be going in the direction we suspect.

REFERENCES

Archer, E. J. Concept identification as a function of obviousness of relevant and irrelevant information. *J. exp. Psychol.*, 1962, **63**, 616-620.

Archer, E. J. On verbalizations and concepts: Comments on Professor Kendler's paper. In A. W. Melton (Ed.), *Categories of human learning.* New York: Academic Press, 1964. Pp. 237-241.

Archer, E. J., Bourne, L. E., Jr., & Brown, F. G. Concept identification as a function of irrelevant information and instructions. *J. exp. Psychol.*, 1955, **49**, 153-164.

Bourne, L. E., Jr. Effects of delay of information feedback and task complexity on the identification of concepts. *J. exp. Psychol.*, 1957, **54**, 201-207.

Bourne, L. E., Jr., & Bunderson, C. V. Effects of delay of informative feedback and length of postfeedback interval on concept identification. *J. exp. Psychol.*, 1963, **65**, 1-5.

Bourne, L. E., Jr., Guy, D. E., Dodd, D. H., & Justesen, D. R. Concept identification: The effects of varying length and informational components of the intertrial interval. *J. exp. Psychol.*, 1965, **69**, 624-629.

Bourne, L. E., Jr., & Haygood, R. C. The role of stimulus redundancy in concept identification. *J. exp. Psychol.*, 1959, **58**, 232-238.

Bourne, L. E., Jr., & Haygood, R. C. Supplementary report: Effect of redundant relevant information upon the identification of concepts. *J. exp. Psychol.*, 1961, **61**, 259-260.

Bousfield, W. A., Cohen, B. H., Whitmarsh, G. A., & Kincaid, W. D. The Connecticut free association norms. *Tech. Rep. No. 35,* 1961, Univer. of Connecticut, ONR—Contract Nonr—631 (00).

Bousfield, W. A., Whitmarsh, G. A., & Danick, J. J. Partial response identities in verbal generalization. *Psychol. Rep.*, 1958, **4**, 703-713.

Bruner, J. S., Goodnow, Jacqueline J., & Austin, G. A. *A study of thinking.* New York: Wiley, 1956.

Bulgarella, Rosaria G., & Archer, E. J. Concept identification of auditory stimuli as a function of amount of relevant and irrelevant information. *J. exp. Psychol.*, 1962, **63**, 254-257.

Dominowski, R. L. Role of memory in concept learning. *Psychol. Bull.*, 1965, **63**, 271-280.

Fitzgibbon, C. Young Dylan Thomas: The escape to London. *Atlantic*, 1965, **216** (4), 63-70.

Harlow, H. F. The formation of learning sets. *Psychol. Rev.*, 1949, **56**, 51-65.

Heidbreder, Edna. The attainment of concepts: VII. Conceptual achievements during card-sorting. *J. Psychol.*, 1949, **27**, 3-39.

Hovland, C. I., & Weiss, W. Transmission of information concerning concepts through positive and negative instances. *J. exp. Psychol.*, 1953, **45**, 175-182.

Hull, C. L. Quantitative aspects of the evolution of concepts. *Psychol. Monogr.*, 1920, **28**, No. 1 (Whole No. 123).

Hunt, E. B. *Concept learning: An information processing problem.* New York: Wiley, 1962.

Kendler, H. H. The concept of the concept. In A. W. Melton (Ed.), *Categories of human learning.* New York: Academic Press, 1964. Pp. 211-236.

Kendler, H. H., & D'Amato, May F. A comparison of reversal shifts and nonreversal shifts in human concept formation behavior. *J. exp. Psychol.*, 1955, **49**, 165-174.

Kendler, Tracy S., Kendler, H. H., & Wells, Doris. Reversal and nonreversal shifts in nursery school children. *J. comp. physiol. Psychol.*, 1960, **53**, 83-88.

Lordahl, D. S. Concept identification using simultaneous auditory and visual signals. *J. exp. Psychol.*, 1961, **62**, 283-290.

Mednick, S. A., & Freedman, J. L. Facilitation of concept formation through mediated generalization. *J. exp. Psychol.*, 1960, **60**, 278-283.

Newman, S. E. Effects of contiguity and similarity on the learning of concepts. *J. exp. Psychol.*, 1956, **52**, 349-353.

Osgood, C. E. Comments on Professor Bousfield's paper. In C. N. Cofer (Ed.), *Verbal learning and verbal behavior.* New York: McGraw-Hill, 1961. Pp. 91-106.

Pishkin, V., & Wolfgang, A. Number and type of available instances in concept learning. *J. exp. Psychol.*, 1965, **69**, 5-8.

Rasmussen, Elizabeth A., & Archer, E. J. Concept identification as a function of language pretraining and task complexity. *J. exp. Psychol.*, 1961, **61**, 437-441.

Reed, H. B. The learning and retention of concepts. II. The influence of length of series. III. The origin of concepts. *J. exp. Psychol.*, 1946, **36**, 166-179.

Russell, W. A., & Jenkins, J. J. The complete Minnesota norms for responses to 100 words from the Kent-Rosanoff Word Association Test. *Tech. Rep. No. 11*, 1954, Univer. of Minnesota, ONR—Contract No. N8-onr-66216.

Sanders, Barbara, Ross, L. E., & Heal, L. W. Reversal and nonreversal shift learning in normal children and retardates of comparable mental age. *J. exp. Psychol.*, 1965, **69**, 84-88.

Sartre, J. P. *La nausée.* Paris: Gallimard, 1938.

Underwood, B. J. False recognition produced by implicit verbal responses. *J. exp. Psychol.*, 1965, **70**, 122-129.

Underwood, B. J., & Richardson, J. Some verbal materials for the study of concept formation. *Psychol. Bull.*, 1956, **53**, 84-95.

Walker, C. M. Concept identification as a function of amounts of relevant and irrelevant information. Unpublished doctoral dissertation, Univer. of Utah, 1958.

CHAPTER 4

SOME RELATIONSHIPS BETWEEN CONCEPT LEARNING AND VERBAL LEARNING

BENTON J. UNDERWOOD

NORTHWESTERN UNIVERSITY
EVANSTON, ILLINOIS

It can be shown that rote verbal learning tasks elicit responses which are conceptual or categorical in nature. Although we sometimes speak of this as concept utilization, the utility of the responses for learning depends upon the nature of the task. If a list of words includes several instances of a given concept, and if several different concepts are involved in the list, it will be acquired more rapidly as a list than will one in which no apparent conceptual relationships exist among the words. For example, a list consisting of *cow, horse, pig, sheep, robin, bluebird, crow,* and *canary* will be learned more quickly than one in which the eight words do not fit easily into categories (Underwood, 1964). On the other hand, if we construct a paired-associate list in which instances of two different concepts are paired, such as *cow-robin, horse-bluebird, pig-crow, sheep-canary,* the task is one of the most difficult ones we can construct by the use of words (Underwood & Schulz, 1961). The fact that free learning is facilitated by the presence of instances of concepts in a list and that paired-associate learning of a list as constructed above is severely inhibited, suggests that the subject has little if any control over the well-learned categorizing responses. It is not the intent of this paper to trace the implications of such findings other than to note that any interpretation of them must assume that the words as presented elicit implicit associative responses which are conceptual in nature (category names). No other interpretation will account for all the known facts.

If the paired-associate list described above is extended so that in addition to having animal names and bird names paired, there are also pairings of names of countries and names of fish, and pairings of names of flowers and names of insects, the subject, to his detriment in learning, acquires three conjunctive concepts the components of which are themselves category names. That is, he learns that animals and birds go together, countries and fish, and as a third concept, flowers and insects. Such higher-order learning in this case is detrimental to the prescribed paired-associate task because it retards the acquisition of discriminatory cues which are necessary to associate specific instances of the concepts. Such studies show that conceptual responses are elicited persistently in verbal-learning studies and they also show that new concepts may be acquired in the act of learning the list.

The above studies are mentioned to show that the research worker in verbal learning must necessarily deal with categorizing behavior of his subjects. It is probably impossible to give the subject a verbal-learning task in which some form of classificatory responding does not occur. It must follow, therefore, that an understanding of verbal learning depends in part upon an understanding of concept learning and concept utilization. In the present paper, the line of argument will be reversed, the thesis being that an understanding of verbal-learning phenomena may aid our understanding of concept learning. At the minimum, we believe it can be shown that the analytical approach being used in rote learning has relevance to approaches which may be taken in studies of concept learning.

A BASIC PARADIGM

One of the frequently used paradigms in the study of transfer in verbal learning is, in the jargon of the field, the A-B, C-B paradigm—a paradigm wherein successive lists have the same responses but different stimuli. It can be seen that this paradigm, and variants on it to be discussed later, satisfies the usual definition of concept learning when there are two instances. When two or more stimuli come to elicit the same response, implicitly or explicitly, we say a concept has been learned. An extension of the paradigm to include more than two instances of the concept presents no problems. However, in concept studies as such, we normally have the A-B, C-B paradigm represented within a single task or list—not across lists, as the paradigm is used in transfer studies. This minor difference, however, need not mask the fact that the A-B, C-B paradigm fits the definitional requirements of concept learning.

The A-B, C-B paradigm represents concept learning in pure form;

there is minimum similarity between the two stimuli. In fact, in the pure form this paradigm represents the disjunctive concept, where the two or more instances given the same name have little if any apparent similarity and are never presented together. For example, the varieties of behaviors which, in the eyes of the law, are classed as misdemeanors, fit this paradigm rather precisely. Concept learning in many laboratory studies as well as outside the laboratory, however, often involves assigning a common name to events or objects which have some common characteristics, either characteristics given in immediate perception or in terms of functional characteristics. Therefore, in thinking about the relationship between verbal learning and concept learning, we must include variants of stimulus similarities in the A-B, C-B paradigm. When some similarity exists between stimuli we usually note this as an A-B, A'-B paradigm. To include the entire dimension of similarity, therefore, we may assert that concept learning of any type falls at some point on the dimension of stimulus similarity identified at the two extremes as A-B, C-B and A-B, A-B, the latter point merely representing the logical extreme where rote learning and concept learning cannot be distinguished.

In rote learning the A-B, A'-B paradigm will produce positive transfer, and the amount of positive transfer is directly related to stimulus similarity (Hamilton, 1943). The A-B, A'-B paradigm when applied to concept learning includes conjunctive and relational concepts. The A-B, C-B paradigm when used in rote learning may produce negative transfer (Twedt & Underwood, 1959) and, as noted above, may be coordinated with disjunctive concepts. It is probably no coincidence that subjects find conjunctive and relational concepts easier to learn than disjunctive concepts (Hunt & Hovland, 1960). When viewed from the transfer studies in verbal learning, relational and conjunctive concepts have the necessary similarity among the positive instances of the concepts to produce positive transfer, whereas the disjunctive concept does not. If within a single task we had both conjunctive and disjunctive concepts, it seems likely that the disjunctive concept would be learned more slowly. Everything we know about the effects of similarity on transfer would predict this, although if such an experiment has been done it is not known to the present writer.

We need to consider briefly the properties of the response term in the A-B, C-B paradigm and its variants. In the usual rote-learning situation the response term initially holds no relationship to the stimulus term, and must be learned as an independent unit. This situation also obtains for the disjunctive concept, although in some cases the concept name may derive from one of the instances of the concept (as the swung-and-missed "strike" in baseball). Any study that uses neutral terms (such as nonsense words) as the concept name fits the A-B, C-B paradigm as used in verbal learning, and many of the concepts we learn are of this nature. Without a knowledge of Latin the concept name "quadriped" is a nonsense word to most students initially. There are other situations in which concept learning is studied, however, in which the concept name (the B term) is given directly by the display. This is true in the studies in which geometrical forms varying in several dimensions are used. In such cases the B response as a response does not have to be acquired, and there is no associative connection required between the instance and the concept name. Analytically, such studies are valuable because they limit behavior to that involved in selection strategies, but they are not representative of concept learning in the "raw." And of course, our more abstract concepts cannot by definition be given immediate sensory representation and, therefore, require names and associations. In the discussion to follow, therefore, our emphasis will be on concept learning which requires the use of an indicator, usually a word, which is not given directly by the display and which, therefore, requires either the acquisition of a new association or the evocation and perhaps strengthening of an old one. This qualification clearly is a matter of convenience when relating concept learning to factors involved in the verbal learning of the A-B, C-B paradigm and the variants thereon.

BACKWARD ASSOCIATIONS

In an earlier article (Underwood, 1952) the present writer developed a rudimentary orientation to direct certain studies of concept formation and problem solving. One of the assumptions of the orientation was that response contiguity was a critical variable for concept learning or concept recognition, and the response referred to is the B response. It was stated that in order for a relationship among stimuli to be perceived (e.g., for a concept to be formed), responses to the stimuli representing different instances of the concept must be contiguous. To state this another way, if the responses to two or more different stimuli occur in close temporal contiguity, and if the stimuli have some one or more properties in common, discovery of the commonality will be directly related to the contiguity of the responses to the stimuli. In terms of the language of the present paper, this reasoning held only for the A-B, A'-B paradigm.

The reasoning was based on the fact that forgetting occurs over time. If at one point in time the subject is presented with a display and is told that a *gokem* is represented, and if several minutes later a different

display is presented and the subject is told that *gokem* is again represented, forgetting may not allow the subject to remember the features
of the first display. An indirect way of manipulating response contiguity
is to vary the spacing of instances of the same concept within a list by
inserting varying numbers of instances of other concepts. Inserting other
irrelevant concepts between two instances of the same concept makes it
more difficult for the subject to bring the responses to the instances of the
same concept into a contiguous relationship. The importance of contiguity,
as indirectly varied in the above manner, seems to have considerable
support from experimental studies (Dominowski, 1965).

The above orientation is incomplete; there is an implicit assumption
which, if not made, leaves nothing but nonsense in the statement about
the role of contiguity. The principle is that the more contiguous the
responses to instances of the same concept the more likely it was that
the subject would detect similarities among the stimuli, hence, learn to
recognize the concept involved. It is clear, however, that contiguity of
responses is of no consequence unless the stimuli associated with the responses can be remembered. We may illustrate the problem in two tasks;
let the successive presentations of the items be as follows:

$$
\begin{array}{ll}
14-Z & 14-Z \\
48-Z & 23-X \\
& 58-Y \\
& 48-Z
\end{array}
$$

In the two-item illustration on the left the common response to the two
stimuli occurs in immediate succession and, according to the principle
of contiguity, the common element in the stimuli (4) should be more
readily detectable than in the illustration on the right where the two
instances are separated by instances of other concepts. The theory must
necessarily assume that if the subject is given the response for a previous
instance of a concept he can remember or reconstruct the stimulus.
Response contiguity has no meaning for concept learning unless it is
related to the ease of recall of the stimuli that go with the responses. In
the above illustrations, when A occurs the second time, we must assume
that the subject, in a manner of speaking, asks himself what stimulus went
with that response earlier. To answer his own question, the subject must
get from Z back to the original stimulus. But, given that this stimulus
term could be remembered, and given the second stimulus term directly,
the contiguity notion said that only under these circumstances would
the subject be able to detect the commonality of the stimulus terms.

The implicit assumption in the notion was that the subject *could* get from Z back to the stimulus, but in 1952 we had no available knowledge which would allow us to say that such an assumption was reasonable. We merely assumed that it was possible. Shortly thereafter, however, studies were undertaken using paired-associate lists to determine if, following learning, the subject could produce the appropriate stimulus term if given the response term. These studies were done initially to see if backward associations, as they are now commonly called, were present following the learning of a forward association. If such associations existed, the mechanisms by which response contiguity influenced concept learning could be considered complete. As is known, backward associations do, indeed, exist following the acquisition of forward associations, and a number of investigators, for quite different reasons apparently, became interested at about the same time in studying backward associations. There is now a rather vast literature on the topic. The only point we wish to make here is that backward associations are operationally real; the subject can recapture the stimulus term in greater or lesser detail following the learning of the forward association. Probably no one was surprised at the demonstrations of backward associations, but the fact that they are relatively strong associations did, perhaps, surprise some. Of course, for any well-learned concept or well-learned association, the reversibility is quite apparent, e.g., *horse* will lead to *animal* and *animal* to *horse*.

As noted above, when the pure A-B, C-B paradigm is used in a transfer study in verbal learning we may expect a small amount of negative transfer. There is inferential evidence that this is caused by the presence of the backward association (B-A) interfering with the learning of a new backward association (B-C). There is no reason why this same interference should not occur within a single task in acquiring a disjunctive concept. The major point, however, is that we must recognize that concept learning at some stage involves the development of a word association between an instance of a concept and the concept name, and that the moment a forward association is developed, a backward association is also present.

STIMULUS SELECTION AND STIMULUS BIAS

If the stimuli of a paired-associate list consist of two or more discrete elements (e.g., two letters, two words), the association may be formed between only one of the elements of the stimulus and the response term. Such stimulus selection may be demonstrated by transfer tests in which the second-list stimuli consist of only one of the stimulus elements. In extreme cases the selection may be complete and nearly universal across subjects. Thus, if a common word and a difficult trigram make up a stimulus compound, the transfer tests show that the performance is nearly perfect when the word is used as the formal stimulus, but nearly zero when the trigram is used (Spear, Ekstrand, & Underwood, 1964). From a certain point of view, the laws of stimulus selection seem quite reasonable, but from another they appear to represent the tapping of biases which do not, in fact, reflect accurately the laws which govern the learning. Two illustrations may be given. We noted that subjects will overwhelmingly select a common word as the functional stimulus when both the word and a difficult trigram are paired consistently with the response. If the trigrams are used as the only stimuli in one list and the words as the only stimuli in another, however, there may or may not be a difference in the rate of learning the two lists. Stimulus meaningfulness has a relatively small effect on learning (and there are investigations which have shown no effect), and yet the subjects when given a choice will "choose" to learn the list with words as stimuli. A second illustration comes from a study in which each compound consisted of a common word and a frame of easily labeled colored paper (Underwood, Ham, & Ekstrand, 1962). In this situation the selection of the word over the color as the functional stimulus was roughly 2 to 1. When other groups learned lists in which either the words or the color frames were stimuli, however, there was no difference in the rate at which the two lists were learned. The usual college-student subject can identify with great accuracy how easy or how difficult a given verbal unit will be to learn as a unit in free learning. However, he seems much less capable of distinguishing the ease or difficulty with which a given stimulus will enter into an association. This suggests, therefore, that certain stimulus biases or preferences must to a certain extent determine stimulus selection.

The study of concept learning *is* the study of stimulus selection. The crux of concept learning is the abstraction—selection—of a common feature, characteristic, or property which is present in a number of stimuli which differ on other characteristics. Indeed, if we were to contrast rote learning and concept learning at the point where a contrast is most meaningful, we would say that stimulus selection is an interesting by-product of rote learning but a necessity in concept learning. At the same time, however, the laws that govern stimulus selection in both cases may turn out to be very similar.

We must first recognize that just as in verbal learning, stimulus selection in concept formation is heavily determined by biases and preferences. In spite of the fact that a subject may know that all characteristics of a stimulus display have equal likelihoods of entering into the appropriate concept, the choices are not random. This is most clearly seen in the study by Wallace (1964). He explained to subjects the nature of two-attribute concepts. He then presented them with cards having four attributes and across cards the attributes had three different levels. All cards were present simultaneously and the subject was asked to emit as many two-attribute concepts as possible. The emissions were not random, and there was considerable agreement among subjects on the order of emission. Subsequently, when Wallace had new subjects discover appropriate two-attribute concepts, the rate at which the discoveries were made was accurately reflected in the order of emission of two-attribute concepts by the first group of subjects. Different attributes or characteristics of stimuli have different degrees of dominance for the subject, and concept learning is difficult when the dominant attributes are incorrect. For any given problem the dominant attributes may be quite irrelevant, but it is unlikely that they are irrelevant in the long run history of the organism. Although some types of attributes may have more direct perceptual compellingness than do others, when considering concepts which are formed without reference to the perceptual characteristics of the instances of the objects, dominance is still found. This must mean, therefore, that the dominance has grown because it has been serviceable; the initial attack on a problem makes use of dominant characteristics because those characteristics have been successful in the past. The organism is quite sensitive to variation in environmental probabilities, and it is reasonable to believe that dominance in stimulus selection represents the end product of probability learning. A problem to be solved or a concept to be learned at the moment becomes difficult when the dominance habits are inappropriate.

The experimental investigation of stimulus selection is a relatively new area in verbal learning, and we do not know very much about the preference habits of our subjects. But, upon the relationship between stimulus selection in verbal learning and stimulus selection on concept formation, two points by way of summary seem relevant. The first is that as the facts grow about stimulus selection in verbal learning, our understanding of the processes of concept formation must also grow since, as was insisted earlier, concept formation is basically the study of stimulus selection. There are many studies that can be done which would be directly relevant to the understanding of concept formation. For example, to the best of the writer's knowledge, no one has investigated stimulus selection habits as a function of an abstract-concrete dimension. Such work might be pertinent to the understanding of the problems that occur in forming abstract concepts. As another illustration, we know little about the development of selection habits, their strength, nor how easily they may be modified. Let us assume that if a study of stimulus selection were performed in which clear preferences were demonstrated for dealing with concrete words, could we, by making it pay, teach the subject to reverse this selection habit and to deal with the abstract initially?

The second general summary point about stimulus selection relates to a problem of method. The experiments studying stimulus selection use a transfer technique, but the technique is concerned with the transfer only because it allows direct inferences about the nature of the learning which occurred in the original task. There seems to be no reason why it should not be an appropriate procedure for studying certain problems in concept formation. For example, we have seen that subjects usually learn conjunctive concepts more readily than disjunctive concepts. But suppose the subject is forced to learn a two- or three-value disjunctive concept in one task and then, on a second task, the attributes defining the disjunctive concept become the relevant attributes in a conjunctive concept. Will the stimulus dominance, hence the stimulus selection, be changed?

As another illustration, assume that four unrelated words are used as stimulus terms and a single word (the concept name) as the common response for all four stimuli. This is a rote-learning task but fits the definitional requirements of concept learning. A critical question, however, is whether or not the four words will "behave" as if they were conceptually related when used in a new task. For example, would there be interference if in a subsequent paired-associate task the subject were required to learn different responses to the four items?

RESPONSE LEARNING AND ASSOCIATIVE LEARNING

The division of the learning of a paired-associate list into two phases, response learning and associate learning, is a fairly gross breakdown but even at the gross level has considerable analytical value. Variables that influence positively the acquisition of responses may influence associative formation negatively although some variables may facilitate both stages. There is a direct application of these stages, and what we know about them, to the study of concept learning. It is the purpose of this section to discuss some of these applications.

The speed at which a verbal unit is acquired as a unit (response learning) is enormously affected by the meaningfulness of that unit. At every level of our educational system we require our students to learn words, often concept names, which vary in meaningfulness from very high to very low. That this is even a tolerable situation stems from the fact that we may often code our technical terms so that the word implies the concept, i.e., it may be generated from an instance or it may be derived from Latin and Greek roots if the student has a knowledge of these languages. Yet there are a great number of technical terms for which this is not possible and there is no recourse for the student but to memorize the concept name, and our best evidence at the present is that this memorization can occur only by practice at emitting the word. Many of the early studies of concept learning required the subject to learn a nonsense word to indicate each concept. These studies were not unrealistic representations of normal concept learning, but it must have been a considerable surprise to some when it was demonstrated (Richardson & Bergum, 1954) that most of the learning time involved in such studies consisted of acquiring the responses and forming the associations with only a small proportion of the total time actually involved in concept learning as such.

The meaningfulness of the response term determines its rate of acquisition, and insofar as concept names differ in meaningfulness, the laws of meaningfulness as determined from studies in verbal learning should be directly applicable. Since, in learning a concept, the class name is used or rehearsed once for every instance of the concept, the response learning should occur relatively fast.

The associative phase in verbal learning is not an extended phase such as that required for the integration of responses. The fact that there can be a disagreement between one-trial and incremental-learning theorists indicates that the associative phase in the usual situation may occur very quickly. As noted above, if in concept learning the coding is such that the stimulus term (an instance of a concept) directly suggests the class name, the associative learning phase should occur very quickly. At the same time, however, there is one variable which profoundly influences the associative phase in verbal learning and which also has been shown to influence the acquisition of concepts as such, and probably for the same reason that it influences verbal learning. This variable is intralist stimulus similarity, and its importance in both verbal learning and concept learning has long been recognized (e.g., Gibson, 1940). For the present purposes, the discussion will be limited to similarity resulting from associative overlap.

We noted at the outset that verbal learning could be seriously retarded if words obviously belonging to the same class were stimuli for different responses. The moment the same response is used for all instances of the class, however, learning will occur in one trial. In acquiring a concept from "scratch," a concept in which the instances do not mediate the concept name directly (as when the concept name is a nonsense word), we presume that when learning is complete the concept name will be elicited implicitly when the subject hears or sees an instance. The word *eagle* will elicit *bird* as an implicit response with very high frequency, but under appropriate instructions it can be shown that *eagle* will also produce a number of other associated words, perhaps *big, remote,* or *bald.* Insofar as the names for other quite different objects may elicit these same associates, there is a basis for the existence of new concepts —concepts which have never been recognized. Such word materials, therefore, provide a means for the study of concept recognition and interference in concept recognition with college students under quite realistic circumstances.

Among the studies done with such materials was one in which we varied what we call concept overlap (Underwood, 1957). When objects are described in terms of sensory attributes, the number of words available for such description is sharply limited. Therefore, when concrete nouns are described by sensory characteristics we discover that many not obviously related objects are occasionally given the same descriptive associates. These associates may be used to devise "new" concepts, i.e., to relate objects in a manner in which they have not been previously related. That *village, crumb, minnow,* and *atom* are related by a common descriptive characteristic (*small*) is an illustration.

Pursuing this line of thought, it can be seen that if the subject is required to learn several such "new" concepts at the same time, we may use stimulus words which "throw out" irrelevant, distracting, and interfering associates. In more technical language we say that, although there is necessarily similarity (defined by common associates) among the instances of a concept, there is, under a high-overlap condition, also high similarity among instances of different concepts. The result is a difficult stimulus selection task for the subject. However, it may be argued that this is a very realistic situation in that it is one faced by all of us when we attempt to draw together seemingly disparate concept instances or disparate phenomena into a new concept based upon commonalities that have not been perceived before. Indeed, some have speculated that the ability to perceive remote commonalities is one of the ingredients in creativity (Mednick, 1962). Whether this is correct or not, the evidence indicates that the ability to detect unusual relationships among objects or events is difficult because of interference from the strong associates defining already recognized concepts.

IMPLICIT ASSOCIATIVE RESPONSES

As a final section to this brief excursion into some relationships between concept learning and verbal learning, we may make explicit an underlying theme. A great many verbal-learning phenomena exist only because verbal units produce implicit associative responses. Mediation, transfer, interference, forgetting, similarity effects, meaningfulness effects, and so on, are based on the elicitation of implicit associative responses. Verbal learning cannot exist as an analytical endeavor without attending to the implications of implicit associative responses. It has been an underlying theme of this paper that the study of concept learning is also vitally concerned with the implicit associative response. In learning a new concept the associative responses to instances of the concept must be identical. The act of learning a new concept is the act of acquiring these identical associates so that they will be immediately and consistently elicited. This is what verbal learning is all about. In detecting new relationships among objects or events, the concept-formation task is essentially a problem-solving task in which there is a search for common associative responses among the many produced by the objects and events. These associations had to be established sometime, and how they are established is the province of verbal learning. That a new instance of a concept can be readily classified can only occur because it elicits an implicit associative response that defines the concept. In short, the study of concept learning is the study of the acquisition and utilization of common associates to different objects and events. The study of the development of associative responses *is* the study of verbal learning as is also the study of the implications of their elicitation after development. Given this orientation, it is sometimes difficult to make a distinction between concept learning and verbal learning.

REFERENCES

Dominowski, R. L. Role of memory in concept learning. *Psychol. Bull.*, 1965, **63**, 271-280.

Gibson, E. J. A systematic application of the concepts of generalization and differentiation to verbal learning. *Psychol. Rev.*, 1940, **47**, 196-229.

Hamilton, R. Jane. Retroactive facilitation as a function of degree of generalization between tasks. *J. exp. Psychol.*, 1943, **32**, 363-376.

Hunt, E. B., & Hovland, C. I. Order of consideration of different types of concepts. *J. exp. Psychol.*, 1960, **59**, 220-225.

Mednick, S. A. The associative basis of the creative process. *Psychol. Rev.*, 1962, **69**, 220-232.

Richardson, J., & Bergum, B. O. Distributed practice and rote learning in concept formation. *J. exp. Psychol.*, 1954, **47**, 442-446.

Spear, N. E., Ekstrand, B. R., & Underwood, B. J. Association by contiguity. *J. exp. Psychol.*, 1964, **67**, 151-161.

Twedt, H. M., & Underwood, B. J. Mixed vs. unmixed lists in transfer studies. *J. exp. Psychol.*, 1959, **58**, 111-116.

Underwood, B. J. An orientation for research on thinking. *Psychol. Rev.*, 1952, **59**, 209-220.

Underwood, B. J. Studies of distributed practice: XV. Verbal concept learning as a function of intralist interference. *J. exp. Psychol.*, 1957, **54**, 33-40.

Underwood, B. J. The representativeness of rote verbal learning. In A. W. Melton (Ed.), *Categories of human learning.* New York: Academic Press, 1964. Pp. 47-78.

Underwood, B. J., & Schulz, R. W. Studies of distributed practice: XXI. Effect of interference from language habits. *J. exp. Psychol.*, 1961, **62**, 571-575.

Underwood, B. J., Ham, M., & Ekstrand, B. Cue selection in paired-associate learning. *J. exp. Psychol.*, 1962, **64**, 405-409.

Wallace, J. Concept dominance, type of feedback, and intensity of feedback as related to concept attainment. *J. educ. Psychol.*, 1964, **55**, 159-166.

CHAPTER 5

MEANINGFULNESS AND CONCEPTS; CONCEPTS AND MEANINGFULNESS

JAMES J. JENKINS
UNIVERSITY OF MINNESOTA
MINNEAPOLIS, MINNESOTA

I was originally asked to write on "the role of meaningfulness in the learning of concepts." I took this to imply concern with the number of associates given to particular stimuli and the role of relevant and irrelevant associates in achieving or delaying concept formation or identification. Such ground has already been well covered by Dr. Archer and Dr. Underwood in their excellent chapters (3 and 4) and they have suggested appropriate directions of attack. Fortunately, for the sake of the reader, I reread the suggestions for discussion that accompanied the topic and decided that my first reading was in error. The questions included "What are the most promising methods of assessing the *meaningfulness of concepts?*" and "To what extent are there differences in the *meaningfulness of concepts?*"

At this point the task became much simpler and much harder. It became much simpler because I think one must argue that "meaningfulness" is *not* a property of concepts. It became harder because it was clear that I would have to make that argument and try to spell out its consequences. In the course of the writing it seemed to me that the basic issue was somehow inverted—that meaningfulness had no direct relation to concepts but that concepts might have a powerful relation to meaningfulness. This idea, I shall attempt to illustrate later in the chapter.

CONCEPTS, STIMULI, AND MEANINGFULNESS

Let us first consider why it is that concepts cannot be said to have "meaningfulness." Meaningfulness is a venerable term in the verbal learning tradition and one with which a writer would tamper only under great provocation. It is ordinarily held to be measured by indices such as the number of subjects reporting an association in the presence of the stimulus, the number of associations to a stimulus per unit time, and the subjective appraisal of associative richness by a subject, objectified by a rating scale. All these measures appeal to responses of subjects in the presence of the stimulus when the subjects have a particular set of instructions. It is obvious that all these operations require a stimulus to be responded to and it is to the stimulus that the meaningfulness attaches. I want it to be painfully clear that I am going to insist that *a concept is not a stimulus*. A concept is, rather, a construct, in every sense equivalent to constructs in scientific theory and no more directly available than such constructs usually are.

Consider the construct "a word in English." How shall I define its meaningfulness? No matter what procedure I choose, I must have a word or a set of words to be rated, and it will be those particular ratings of those particular stimuli rather than "the concept" that is summarized in the meaningfulness measure.

Alternatively, I might seek the meaningfulness of more traditional concepts such as those Heidbreder used in her classic experiment. Any particular instance I choose can be appraised—say I choose the card showing six birds—and the meaningfulness of the stimulus will be specified by that appraisal but the meaningfulness of the concept "six" is beyond my reach. It must be presented in particularized form. If I present the word "six" instead of six items, I only appear to solve the problem. An association to "six" such as "bricks" makes clear the fact that the word, too, is a particular stimulus with properties of its own which affect the associative distribution.

It may be helpful to approach this problem from still another point of view. Elementary textbooks sometimes talk of concepts as being represented in stimuli or being identifiable in different sets of stimuli. The concept *a red patch* is presumably represented in every red patch but it is clear that it is not identical with any particular one of them nor could it be. The issue here is readily seen to be the same as that involved in the older discussions of "images." "What triangle is *the image* of triangle?" The answer, of course, had to be that no particular image could serve, precisely because it *was* particular and, therefore, could not be the image that was "matched" when one said some other stimulus was a triangle. The fruitlessness of the debate on images should suggest to us that this is the wrong way to approach the problem. Surely, we must consider more complex notions of what a concept is than the notion that it is some stimulus invariant, isolated as a cue by some process that stores a family of instances and then somehow identifies what is common to the physical display of all of them.

To say that the concept is in some way "available" or identifiable in the stimulus attributes of any particular exemplar is false, I suspect, not only in special cases but in the usual and general case. When I see a colleague, I may say that he is an example of a *bearded man*. This chooses an intersection of concepts each of which is more or less identifiable on the basis of physical properties (although we may have a terrible time specifying what the sets of stimulus cues are supposed to be). In addition, I have chosen classes or concepts which are supposed to combine in a known and unambiguous fashion (note that I might not be sure what was meant by "bearded lion" or "lion man"). This is the kind of example that encourages one to continue with the struggle of assigning physical attributes to the delineation of a concept. But the inappropriateness of the approach can be immediately sensed when I go on to point out that he is a psychologist, a Unitarian, a father, a musician, or, indeed, as I said at the outset, a colleague. These kinds of concepts are not to be identified in the stimulus but rather in *my knowledge* of the stimulus person.

At this point it is fashionable to say that I ought not to talk in this careless fashion, that I should not say "my knowledge of the stimulus" but rather I should say that the important properties are not in the stimulus but rather in my "responses to the stimulus." This is, of course, the approach taken by all mediation theories and to the extent that any theory deals with "concepts" currently it must *at least* be mediational. But even here there is disappointment. It must also be clear that it is the "potential response" rather than the actual response that identifies an instance of a concept. In the case of my colleague, you may well seek to exhaust my possible responses to his name, his picture, or to him, physically present as a stimulus object. Having worn yourself out you may not yet have discovered that he belongs to the class, member of Democratic-Farmer-Labor party, friend, nearsighted people who hate fat meats, or arbitrarily many other classes to which he may belong and of which I have knowledge and might admit him as an instance if you had asked me. Certainly, his membership in a class and my recognition of it is not contingent on my volunteering the information under some general set of instructions to respond. Indeed, I may recognize his membership in a class which had never before been defined for me if you create such a class in terms which I can understand (e.g., tank commanders of World War II who were wounded in the right knee in France in 1944).

My actual responses may further be positively misleading as to the relevance of the stimulus to some particular concept. In the course of responding to the stimulus of my colleague, it is quite likely that I would be led to name his wife and the art in his home which she collects. In the uninterpreted responses there is nothing to guide one as to the properties that he possesses and those possessed by his surround and thus "merely associated" with him. The brute fact is that until my responses are utilized or put to work in some as yet unspecified way I do not know what bearing they have on any concept. *Tables* are not *chairs* and *black* is not *white* yet these are strong bidirectional associates. Whether they are instances of the same concept depends on what concepts are employed. Then, depending on the task at hand, the observed behavioral relationship, i.e., the fact of their association, may be facilitating, interfering, or irrelevant. Associative networks provide an important part of the material on which other orderings and relationships can be imposed and against which requirements and specification may be checked. This does not mean that "checking" is easy. To see a stimulus as an instance of a particular concept or to see how it relates to a more general conceptual scheme may be a great intellectual feat or a trivial exercise akin to running a batch of cards through an IBM machine to pick off all that have a "9" in the second column. But, surely, it is not *merely* the latter.

THREE KINDS OF CONCEPTS

Perhaps, the orientation of this paper can be made clearer by considering concepts to belong to three general classes. The first class is that of concepts that depend on the isolation of some aspect (or set of aspects) of the stimuli which are instances of that concept. The second class is that of concepts that depend on community or agreement of particular responses to the stimuli. The third class is that of concepts that are constructs in general systems of relationships. Instances may be recognized by submitting them to some test procedure or set of procedures. Neither the test procedures nor the rules of the concept system may be clear to the subject who possesses the concept.

Consider the first class. At the first level, so to speak, we can talk of concepts that are dependent on shared characteristics of the physical stimulus. This kind of concept-formation study began to appear in the literature in the 1920's. Concepts of this class may be very complex in expression (as in taxonomic zoology) or very simple (as in the psychologists' concept identification experiments with children and animals). The important aspect for our purpose is that these concepts may be made *explicit* in the form of physical characteristics present in the stimulus display itself. Presumably, the subject needs to learn what to look for and where and how to look; in extreme cases he may even need an elaborate check list to work from and require special apparatus. But the psychological problem involved in such concept identification does not seem particularly deep. (The parallel "simple process" is presumably primary stimulus generalization.)

The second kind of concept is seen emerging in the literature in the late 1930's and early 1940's. This concept is defined in terms of a common response or set of responses which the subject makes to disparate physical stimuli. In this case the invariance is moved from the stimuli to the subject's behavior (and sometimes right out of sight). The simplest case is mediation through "naming" or "labeling" responses. The parallel simple process is secondary stimulus generalization.

The third kind of concept, and the one that I want to call to your attention, is that based on systematic relations; a concept that has its existence in a body of rules and that can be identified by testing procedures involving these rules in some fashion even though no simple labels or common features can be identified. Examples abound, I believe, for I think these are the most common of all concepts, but I must choose from those with which I am best acquainted. A very complex concept might be illustrated by the following:

S_1 The boy hit the ball
S_2 Elephants trumpet at midnight
S_3 of Soldiers the street down march

The first two stimuli exemplify a particular concept; the third does not. The first two are English sentences; the third is not. *Why* this is so is difficult to say, but *that* it is so is readily agreed. Any bypassing of the problem by saying the concept is simply a function of the tendency to label familiar sequences as English sentences can be refuted by "odd" sentences that we all agree are sentences but have low probability values (e.g., "The green cows on the cloud are eating pancakes") and relatively high probability sequences which are not (e.g., ". . . boy and girls are always doing what you please is a word of . . ."). Nor is it fruitful to say that the concept is the result of the common mediating response which one makes to these stimuli, e.g., "That is a sentence in English," since we cannot explain how that response comes to be made to an infinite variety of stimuli. The same argument holds for identification of parts of speech, sentence types, intersentential relations, awareness of underlying linguistic structure, perception of speech sounds, etc.

It must be clear that all three kinds of concepts are important (indeed, they are distinct kinds only for purposes of pedagogy). The first two are neither unnecessary or trivial though they could be subsumed under the third kind. The first involves important orderings of the world and the second mediates many kinds of thinking and problem solving. But the time has come when we must seriously attend to the third kind of concept, difficult though it may be for present psychological theories. This kind of concept has precisely the same status as a construct in a scientific theory. It need not be immediately available, nor directly observable but may rest on an inferential base specified only by its systematic relationships.

LINGUISTIC CONCEPTS AS DETERMINERS OF MEANINGFULNESS

The notion of a concept as being identified by a set of rules can lead one to a rather interesting consequence. Although we must argue that concepts do not have meaningfulness as it is usually defined, conceptual systems may, nevertheless, play an important role in determining the meaningfulness of stimuli. This can be illustrated by examples from research on language.

The work that follows was performed in collaboration with Joseph H. Greenberg, the distinguished anthropologist–linguist whose penetrating insights into linguistic structure and indefatigable analytic zeal made these studies possible. The research began in 1958–1959 when Greenberg was concerned with the problem of the "virtual syllable." This is an old linguistic problem. When one has written the rules for syllable formation in a particular language one is always confronted with the fact that not all possible entries exist (or rather one usually does not know whether they exist or not; one must say he has not yet found them). This is not surprising to the psychologist but it is troublesome to the linguist since he cannot be sure he has written his rules "tightly" enough, unless he finds instances of everything that is possible. But this creates an interesting psychological problem—given that two sequences of sound are not English words, what meaning does it have to say that one of them *could* be and the other one *couldn't* be? Or given two sequences, neither of which could be English words, what does it mean to say that one of them violates fewer rules and thus is more like English than the other?

In the psychological literature, Ebbinghaus (1913) struggled with exactly the same problem (though he did not guess its linguistic foundation) as he studied the nonsense syllables he had invented.

". . . the homogeneity of the series of syllables falls considerably short of what might be expected of it. These series exhibit very important and almost incomprehensible variation as to ease or difficulty with which they are learned. It even appears from this point of view as if the differences between sense and nonsense material were not nearly so great as one would be inclined *a priori* to imagine" (Ebbinghaus, 1913, p. 23).

Greenberg's general hypothesis was that the variations in response to "the probability of something being a word" as well as the variations of meaningfulness of nonsense syllables were attributable to the degree to which the novel stimuli accorded with or departed from the rule structures of syllable and word formation in English.

In English, and probably in all languages, the sequences of phonemes (elementary speech sounds) which may occur are subject to powerful constraints. Let us suppose that we are playing a game, such as anagrams, where we draw at random a sequence of English phonemes. If we draw sets of six symbols and keep the order in which they are originally drawn, the overwhelming majority will not be existent English sequences. As an example, we might well draw a sequence such as *g v s u r s*. This is, of course, a nonexistent sequence in English. (It should be noted that this sequence is not "impossible" in any universal sense. It is, in fact, a word in Georgian.) Something further can be said, however, for in a certain sense it is an "impossible" combination. Thus we would not be tempted to look it up in a dictionary to discover whether it might be a rare word that we just happened not to know. We would, further, feel safe in predicting that no soap manufacturer would use it as a brand name for his product.

Let us draw a second time, this time taking three phonemes. Suppose that we draw *d i b* in that order. Let us further suppose that we are unacquainted with any word *dib*, just as was the case with *gvsurs*. There will be this difference, however; in the case of *dib* we would be quite willing to look it up in the dictionary or assume its possible coinage as a brand name or slang expression in the future. Indeed, *The Oxford English Dictionary* does list a word *dib* meaning, among other things, a counter used in playing at cards as a substitute for money.

Let us now draw a third time, taking three phonemes. On this occasion we obtain the sounds that we would represent in spelling as *lut* or *lutt*. Surely we would be willing to look this up and would half expect to find it in a large dictionary. But even the unabridged Oxford dictionary in this case gives no such word. It seems, then, that some things which are not in English, such as *lut*, are more "possible" than others which are not, such as *gvsurs*.

Linguists have established a set of rules regarding such possible combinations. These are rules of patterning for the English syllable which have been constructed on the basis of sequences found in existent forms. Thus, *gvsurs* would immediately be declared impossible, among other considerations, because all existent English syllables that begin with as many as three consonants (the upper limit) have an initial *s*, a medial unvoiced stop (*p*, *t*, or *k*) and final liquid or semivowel (*r*, *l*, *w*, or *y*). Thus another nonexistent sequence, such as *strab*, would not have been ruled out by these considerations because it contains an initial consonant sequence *str-* which conforms to this rule. In fact, *strab* obeys this and all other rules for the patterning of English syllables, though it, like *lut*, happens not to exist.

On the basis of the rule set we have a simple threefold division of sequences we might draw. Every sound sequence will be "possible" if it conforms to rules such as the above [which are to be found in Whorf (1956)] or "impossible" if not. Among the "possible" ones some will be found in a dictionary and some will not. Thus, we have (1) impossible sequences, (2) possible but not actual sequences, and (3) actual sequences. These are illustrated by *gvsurs*, *strab*, and *struk* (struck), respectively.

But the situation is not merely one of such gross categorizations. Pursuing the same general line of attack we can discover still finer divisions which are reasonable. Going back to our game, let us suppose that we now draw *stwip*. Here the first consonant group, *stw*, conforms to the general rule for initial sequences described above; *s*, followed by unvoiced stop (in this case *t*), followed by liquid or semivowel (in this case *w*); yet in this instance we will in all probability not be tempted to look it up in a dictionary. This is because *stw* does not occur as an initial sequence in any English word whatsoever. It can, however, be educed by analogy from *skr*: *skw* :: *str* : ? , where *skr*, *skw*, and *str* all occur (e.g., in *script*, *square*, and *strap*). Here we evidently have a case which is, so to speak, not quite so possible as *strab* but certainly more possible than *gvsurs*.

As these examples suggest, we can go on to construct a scale of "distance from English" depending on degree of conformity to permissible English sequences of sound structure. At one extreme we have sequences actually found in English and at the other those which we know deviate most drastically, with impermissible sounds and orders. Greenberg did exactly that, developing a 16-step scale by the systematic use of the common linguistic procedure of sound substitution. The linguistic details of the scale need not concern us here except to note that the scale was a rational one, developed from the logical base of the linguistic rules for syllable construction in English.

Following the development of the scale, Greenberg generated instances (i.e., particular monosyllables) at various points on the scale. We then tested these instances for perceived psychological distance from English as judged by native English speakers. The research, reported elsewhere (Greenberg & Jenkins, 1964), is a dramatic demonstration of the mapping of a psychological dimension (judged distance from English) by a logical–rational dimension. For every additional linguistic step away from English, the psychological distance increased by one unit as shown in

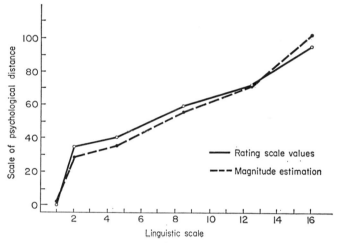

Fig. 1. Relation between linguistic and psychological distance.

Fig. 1. It turned out, in addition, that this correspondence between psychological judgment and linguistic rationale was extraordinarily robust in terms of the kinds of psychological measurement employed, magnitude estimation, or category rating scales.

The results from the magnitude estimation experiments correlated + .94 with the linguistic scale whereas the results from the category scale correlated + .95 with the linguistic scale. The two psychological techniques correlated + .99.

We then went on in a separate experiment to evaluate the meaningfulness of the test stimuli. We presented the stimuli in the same fashion as in the scaling experiment and allowed the subjects 15 seconds to write down associates to each stimulus. The median number of associates per syllable correlates with the magnitude estimation values — .84, with the rating scale values — .84, and with the linguistic scale itself — .75. In this case, then, meaningfulness appears to be a derived value that reflects how well a stimulus fits into the linguistic–conceptual–logical net which defines a syllable in English.

It should be noticed that this study reverses the usual psychological pattern. Rather than determining meaningfulness in order to structure a stimulus domain, it ordered a stimulus domain on extrapsychological grounds and then observed the resulting meaningfulness. Similarly, this study implies a change in emphasis in interpretation. Perhaps meaningful stimuli are not related to a host of concepts because they have many associates; the reverse may be true. Stimuli which are systematically related to a host of concepts (i.e., which readily enter into the rule sets which define concepts) have more associates as a consequence.

LINGUISTIC ANALYSIS OF NONSENSE SYLLABLES

But it may be argued that these experiments constitute special cases in which only a few stimuli are generated and that there may be all sorts of biases working in the generation and selection of instances which predetermine the outcome of the experiments. A much more general case is posed by the body of data existing on the set of all consonant-vowel-consonant "syllables" collected by psychologists as part of the operation of norming materials for learning experiments. These materials are, of course, biased in other directions: orthography has been allowed to determine what a vowel or a consonant is; not all combinations are actually used (e.g., syllables which begin and end with the same consonant are avoided and sometimes all real words are avoided); visual presentations are employed; etc. Nevertheless, if one is willing to make a set of simplifying assumptions, it is possible to arrange at least an approximate linguistic analysis of the data.

We began with the assumption that the subject applies normative rules to the orthographic stimulus to attempt pronounciation. If he can pronounce it, he checks it against his knowledge of English words. If it is an English word, he checks the spelling to make sure that it is acceptable. Thus when the subject sees *KOT* we assume that he attempts to pronounce it and comes up with "*k o t*" which he recognizes as an English word (cot) but which he must also realize is incorrect orthographically. When he sees *COT* we assume that he goes through the same operations but that the orthography conforms to the norm and thus the combination achieves a higher rating. Archer's norms (1960) show that *KOT* is judged meaningful by 86% whereas *COT* is judged meaningful by 100%. Proceeding in this fashion, we can readily recognize a four-step scale such as the following:

1. COT   pronounceable, an English word, spelled correctly
2. KOT   pronounceable, an English word, spelled incorrectly
3. BOD   pronounceable, not a word
4. XYM   not pronounceable

This almost seems to be what Archer had in mind when he instructed his subjects: "Is this a word? Does it sound like a word? Does it remind me of a word?"

This scale can be expanded by introducing an additional distinction for words that are analogically pronounceable (e.g., SAF can be pronounced but it has no strict parallel in written English since there are no CVCs which end in F). A five-step scale built on this simple model showed

TABLE I

RELATION BETWEEN THE FIVE-STEP SCALE AND ARCHER'S NORMS FOR
ASSOCIATION VALUE OF CVCs

Mean association values for linguistic scale classes		
Linguistic scale	Example	Mean Archer value
Real English words	CAT	96.05
Pronounceable as words	KOT	72.19
Pronounceable but not words	BOD	50.22
Only analogically pronounceable	SAF	38.68
Unpronounceable	XYM	23.48

Mean linguistic scale values for association scale classes	
Archer deciles	Mean linguistic scale value
1–10	4.63
11–20	4.27
21–30	4.00
31–40	3.82
41–50	3.46
51–60	3.10
61–70	2.87
71–80	2.62
81–90	2.31
91–100	1.81

very convincing orderliness over the Archer data as Table I shows. Each linguistic class differs by a large amount in rated meaningfulness from the next and each decile of the Archer norms is distinct from the next in terms of mean linguistic scale value. There are no reversals in either set of means.

Encouraged by these findings we went on to split apart the variables of pronunciability and identification with a meaningful word as being of particular interest. Pronunciability was developed as a substitution scale directly analogous to the scale described earlier. In essence it asked how the CVC had to be treated to make it pronounceable. Meaning was then treated by taking the closest target word in English and asking what one had to do to the orthography to achieve a match with the CVC. These procedures depended on the development of explicit pronunciation rules for CVCs; a standard for what counted as a word in English, and a

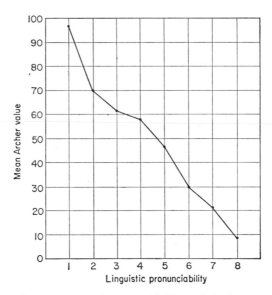

FIG. 2.   Relation between ease of pronunciability and Archer association values.

scoring procedure to bridge the correspondence between the CVC with which one started and the specified English word. Although some of the decisions that were made were arbitrary, particularly with respect to the weights given to spelling changes, the rules have been made clear and detailed and are completely objective (see Greenberg & Jenkins, forthcoming). The final product was two scales: one, ranging in value from 1 to 8, specified the pronunciability of the CVC, the second, ranging from 0 to 9, evaluated the amount of change that was required to move from the CVC to the English orthography of the phonemically closest English word.

Figure 2 shows the mean Archer value for each value of the first variable, and Fig. 3 shows the mean Archer value for each value of the second variable. Taken together in a multiple regression equation, the two variables correlate $+ .857$ with the Archer values of each CVC. When correlated against Nobel's m' values (independent ratings of association for the nonsense syllables; 1961), the relation is virtually the same, $+ .824$.

When one considers that our systematic procedures allow us no judgment about English words that are "known" versus those that are "unknown" by the subject and that we have taken no advantage of our knowledge of other sources of meaningfulness of these materials (XYZ

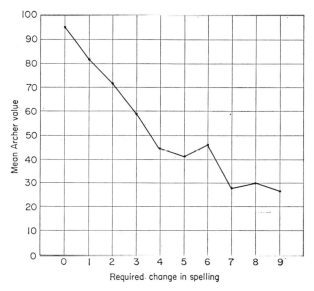

FIG. 3.   Relation between spelling change required and Archer association value.

is an outstanding example), it seems fair to claim an outstanding degree of success for a systematic linguistic approach to the meaningfulness of nonsense syllables.

Perhaps it is time to return to the main purpose of the paper, the relation between meaningfulness and concepts. The findings just reported can be used to support the notion that stimuli achieve meaningfulness through their relationship to powerful general conceptual systems which bestow meanings or provide routes to meanings for these previously unexperienced assemblies of elements.

The language case is a particularly fascinating one because at least part of the linguistic rules are known. Knowing the conceptual scheme suggests ways one can analyze performance on related materials and affords some insights as to the operation of the subject when he is called on to respond to or judge new material. In this important sense, studies of conceptual schemes may lead to better descriptions of behavior and more understanding of the nature of tasks than any particularistic exploration of the surface nature of the stimulus or the response. In the specific case of nonsense syllables, psychologists usually ask whether a complete account of association value could not be accomplished by an analysis of the letter frequencies involved, the subject's reading habits, etc. From our experience in the analysis of letter frequency data, it appears to us that this kind of approach is ineffective when taken by itself. Raw letter frequencies are of little predictive value in appraising nonsense syllable meaningfulness. They improve only as one tempers them with explicitly linguistic considerations, i.e., frequency counts become more closely related to judgments of meaningfulness as one counts frequency of a letter in syllable initial position, syllable final position, in conjunction with this particular vowel, etc. As a supplement to linguistic analysis it appears that frequency has some value (as, for example, in selecting words which are known as opposed to words which are unknown) but *what it is that one is to count* is a question that must be determined by systematic concerns related to conceptual systems; it does not emerge in any automatic fashion from the frequency notion itself.

SUMMARY

This paper began by denying that meaningfulness was a property of concepts and ended by asserting that the meaningfulness of stimuli might be determined by the rules of the conceptual frameworks in which they could be imbedded. In between it was argued that some, if not most, concepts are not to be found in stimuli or even in responses but rather in sets of systematic relations or bodies of rules. An especially clear case involving the rules of language having to do with the formation of syllables in English was chosen for elaboration. Experiments were discussed in which the set of rules provided a metric on which a psychological distance metric was found to depend. Further, the linguistic scale predicted meaningfulness of the stimuli concocted to test the theory. The more general case of accounting for the meaningfulness of CVC nonsense syllables was briefly treated and shown to be amenable to the same kind of analysis. The final thought was that meaningfulness of stimuli might be accounted for in terms of concepts but that concepts were not to be found in any simple way in the raw elements of the stimuli or responses.

REFERENCES

Archer, E. J. A re-evaluation of the meaningfulness of all possible CVC trigrams. *Psychol. Monogr.*, 1960, **74**, No. 10 (Whole No. 497).

Ebbinghaus, H. *Memory: A contribution to experimental psychology.* Transl. by A. H. Ruger & C. E. Bussenius. New York: Columbia Univer. Teachers Coll., 1913.

Greenberg, J. H., & Jenkins, J. J. Studies in the psychological correlates of the sound system of American English. *Word*, 1964, **20**, 157-177.

Noble, C. E. Measurements of association value (a), rated associations (a'), and scaled meaningfulness (*m'*) for the 2100 CVC combinations of the English alphabet. *Psychol. Rep.*, 1961, **8**, 487-521.

Whorf, B. L. Linguistics as an exact science. *Technological Rev.*, 1940, **43**, 61-63, 80-83. Reprinted in J. B. Carroll (Ed.), *Language, thought, and reality.* Cambridge, Massachusetts: M.I.T. Press, 1956. Pp. 220-232.

CHAPTER 6

THE LEARNING OF PRINCIPLES

ROBERT M. GAGNÉ
UNIVERSITY OF CALIFORNIA
BERKELEY, CALIFORNIA

It would surely be agreed by all investigators of learning processes that "conceptual learning," as opposed to other, presumably simpler, forms of learning, constitutes by far the major portion of the learning associated with what is supposed to go on in schools. Most of us have, in fact, fallen into the habit of using the word *conceptual* in a pretty broad sense to refer to the kind of behavioral change that is often verbal in its expression, but actually is a change in the symbolic or representational capabilities of the human learner. Thus, we tend not to think of acquiring capability to tie a shoelace or print a letter as conceptual. However, we do think of the performance of answering the following question as conceptual: "What must I do if my shoelace comes untied?" Bartlett (1958), however, reminds us that these two categories may not be so entirely different as we sometimes like to think.

Beyond these specific classes of human activity, we are also used to referring to the *content* of school subjects as conceptual, without necessarily considering the nature of behavioral change that may be involved. Thus, we often refer to the body of knowledge called physics as "the concepts of physics," or the body of knowledge called genetics as "the concepts of genetics." If forced to say what we mean by the concepts of physics, we are inclined to reply by naming such things as mass, energy, work, gravitation, and atom. In the case of genetics, the entities named might be genes, chromosomes, DNA, RNA, and perhaps many others. We speak of students learning the concepts of physics and the concepts of genetics, and by so doing we surely mean to imply that what is learned is conceptual.

When *concept* and *conceptual* are used in these ways, it seems to me very important to recognize that they are being employed in a most general, rough, and imprecise manner. There is nothing wrong with this, because such imprecision is often required for communication in the English language. Conceptual in this sense refers to the general class of human activities that we infer to require internally stored symbolic or representational processes (cf. Hunter, 1924), as opposed to those that seem to require routine or habitual processes.

The requirements of ordinary everyday communication, however, are by no means the same as the requirements of scientific inquiry. In conversation, we may be satisfied to speak of the *particles* of matter; but a physicist would demand to know how such particles were defined, whether there were different varieties, and what observations were required in studying them. Similarly, the investigator who approaches concepts scientifically is bound to want to know what operations define them and whether one kind can be distinguished from another.

Eventually, I intend to talk about *principles*. The reason I lead up to it in this fashion, though, is this: If I am speaking conversationally, I have absolutely no objection to talking about the concepts of physics or the concepts of meteorology, or any other subject. I would not even insist that one speak of the principles of physics or the principles of meteorology, since the word *principle* in this conversational sense might be more restrictive in meaning. In contrast, though, if you invite me to study conceptual kinds of learning as a scientific investigator, the first thing that is apparent—strikingly so—is that there are several different kinds of things which may be referred to as concepts. And operating with this point of view, I should insist that insofar as they can be given precise scientific meaning, a concept and a principle are very different things indeed.

I am not at all confident that I could distinguish *all* of the behavioral entities that might be called by the name *concept*. Some of them, at least, have been discussed in previous papers. But in order to proceed with the job of saying more about principles, I shall first need to distinguish these, at least, from concepts in their scientific meaning.

THE SCIENTIFIC MEANING OF CONCEPT

Despite differences in the language used to describe a concept, there is considerable agreement among research psychologists as to what this word means. Let me give some examples.

Berlyne (1965) believed that a concept is formed when overt behavior comes to depend on certain properties of a stimulus pattern while disregarding other properties. "It means forming what logicians and mathematicians call an 'equivalence class' of stimulus situations, which share some characteristics but are distinct in other respects, and performing the same response to all members of the class" (p. 45).

Kendler (1964) defined concept learning as the acquisition of a common response to dissimilar stimuli. But he also went on to say that concepts are associations, and that they function as cues or mediators of learned behavior. This conception of the concept is basically similar to that of Osgood (1953) who emphasized the acquisition of a mediating process that can be "detached" or "abstracted" from the stimulus objects with which it may initially have been associated. From a somewhat different point of view, Carroll (1964) defined a concept as an abstraction from a series of experiences which defines a class of objects or events.

Although these examples of the definition of a concept are not exhaustive, they nevertheless derive from a sample of research people who are prominent in this field, and therefore cannot with wisdom be ignored. All these definitions have some general properties in common, and I judge these to be as follows.

(1) A concept is an inferred mental process.
(2) The learning of a concept requires discrimination of stimulus objects (distinguishing "positive" and "negative" instances).

(3) The performance which shows that a concept has been learned consists in the learner being able to place an object in a class.

The common examples of concept learning which would presumably be acceptable to each of these investigators might include the following: learning *chair* as a class of objects; learning *red* as a property of objects detachable from particular objects; learning classes of direction or position, such as *up, down, middle, right,* and *left,* as classes of position or movement not invariably associated with particular positions or movements.

From the standpoint of the investigator of behavior, therefore, the notion of a concept as an "inferred process which enables the individual to classify objects" is both prominent and widely accepted. The next question is, according to such a definition, what could possibly be the meaning of the "concepts of physics," the "concepts of mathematics," the "concepts of biology."

Certain examples can perhaps be considered. In physics, for instance, one deals with lengths, times, distances, and directions, and each of these needs to be learned as a concept, in rather precise form, by the beginning student of physics. One also deals with many classes of objects in physics—levers, gases, liquids, conductors, resistances, waves, lenses, and many, many others. These could certainly be called concepts in accordance with the definition previously given. One might even include such concepts as force, volume, density, rotation, particle, frequency, refraction. Although these latter terms appear to have a somewhat greater degree of abstractness than the ones mentioned earlier, they can without too much of a strain be considered as concepts in the sense of classifiers of sets of objects or events. Similar examples could readily be given for mathematics and biology.

A physicist, or a physics teacher, would perhaps agree that what we have called concepts might be so designated, if one wants. However, he is likely to protest that they are somewhat trivial, and do not begin to include what he means by the concepts of physics. What about Newton's second law? What about potential energy? Work? Universal gravitation? Archimedes' principle? Heat? The structure of the atom? Similarly, were we to apply the suggested definition of a concept to mathematics, we should undoubtedly find that it failed to include many things the mathematician would like to think of as concepts of mathematics, such as integers, rational numbers, irrational numbers, functions, and many others. In biology, it seems doubtful that this definition of concept could include such things as reproduction, mitosis, homeostasis, evolution, and messenger and coding functions of cell components. All these concepts appear to be altogether too complex to be viewed as object classifications. They will not fit the definition derived from experimental studies of behavior.

The implication of this discussion is, then, that one cannot generalize from scientific or laboratory findings about concept learning to all of the varieties of content which may be found in school subjects. Certain fundamental classifications of objects and events do, in fact, seem to fit the conception of concept derived from experimental studies. These should by no means be ignored, because they do have to be learned in order to proceed with the study of these subjects. But the concepts of physics (as an example) includes a great many instances of capabilities to be learned which, even superficially, appear to involve more complex kinds of behavior than are implied by a definition based on object classification.

PRINCIPLES

The next question is, then, how can these more complex capabilities be defined? How can one distinguish the kind of learning situation in which the capability acquired is simply one of being able to classify objects or object properties, and the kind of learning situation in which these apparently more complex entities, sometimes called concepts, are involved?

The clue to the added complexity may come from a consideration of the criterion performance in each case. As has been said, the performance that reflects the learning of a concept is one of identifying a class of things, or any member of the class. If the concept is a *radius* of a circle, we expect the student to be able to answer questions such as "Show me a radius" or "Draw a radius" when confronted with any drawing of a circle; in addition, we expect him to be able to "pick out a radius" when confronted with drawings of circles containing a number of internal lines, some of which are radii and some not. We do not necessarily expect him to answer the question "What is a radius" by means of a verbal definition, nor do we necessarily expect him to be able to tell us why a particular line is a radius. The performance for a concept, in other words, is simply one of identifying an object, or distinguishing it from other objects. It is an operation very close to "stimulus discrimination," except that what is distinguished is a class, rather than a specific object.

An entity such as *work*, however, doesn't have this point-at-able quality. We do not think of asking a student to point to objects or situations in order to tell us which is work and which isn't. We may ask him to define work, to be sure, and this possibility will be discussed in a moment. Mainly, however, the performance that goes along with knowing what *work* is, is one of *demonstrating* that some particular situation involves work. *Demonstrating* involves more than pointing at, or *identifying*. That is why we say we are dealing with a capability that is more complex than is the case with a simple concept. My suggestion has been (Gagné, 1965a) that this more complex learned capability be called a *principle* (or *rule*). In accordance with this idea, *work* is a *principle*. One would speak of *demonstrating* a principle, whereas one can ask for *identifying* a concept.

The principle of work under discussion here is

$$\text{work} = \text{force} \times \text{distance}.$$

That is, the work done is the product of the force acting on a body and the distance through which the body moves while the force is acting on it. What must the student do to demonstrate this principle? The answer is, he must identify not one, but several concepts and their proper sequence. To get *work*, he must identify a member of the class *force* (a concept), a member of the class *distance* (another concept), and an instance of the class *product* or *multiply* (a third concept). Their sequence must also be identified, in order to obtain the product (this would be more readily evident were division the concept involved rather than multiplication). In other words, the situation is more complex because there is not one concept, but several. Demonstration of a rule involves the simpler performance of identifying each concept and the sequence that relates them. There are many ways of saying this. For example, one could say a *principle is a relationship among two or more concepts.* This is all right, so long as it is understood by being referred back to performances.

Perhaps I need to clarify the meaning of "demonstrating a principle." I do not mean to imply by this a single measure of performance such as the question which verbally says to the student "Demonstrate work in the following situation" and then describes the situation. Instead, it seems to me that there are a number of different questions that might be asked in order to determine whether a student has learned a principle. One might say "What is the work done in pushing a body of 1000 grams a horizontal distance of 30 centimeters" or "Show how to calculate the work done by a force of 50 pounds pushing a trunk along a floor for 10 feet." Any of these questions may be considered to reflect what is meant by "demonstrate."

Returning to the main thread of the argument, the distinction between a concept and a principle, the ideas of Berlyne (1965) may have both relevance to and compatibility with the present description. According to Berlyne, there are two types of concepts, or mediators, that occur in chains of thought. One is called situational, because it represents some aspect of a situation, whereas the other is transformational and represents an operation. It may be noted that, in these terms, concepts of *force* and *distance* occurring in the principle of work are situational mediators, whereas *multiply* is obviously a transformational mediator. It is possible to suppose that a principle must include both a situational concept and a transformational concept. I have not followed this line of thinking very far, but it is a very appealing notion at first glance. And, of course, it is quite consistent with the idea that a concept is typically a single mediator, whereas a principle is composed of several mediators in a sequence or chain.

It would appear, then, that principles can be distinguished from what have previously been called concepts in two ways. First, the performance required to demonstrate that a concept has been learned is simply an identification, that is, a choice from a number of alternatives; a principle, in contrast, must be demonstrated by means of performances that identify its component concepts and the operation relating them to one another. Second, this means that the inference to be made about mediating processes is different in the two cases. A concept is a single mediator that represents a class of stimuli (or objects), whereas a principle is a sequence of mediators each of which is itself a concept.

Naturally enough, these two kinds of differences imply a third—namely, the difference in conditions required for learning the concept and the principle. I have previously described this difference in a couple of other places (Gagné, 1965a; 1965b). To summarize briefly, learning a concept is a matter of presenting a variety of positive instances of the class together with the common response, and contrasting these with negative instances of the class. Thus the concept *three* may be learned by a child who makes the response "three" to several different sets of objects, let us say, three marbles, three dots, and three tables, while he is negatively reinforced for making this response to sets of objects numbering two or four or five.

Learning a rule such as "three plus two equals five" requires quite a different set of learning conditions. First, it requires that the child already know the concepts contained in this sequence, namely, three, two, plus, equals, and five. (Note that I do not speak here of learning the verbal sequence "three plus two equals five," but the principle of which the verbal statement is merely a representation.) Second, it requires that these concepts be reinstated by him in the proper sequence. There are several ways of accomplishing this latter event, perhaps the simplest being by means of verbal instructions which name the component concepts in the proper sequence. Alternatively, if one is fond of "discovery learning," the correct sequence may be hinted at or partially prompted, using the technique often referred to as "guided discovery" (cf. Gagné, 1966; Wittrock, 1966). Finally, in order to promote recall, and also to determine whether the principle has truly been learned, the child may be asked to demonstrate that two plus three equals five, in any of the specific ways previously mentioned.

To complete the examples previously mentioned, it is evident that *radius* as a concept is learned under a different set of conditions than is a principle such as *work*. To learn *radius,* the student is presented with a number of different drawings of circles having straight lines within them. Some of these straight lines are radii, while some are not. He learns to point to the correct ones, and it is shown that he can point to a new and different radius that he has not seen before. For the principle of work, the conditions are quite different. First, one must make sure that he does, indeed, know what is meant by "force," "distance," "equals," and "multiply." Verbal cueing may then be provided by the statement "the work done is equal to the distance a body is pushed times the force acting on it." This is followed by an example, such as "How much work is done on a block of wood pushed 2 feet by a force of 10 pounds," and, perhaps, by one or two more. The determination that the student is able to apply the rule to one or more specific problems constitutes evidence that the rule has been learned. (Whether the student can state the principle in formal terms is a different matter, which may be of some importance for other purposes.)

In summary, a principle (or rule) is composed of two or more concepts having an ordered relationship to each other. A principle has been learned when it can be shown that a problem involving specific concepts can be solved by identifying these concepts correctly and placing them in the correctly ordered relationship with each other; in other words, by "applying the rule."

CONCEPTS BY DEFINITION

It seems to me to be quite important to maintain as clear as possible a distinction between a concept and a principle, and I have tried to show why. An additional reason is that there is a strong tradition in experimental psychology relating concept to discrimination learning (e.g., Fields, 1932; Hull, 1920; Oseas & Underwood, 1952), and there are good theoretical reasons for keeping this relationship clean and unfuzzy. Within such a tradition, the principle becomes a kind of learned capability which goes a step beyond the concept in complexity, and, therefore, in theoretical sophistication.

Unfortunately, I have to face the fact that things are not this simple, and, in fact, in danger of being a little fuzzy. The difficulty arises from the fact that the term *concept* is used by educators, psychologists, and others to include something other than just "classes of concrete objects or object-qualities." Even if I call *work* a principle, others will insist on calling it a concept. What about an *uncle*? Could this concept possibly have been learned by means of a set of contrasting examples? I am forced to agree that it cannot. Another example is a concept such as *mass*, encountered in physics. One of the main reasons why this concept gives beginning students so much trouble, I venture to guess, is that in contrast to many other concepts in physics (such as force, distance, liquid, gas) it cannot be learned by means of the direct observational method previously described. The concept *weight* (or heft) can be acquired in this way, and therein lies a difficulty that bothers many physics teachers.

It appears, then, that many concepts must be learned, not by direct observation (contrasting concrete examples), but *by definition*. *Mass* can be learned by means of the definition "that property of an object which determines how much it will be accelerated by a given amount of force." *Uncle* can be learned via the definition "brother of a parent, or husband of a sister of a parent."

But what is being learned when one undertakes to acquire such concepts by definition? I should like to say that what is being learned is a *principle*, in accordance with what has been described previously. *Mass* is learned when one is able to demonstrate that the principle relating the concepts *force* and *acceleration* depends upon *mass* in an inverse way (the greater the mass, the smaller the acceleration). *Uncle* is learned when one is able to demonstrate specific examples of the relationships involving the concepts brother, parent, and husband, sister, parent.

It should be pointed out that some experimental investigations of concepts have dealt with this kind of concept—the *concept by definition*, rather than with the more basic kind, the *concept by observation*. One of the best known examples occurs in the work of Bruner, Goodnow, and Austin (1956). These investigators studied the acquisition of conjunctive concepts (e.g., "all cards with three red circles"), disjunctive concepts (e.g., "cards having red figures, *or* circles, *or* three figures"), and relational concepts (e.g., "cards having the *same* number of figures and borders"). It would appear that conjunctive concepts could be learned by contrasting positive and negative instances, since what are being combined are simply stimulus attributes. In other words, these are *concepts by observation*. Disjunctive concepts and relational concepts are quite different, however, since they require the combining of concepts. In other words, learning them requires learning a rule—they are *concepts by definition*. In the study cited, the latter two categories of concept were found to be considerably more difficult to learn than conjunctive concepts, under a particular set of learning conditions.

Another excellent example of the learning of concepts by definition (that is, by rule) is in the work of Shepard, Hovland, and Jenkins (1961). These investigators arranged stimulus objects having the dimensions triangle–square, large–small, and black–white in various combinations so that some figures had to be sorted into a pile on the right, others into a pile on the left. The complexity of the classification that was to be learned could thus be varied. A Type I classification, the simplest, could be represented by such a rule as "all circles on the left; triangles on the right," in other words, there were two *object classes*. A more complex rule was required for a Type II classification, such as, "small triangles and large circles on the left; large triangles and small circles on the right." Other more complex classifications were employed in addition. The results leave no doubt that there are marked differences in ease of learning of a concept of the simple Type I sort and those which are more complex.

Other examples can be cited of studies investigating the learning of concepts which are rule-like (Hunt, 1962). The key to the difference between the two varieties, concepts by observation and concepts by definition, appears to be, in Berlyne's (1965) terms, that the latter require both transformational and situational concepts, whereas the former involve only one of these.

Differences between these two varieties of concepts can probably be established by experiment, as has been suggested. This does not, however, solve the semantic problem that there *are* two types, both called concepts. I confess I do not know how to change people's highly practiced language habits, even though I know they should be changed. The best I can do here is to summarize the following conclusions.

(1) There are two types of learned capabilities called concepts.

(2) One is a concept by observation, the simpler type, whose learning conditions require contrasting presentation of positive and negative instances.

(3) The other is a concept by definition, which is in a formal sense the same as a principle. It is a combination of simpler concepts, and is typically learned by human beings via verbal statements that provide the cues to recall of component concepts and to their correct ordering.

RESEARCH QUESTIONS RELATED TO PRINCIPLE LEARNING

If one is clear about this distinction between a concept and a principle, one is in a good position to ask some questions about factors in the learning situation that affect the acquisition of principles.

THE PREREQUISITES OF PRINCIPLE LEARNING

It is hypothesized that principles are learned when previously learned concepts are combined in some particular order. In order to enter into such a newly ordered relationship, the concepts themselves must be recalled. The student who hears for the first time the statement of the principle, "the cotangent is the reciprocal of the tangent," cannot be expected to learn anything from this statement unless he can, in fact, remember what a reciprocal is and what a tangent is. The problem is, how well or how vividly must these subordinate concepts be recalled, at the time of learning, in order for the learning to be most effective? Is there a difference in rate of learning the principle, depending on how recently the component concepts have been recalled? This question may be related to the suggestion once made by Underwood (1952) regarding the importance of *contiguity* of concepts in complex learning. At any rate, the basic approach to investigation seems clear. Variations in the recency of recall would be made in specific component concepts, as independent variables. These would be related to the rapidity of principle learning under standard learning conditions, or alternatively, to the number of principles successfully acquired.

Another characteristic of component concepts that might be systematically varied is their *generalizability*. It is apparent that concepts may be more or less "narrow" with respect to the class of specific instances they include. Thus, the concept "number" is much more highly generalizable to a student of tenth-grade mathematics than it is to the student of third-grade mathematics. The specific instances that can be included as members of the class are much greater in the former case. How does this property of concepts affect the learning of principles in which these concepts are involved? The experimental approach suggested is one of deliberately varying the "breadth" or "generalizability" of concepts originally learned, and testing the effects of this variation in the subsequent learning of principles.

INDIVIDUAL DIFFERENCES IN PRINCIPLE LEARNING

Other kinds of prerequisites for principle learning may be conceived as more enduring characteristics of the individual learner. The *size of the store of concepts* available to the individual probably should be placed in this category. Studies too numerous to mention have demonstrated significant relationships between the size of vocabulary of individuals and their facility at meaningful learning. What is the psychological meaning of such a relationship? The particular hypothesis suggested here is that principle learning using typical printed text presentation of material will be more rapid in those individuals who have a greater store of relevant concepts. Testing such a hypothesis would, of course, require that individual differences in availability of relevant concepts be carefully measured—just any old vocabulary test would not necessarily do the job.

The conception of principle learning described here suggests still other kinds of individual differences that would bear looking into. For example, if the facility of principle learning is affected by the recall of component concepts, then individual differences in such *recall* might show a significant relationship. It has also been pointed out that the method of teaching principles to human beings usually involves verbal statements that provide cues to the desired ordering. Are there differences among individuals with respect to their ability to respond to such cues to sequence, or perhaps to "hold in mind" such sequences when verbally cued? Still another individual difference pertains to generalizability again. As stated previously, one can think of a deliberate manipulation of the breadth of concepts which make up a principle. The additional possibility, however, is that individuals may vary in the amount of self-generated generalization that occurs when a concept is acquired. If this could be measured with suitable controls, it might turn out to be an important kind of individual variation related to principle learning.

CONDITIONS OF PRINCIPLE LEARNING

Some of the conditions relevant to the learning of principles have already been mentioned, namely, those prerequisites that precede the act of learning itself, whether they are conceived as previous learning occasions, or as states within the learner. The remaining set of conditions centers upon the event of combining and ordering the concepts that make up the principle. By far the most common way of bringing this about is with the use of verbal statements, whether printed or oral.

There are some intriguing research problems here, which may be summed up in the question "What is the most effective way to use words to guide the learning of principles?" Certain active lines of research can be identified which bear upon this question. First, one thinks of the work on programmed instruction that is more or less specifically oriented to this problem (cf. Glaser, 1965), including work on cueing and prompting, size of step, and response requirements. Second, there is the somewhat scattered but nevertheless important research on learning by discovery (cf. Keislar & Shulman, 1966). Broadly speaking, this area of investigation deals with the amount and kind of cueing provided by words in principle learning. Discovery learning may be said to occur under conditions in which minimal cueing is given, whereas reception learning (Ausubel, 1963) takes place when words are used to state the principle fully. Various intermediate amounts of cueing represent "guided discovery" (cf. Gagné, 1965a; Gagné, 1966). The question of the effectiveness of different kinds and amount of guidance in discovery continues to be an important one for research.

There is also an interesting research problem, not as yet very well investigated, which may be stated as "What kind of word or symbol ordering will produce the most effective principle learning?" Most printed texts use English sentences. Although these are effective for some communication purposes, they are not the only possibilities, as the works of Virginia Woolf and James Joyce demonstrate. In mathematics and some forms of science, English sentences get to be altogether too space-consuming, and possibly also time-consuming for the learner. Over a period of years, the advocates of symbolic logic have recommended this form of symbolic communication as a means of cueing the learning of principles. From the standpoint of research, it is evident that we have as yet too few experimental results on this problem of how words and symbols may be used to guide the learning of principles.

SUMMARY

In its common meaning, the word *concept* refers to a broad class of inferred representational capabilities of the learner. In this sense, we speak of the concepts of biology, for example, as the entire set of knowledge components of an academic subject. This usage contrasts markedly with the meaning of concept as a technical term derived within a context of experimental studies of learning. In the latter sense, concept means an inferred process enabling the learner to identify classes of objects, object-qualities, or events, despite variations in the particular stimuli used to form these classes.

Technically speaking, *concepts* are distinguishable from *principles*. The former are inferred as capabilities when the learner is able to identify an object class. The latter, however, require that the individual *demonstrate* one or more particular instances of application of the principle. The more complex performance associated with the principle leads accordingly to an inference of a more complex form of internal processing. A single mediator can be inferred to represent a class such as *radius* or *middle;* but a principle such as "square the numerator" seems to demand a *sequence* of mediations, each of which is itself a concept. The principle, then, is a capability that makes possible the demonstration of a sequence of behavior, each element of which may involve a concept.

Many concepts (such as *red, circle,* or *liquid*) may be learned by methods requiring the observation of differences among stimuli that represent a class and stimuli that do not (negative instances). These have been extensively studied by experimental means; they may be called "concepts by observation." Other concepts (such as *mass, uncle, work*) require conditions of learning which are different from these observational techniques. These may be called "concepts by definition," since they are usually learned, in the human being, by means of a carefully constructed sequence of instruction involving verbal communication. In other words, learning of these latter concepts is indistinguishable in a formal sense from learning principles.

Principles are learned under conditions that have two major requirements: (1) the component concepts of which they are composed must be previously learned and readily recallable; and (2) a communication, usually verbal, must be made to the learner indicating the correct sequence of these components.

These two conditions of principle learning suggest a number of research questions which have as yet not received adequate answers. For example, does the recallability of component concepts affect principle learning? Does the generalizability of these concepts have an effect on learning and transfer of principles? What sorts of individual differences may be related to principle learning, such as differences in the availability and recallability of relevant concepts? How can the communication of the correct sequence of concepts in a principle be designed for most effective learning? What does this have to do with discovery learning, and with "learning guidance?"

There is much to be done in conducting scientific research on the learning of principles as well as on the learning of concepts. It seems evident that the planning and execution of such research will be helped by the maintenance of as clear as possible a distinction between principles and concepts, despite the blurring of this distinction produced by common language.

REFERENCES

Ausubel, D. P. *The psychology of meaningful verbal learning*. New York: Grune & Stratton, 1963.

Bartlett, F. C. *Thinking: An experimental and social study*. London: Allen & Unwin, 1958.

Berlyne, D. E. *Structure and direction in thinking*. New York: Wiley, 1965.

Bruner, J. S., Goodnow, Jacqueline, J., & Austin, G. A. *A study of thinking*. New York: Wiley, 1956.

Carroll, J. B. Words, meanings and concepts. *Harv. educ. Rev.*, 1964, 34, 178-202.

Fields, P. E. Studies in concept formation: I. The development of the concept of triangularity by the white rat. *Comp. Psychol. Monogr.*, 1932, 9, No. 2 (Whole No. 42).

Gagné, R. M. *The conditions of learning*. New York: Holt, Rinehart, & Winston, 1965. (a)

Gagné, R. M. The learning of concepts. *Sch. Rev.*, 1965, 73, 187-196. (b)

Gagné, R. M. Varieties of learning and the concept of discovery. In E. Keislar & L. M. Shulman (Eds.), *Learning by discovery*. Chicago: Rand-McNally, 1966.

Glaser, R. (Ed.) *Teaching machines and programed learning, II: Data and directions.* Washington, D.C.: National Education Association, 1965.

Hull, C. L. Quantitative aspects of the evolution of concepts. *Psychol. Monogr.*, 1920, 28, No. 1 (Whole No. 123).

Hunt, E. B. *Concept learning: An information processing problem.* New York: Wiley, 1962.

Hunter, W. S. The symbolic process. *Psychol. Rev.*, 1924, **31**, 478-497.

Keislar, E., & Shulman, L. M. (Eds.), *Learning by discovery.* Chicago: Rand-McNally, 1966.

Kendler, H. H. The concept of the concept. In A. W. Melton (Ed.), *Categories of human learning.* New York: Academic Press, 1964. Pp. 211-236.

Oseas, L., & Underwood, B. J. Studies of distributed practice: V. Learning and retention of concepts. *J. exp. Psychol.*, 1952, **43**, 143-148.

Osgood, C. E. *Method and theory in experimental psychology.* London & New York: Oxford Univer. Press, 1953.

Shepard, R. N., Hovland, C. I., & Jenkins, H. M. Learning and memorization of classifications. *Psychol. Monogr.*, 1961, **75**, No. 13 (Whole No. 517).

Underwood, B. J. An orientation for research on thinking. *Psychol. Rev.*, 1952, **59**, 209-220.

Wittrock, M. The learning by discovery hypothesis. In E. Keislar & L. M. Shulman (Eds.), *Learning by discovery.* Chicago: Rand-McNally, 1966.

CHAPTER 7

A DEVELOPMENTAL APPROACH
TO CONCEPTUAL GROWTH[*]

JEROME KAGAN

HARVARD UNIVERSITY
CAMBRIDGE, MASSACHUSETTS

A pair of propositions dominates inquiry into the componentry of human mentation. A first article of faith states that *concepts* are the fundamental agents of intellectual work. The theoretical significance of cognitive concepts (or, if you wish, symbolic mediators) in psychological theory parallels the seminal role of valence in chemistry, gene in biology, or energy in physics. Concepts are viewed as the distillate of sensory experience and the vital link between external inputs and overt behaviors. The S-O-R model of a generation ago regarded O as the black box switch that connected behavior with a stimulus source. The O is viewed today as a set of concepts or mediators.

The theoretical importance of concepts stretches beyond the domain of inquiry that includes problem solving and language learning, and intrudes into the territory that we normally label personality. Schachter's fresh description of affects (Schachter & Singer, 1962) joins the older Whorfian ideas and argues for the directing role of concepts in emotional and interpersonal phenomena. Our recent studies of infant–mother interactions suggest that a mother's behavior toward her infant derives more from the conceptual label she applies to the child than to his stimulus properties as viewed by an observer. These observations, together with other developments in the field, place the idea of "conceptual structure" in a central explanatory position.

The second basic proposition states that an individual's conceptual structure passes through different stages over the course of development. The stages are characterized by qualitatively different structures, not by

[*] This research was supported, in part, by research grant MH-8792 from NIMH, USPHS.

mere accretion of more or richer concepts. The process of conceptual growth is akin to the growth of a butterfly from egg through larva and pupa to mature form, in contrast to the growth in weight of a group of muscles.

There is a considerable body of data to rationalize a commitment to these two principles, but our knowledge contains two serious lacunae. First, we have no intuitively commanding or attractive theories to help us understand how concepts are formed or how structures change. The noteworthy flaw in Piaget's prodigious output is the absence of any set of theoretical statements that accounts for how or why a child passes from one stage of operations to another. A second void is the absence of a systematic description of the nature of the conceptual structures the child possesses at any one stage in development. What is the hierarchical organization of concepts at age 6 in contrast to age 2 or 12?

This paper addresses itself to these issues. It does not presume to solve them, but hopes to clarify two problems: (1) how and why do conceptual structures change with experience, and (2) what is the organization of conceptual units at different developmental stages.

TERMINOLOGY

In order to continue this discussion, we must first agree on a vocabulary. The generic headings in this vocabulary list include the concepts of *cognitive units, cognitive processes,* and *determinants of attention.*

Cognitive units are the hardware of mental work; the things that get manipulated in mentation. Three basic classes of cognitive units include *perceptual schema, language units,* and *rules of transformation* or principles. Cognitive processes refer to the more dynamic events that act on the cognitive units, much like catalysts act on basic compounds in chemical solution. The processes of *labeling, evaluation, hypothesis production,* and *transformation* are fundamental. Consider a typical problem-solving situation in which the child is confronted with a set of initial thoughts that are problematical or external information which he has to resolve. The first task is to label the information presented, a phase that Guilford calls "cognition." The child then generates hypotheses in accord with these labels. At this point the process of evaluation becomes relevant. The child should pause to evaluate the validity of his hypotheses and initial labels. Finally, the child implements the hypothesis he decided on with appropriate transformation rules. Labeling, hypothesis generation, evaluation, and implementation of transformations are basic cognitive processes. Perceptual schema, language symbols, and rules are the units that are acted on by these cognitive processes.

The final category in our vocabulary list includes determinants of attentional involvement. Problems of learning, relearning, recall, and problem solving require attention to the task at hand. Attentional involvement is the basic medium in which cognitive activity occurs, and degree of attention governs the accuracy and efficiency of the final cognitive product. Without attentional involvement, these processes are not effectively activated and new information is not assimilated. The basic determinants of attention fall into two categories: violations of expected events and personological variables which we usually call motivation and conflict. Let us consider this latter group of variables.

THE MOTIVE FOR DIFFERENTIATION

There is a general human tendency to accrue attributes that differentiate the self from peers and siblings, to develop characteristics that allow the child to label himself in some unique way. The child's understanding of who he is derives in part from the skills he has mastered, and the specific skills chosen are determined by the values of his subculture. Since our social community places emphasis on intellectual mastery, most children choose this route for self-definition, and their striving for excellence in the academic milieu is partially in the service of the desire for differentiation.

THE MOTIVATION TO MAXIMIZE SIMILARITY TO A MODEL

Children and adults want to maximize similarity to adults who command power, status, and instrumental competence. The child desires these intangible goals but does not know how to obtain them. He believes that if he made himself similar to the adult models who appear to possess these resources he might share vicariously in their power, status, and competence. If these models display an interest in the mastery of intellectual skills, the child will attempt to mimic such mastery in order to maximize similarity with the model and increase the probability that he will share in these intangible goals. The absence of this dynamic in many lower-class families is partially responsible for the fact that lower-class children are less highly motivated to master intellectual skills. The lower-class child's inadequate performance in school is not solely the result of his parents' indifference to his school performance. Lower-class parents often exhort the child to work for grades and punish the child for failure. The lower-class parent, however, is not perceived by the child as a person who values intellectual mastery. The child does not view intellectual mastery as a likely way of gaining the adult resources of power and competence that he perceives his parent to possess. It may seem inconsistent to state that the child has a strong motive for differentiation and an equally strong motive for maximizing similarity to an adult model. One of the basic characteristics of man is an attempt to maintain a balance between a desire to differentiate himself from a larger group with less resources than he commands and an equally strong desire to make himself similar to a group which he believes possesses more resources.

EXPECTANCY OF SUCCESS OR FAILURE

Children quickly develop different expectations of success or failure in intellectual tasks. Unfortunately, the most frequent and prepotent reaction to an expectancy of failure is decreased involvement in the task and subsequent withdrawal. Educators have been guilty of minimizing the critical role which a child's expectancy of failure plays in shaping his behavior in a school situation. The child's motives are contingent on expectation of success or failure, and motives are sloughed or adopted with zeal depending on the degree to which the child believes he can attain the goals that gratify the motive. Growth of specific motives and persistence at task mastery hang delicately on the balance between hope and fear.

ANXIETY DERIVED FROM CONFLICTS OVER LEARNING

There are many relevant conflicts that inhibit the learning process. These include excessive competitiveness, desire for power over others, assumption of a passive posture with teachers, anxiety over dependency, and sex-role conflicts. Let us consider each of these briefly.

The school situation in most public-school settings is essentially a competitive enterprise. The child who desires good grades, for whatever reason, is in competition with his peers. In such a context the child with a strong desire for excellence will entertain wishes that those who are his closest rivals suffer some misfortune. The child who is vulnerable to guilt over these hostile thoughts may become anxious and place inhibition on his attempts at excellence. This conflict over the hostile flavor of competitive wishes is one reason why young adolescent girls perform less well in high school and college than they should. The female in our culture is more disposed to guilt over hostile wishes and inhibits intense academic effort as a result of this conflict.

An equally forceful conflict is experienced by boys during the elementary-school years. The primary grades are characterized by a pressure for conformity and for a passive posture vis-à-vis the teacher. The 6- or 7-year-old boy is in the process of identifying with adult males and experiences some conflict over assuming an overly conforming or passive attitude with the female teacher. The imposition of the passive role creates anxiety and conflict and he fights assumption of this behavioral posture. The unruliness and mischievous behavior of second-grade boys is related in part to conflict over the passivity imposed by the school situation.

A final conflict is more pervasive and touches the relation between sex-role identification and academic products. Problems requiring analysis and reasoning, especially spatial reasoning, in science and mathematics, are viewed by both sexes as more appropriate for boys than for girls and girls perform less well on such materials. The typical girl believes that the ability to solve problems in geometry, physics, logic, or arithmetic is a masculine skill and her motivation to persist with such problems is low.

The sex-typed character of knowledge is most evident in the vocational choices of young adolescents. An additional reason for the lowered motivation and performance of girls in science and mathematics rests with the fact that a girl's sex-role identity is more dependent on her ability to attract and maintain a love relationship than it is on her academic skills. The male views academic excellence as a necessary antecedent to vocational success, and since success is an essential component of the masculine sexual identity, the adolescent male should be more highly motivated to master those tasks that are linked to his vocational choice.

Although intense involvement in academics is more characteristic of the adolescent and adult male than female, this differential motivation is not so in the primary grades where girls typically outperform boys in all areas and the ratio of boys to girls with reading problems varies from 3:1 to 6:1. How can we understand the fact that the academic performance of girls is superior to that of boys during the primary grades but gradually becomes inferior during adolescence and adulthood. We have suggested that boys link vocational success with academic performance, and their lower anxiety over competitiveness frees them to strive for superiority over peers (Kagan, 1964a). A final reason for the increasing academic superiority of boys rests with the change in perception of the sex-typed character of school and academic work. Primary-grade boys have more difficulty than girls in mastering reading and arithmetic because the boy perceives the school atmosphere as essentially feminine. The 6-year-old boy is striving to develop a masculine sex-role identification and he resists involvement in feminine acts. The atmosphere of the primary grades is generally viewed as feminine because the child's introduction to school is mediated by women who initiate the activities of painting, coloring, and singing. Most teachers place a premium on obedience, decorum, inhibition of aggression, and restless motoricity. These values are better tailored to girls than to boys, and it is not surprising that most children view the school situation as more feminine than masculine (Kagan, 1964b).

In the above discussion we dealt with some of the major motives and conflicts that exert strong control over the attentional involvement of children in learning new materials. Now let us turn to a developmental description of conceptual growth.

A DEVELOPMENTAL APPROACH TO CONCEPTUAL GROWTH

INFANCY

The major schism in conceptual development is the break between preverbal and verbal functioning that occurs between 18 and 24 months of age. No other change of stage is as important as this discontinuity. The reason for differentiating the first 18 months from what comes later is because after 2 years language becomes a primary mode of operating upon the world. Piaget singled out the first 18 months as the period of sensory–motor development, and Bruner, borrowing from Piaget, labeled it the enactive period. Since this era is critical, let us consider it in some detail.

DEVELOPMENT DURING INFANCY

The primary events of the first 18 months involve the acquisition of schema and learning to orient to the external world. The basic variables controlling attentional investment in external stimuli are (a) movement and contrast characteristics of the stimuli, (b) the acquired reward value of the stimuli, (c) the degree to which the stimuli violate earlier learned schema, and (d) the degree to which the stimuli are conditioned to fear. A fifth determinant of degree of attention to the external environment comes not from the outside but from within the infant and is derived from his level of excitability. A final determinant involves the environmental context in which the stimuli occur. In sum, qualities of external stimuli, the infant's temperamental attributes, and context are essential ingredients in controlling attentional investment. Several bases for attention have been postulated for the infant, but individual investigators have chosen to emphasize different ones. Let us acknowledge immediately that during the opening weeks of life certain stimulus patterns, without prior learning, have some power to attract the infant's attention. We know most about the visual mode, and in this mode movement and high brightness at a contour (black–white contrast) seem to be unlearned attractants of the infant's attention. I am not sure that I wish to admit any more than these two members into this sacred club. Some argue that complexity affects attention. It must be clear that this assumption states that stimulus complexity, independent of prior learning, movement, and contrast contour, influences attention. No paper that I have studied on this issue has been able to demonstrate that infants attend more to a low-, moderate-, or high-complex stimulus where movement, black–white contrast, and prior learning were completely and unambiguously controlled. Some investigators allow themselves or their colleagues arbitrarily to decide which stimuli should be called complex. To give you an idea of how silly this research can be, consider a recent paper by Hoben Thomas (1965). Thomas had students judge whether a series of stripes or bars in contrast to human face or human form was more complex. It should come as no surprise that the human face and form were judged to be more complex by the students and Thomas found that infants attended more to them than to the bars. Thomas felt justified in concluding that more complex stimuli attract the infant's attention. We shall argue that the most important determinant of attention in the human infant is based on prior learning and varies with the degree to which external stimuli match or mismatch the familiarity of the schema that the infant has developed. I apologize for not being able to do much better than Piaget in defining the word schema. It would be easy but glib to say that a schema is a set of neurons developed to match a stimulus that has been presented repeatedly. Let us view a schema as the analog of a concept and as a cognitive representation of an external stimulus. This representation contains an *arrangement of elements*. Both the arrangement and the elements are critical. Let me summarize some recent data to amplify this last statement.

In a set of experiments on infants under 1 year, we presented four different three-dimensional, flesh-colored sculptured faces to the infants, one at a time (Kagan, Henker, Hen-Tov, Levine, & Lewis, 1966). One face is a representation of a regular male face; the second is a collaged version of that face in which the eyes, nose, and mouth are rearranged in random order but all the elements are present. The third form is the same face with the eyes absent but the nose and mouth in proper arrangement, and the fourth is a completely blank face. We studied four major behavioral variables in evaluating the infants' differential reaction to these facial patterns: fixation time (orientation toward the stimulus), smiling, degree of cardiac deceleration, and vocalization. Previous work has demonstrated that there is some covariation between a child's level of attentional involvement with a stimulus and these four dependent variables. When the facial components were held constant and the arrangement was varied, as in the regular versus the scrambled face, there was more smiling and more cardiac deceleration to the regular than to the scrambled face, although fixation times were equivalent. When the arrangement was regular, but some components were missing, as in the regular versus the no-eyes patterns, we obtained longer fixation time to the regular than to the no-eyes face, and, of course, more smiling and greater cardiac deceleration to the former than to the latter. Thus, both the arrangement and the components are important in influencing the attentional behavior of the infant. I suggest further that changing the arrangement represents a moderate violation of a perceptual schema, whereas changing the components represents a more serious violation. When the infants are 13 months of age there are longer fixation times and greater decelerations to a three-dimensional form in which 3 human heads are placed on a human body or an animal head on a human body (alterations involving a change in components) than to forms in which the parts of the human form are rearranged. Our basic assumption is that moderate uncertainty creates maximal attention and at 4 months of age a change in arrangement is a moderate violation whereas at 13 months of age, when the infant is more mature, a change in components represents a moderate violation. Let us now return to the main thread of the discussion.

The most important determinant of attention is the age of the schema in the child's mind. With age a child comes to know a stimulus more completely, which is another way of saying that a schema for a stimulus pattern becomes firmer. If we were able to slice into the child's mind at any time and study the collection of schema and the rate of development of each, we would see some very old schema, some moderately old schema, and some emergent schema. An emergent schema today (one that has just been freshly formed) may be an old one next week or next month. As schema mature, the child becomes capable of assimilating new related stimulus patterns and the process proceeds. A basic principle of attentional involvement states that well-established schema and extreme violations of schema will elicit minimal attention because they have too much or too little uncertainty in them. When recognition is immediate there is minimal uncertainty, for the stimulus matches the schema perfectly and attention is not necessary. *Attention will be maximal to mod-*

erately uncertain stimuli that match emergent schema or stimuli that elicit moderate uncertainty. When the stimulus does not match the schema at all, attention wanes. There is, therefore, a curvilinear relation between the age of schema and the amount of attention investment in a related stimulus. We acknowledge the essential truth of this statement for older children. Material that has already been learned is regarded as boring to the child; material that is too difficult is also avoided because the child has no cognitive structures to assimilate the information. It is of importance to note that this curvilinear relation between age of schema—or age of conceptual structure—and attention holds as well at 16 weeks of age as it does at 16 years. The suggestion that an arrangement of components is less of a distortion than a change in components is implicitly recognized by experienced school teachers. After a principle has been presented to a fifth grader there is often a drill on different arrangements of that principle before new components are added. The infant data validate the implicit wisdom of this approach. Perhaps it should be made more explicit.

A second important governor of attention, besides violations of formed schema, lies in the secondary reward value of the stimulus. An infant's attention is attracted to those stimuli that have been associated with primary gratifications. It is for this reason that the face is probably the first schema to emerge, rather than stimuli in the child's bedroom that might be more attractive. A third set of determinants comes from within the child and deals with his threshold for attentional investment in external stimulation, on the one hand, and his rate of processing information, on the other. We have been struck with the dramatic individual differences among children during the first year of life in the rate at which they appear to assimilate external stimulation, especially in the visual and auditory modes. The operational indexes of rate of information processing include rapid habituation or adaptation to stimuli and refined differentiation. Rate of adaptation is obtained by measuring the decrease in indexes of attention from the first third of a series of trials to the last third. Children with fast adaptation or habituation rates showed dramatic decreases in fixation time or amount of cardiac deceleration over the course of the stimulation episode.

RELATIONSHIP TO BASIC EDUCATIONAL PROBLEMS

One might ask what this information on infant development has to do with the problems educational psychologists and educators confront daily. Recent work in our laboratory suggests that the implications are strong and significant. It appears that lower-class children, as early as 8 to 12 months of age, show slower rates of information processing than middle-class children of the same ordinal position. Lower-class children show less rapid habituation, less clear differentiation among visual stimuli, and, in a play situation, show a high threshold for satiation. The latter measure is obtained by placing the child in a standard playroom with a standard set of toys (quoits on a shaft, blocks, pail, mallet, peg board, toy lawn mower, and toy animals) and by noting the time involved in each activity. Some children play with the blocks for 10 seconds and then skip to the quoits or the lawn mower, playing only 10–20 seconds with each individual activity before shifting to another. A second group of children, called "high threshold for satiation infants," spends 1 or 2 minutes with an activity without interruption before changing. We do not believe the latter group of infants is taking more from the activity; rather it seems that they are taking longer to satiate on this action. It is important to note that the observation that lower-class infants show high threshold for satiation contrasts sharply with the observation that 4-year-old lower-class children are distractible and hyperkinetic. We believe both descriptions. The paradox to be explained is why these lower-class children are pokey and lethargic and nondistractible at 12 months of age, yet display polar-opposite behaviors at 48 months of age.

RELATIONSHIP TO PIAGET

It is useful and important to relate any theory and set of empirical findings to Piaget's basic hypotheses about cognitive development, whenever this is possible. Later in the paper we shall do this in detail. Some introductory comments, however, are relevant in this context. Piaget conceptualized the first 18 months as the sensory–motor stage, a stage during which the child learns schema for overt responses. The emphasis on the prefix *sensory* in the phrase *sensory–motor coordinations* should be altered and the emphasis placed on *motor*. The responses that Piaget grouped under sensory coordinations may be irrelevant or at least orthogonal to perceptual and cognitive development. The overt skeletal response system is, in many ways, a distinctly different system from the perceptual–afferent structures. This fact has long been known to experimental psychologists, and it has been validated by the classic experiment which demonstrated that an organism does not have to make an overt skeletal response in order to learn an action involving that muscle group. The classic experiment involves curarizing the dog's hind paw, pairing shock to the paw with a conditioned signal such as tone. The animal feels the pain but can never make the overt response of foot withdrawal. Does the animal learn anything even though he cannot make the overt foot withdrawal response? The answer is an overwhelming yes, for when the curare wears off and the conditioned stimulus is sounded the dog flexes his paw with the same alacrity as an animal who did make the overt response during the learning trials. At a simpler level, one can tell a child to watch the action of a teacher but not make any overt rehearsal himself and then the next day ask the child to act out a response he learned through attention but never issued during the attentional phase. We have been struck with the fact that although 8-month-old infants show minimal variability in so-called sensory–motor behavior (the kinds of acts displayed and the frequency with which they suck, touch, or manipulate objects), they show marked variability in rate of habituation and differentiation to visual and auditory inputs. It is tempting to speculate that these latter processes are more critical and more predictive of future cognitive performance than the sensory–motor coordinations to which psychologists and educators have given heavy emphasis in theory and in standard infant intelligence tests. Motor coordinations have been studied because they are the most public and, therefore, the easiest to describe and measure. This is not the best reason for focusing energy on a response system. It is more delicate and difficult to study the dynamics of the perceptual system, but individual differences in these variables, in the rate of habituation and differentiation and information processing, may be more prognostic of future levels of cognitive development than the motor coordinations that are so public during the first year and a half.

SUMMARY

The first 12–18 months are characterized by growth of perceptual schema. The first schema to develop are related to those stimuli that have natural attention-getting qualities (such as high contrast and movement) and those that have been associated with reward (primarily food and tactile contact). Rate of growth of schema is related in part to variability of input from the human beings who are sources of reward. This assumption finds support in the fact that lower-class infants show less precocious schematic development during the first year than middle-class children, and these children tend to be subject to less variable inputs for a primary caretaker. Second, a fast rate of information processing, characterized by low threshold for satiation in play, sharp perceptual differentiation of facial stimuli, and rapid habituation tend to be positively correlated and may be indexes of precocious cognitive growth. Finally, one of the important habits being learned during the first year is focusing attention on the external environment. Learning to perceive, attend, focus, and assimilate a stimulus to a schema, as well as attending to violations of that stimulus, are the major cognitive developments in this first stage of human growth.

EIGHTEEN MONTHS THROUGH THE PRESCHOOL YEARS

The second period of cognitive growth is marked by the onset of expressive language and a rapid increase in capacity for comprehension of speech which occurs usually between 13 and 18 months. The most important development during this time is the growth of a labeling vocabulary. The child acquires a set of symbols that allows him to categorize and conceptualize aspects of his environment. Responses are attached, in turn, to these categories. There are also some basic rules of organization, so-called transformation rules, that are being established and these tend to describe a functional–relational basis between objects, in contrast to an analytic or categorical basis. We have suggested before that there are three fundamental ways in which stimuli can be organized. The first is a functional–relational dimension in which objects are regarded as similar because they are functionally related to each other in terms of their action upon one another or their geographical or temporal contiguity. A hole is to dig, an envelope is to mail, and an orange is to eat are good examples of a functional categorization. Analytic or categorical bases classify an orange as an object with skin or as a fruit. The recent studies carried out by Irving Sigel at the Merrill-Palmer Institute indicate that at 4 years of age middle-class children are shifting from a functional–relational basis for categorization to either an analytic or categorical one. Lower-class children, especially nonwhite lower-class children, are still functional or relational in their preferred mode of organization. One of the reasons for this functional preference is their extreme impulsivity which facilitates a functional approach. It should be noted that the categories *functional–relational, analytic,* or *categorical* are formal characteristics of concepts and say little about substantive content. I suspect that the content categories first to be learned are those that are emphasized most frequently to the child and those that have the most salient stimulus characteristics. On this basis we would predict that the concepts *big–small, adult–child, male–female,* and *good–bad* would be the four basic conceptual dimensions typically learned by the Western child—perhaps by children in all cultures. This prediction is based on the fact that these four dimensions are perceptually salient. Size has high natural contrast for the preschool child. The differences between males and females, fathers and mothers, and boys and girls also have high salience. Finally, good–bad is a verbal label typically applied to the child and his behavior by many of the social agents surrounding the child. Empirical investigations of preschool children and their cate-gorizations of people and events confirm the prediction that good–bad, male–female, large–small, and adult–child are four fundamental con-ceptual dimensions the preschool child uses in organization of his world.

THE EARLY SCHOOL YEARS, AGES 5–10

The early school years are witness to a flowering and crystallization of the basic cognitive structure of the child. Although the growth of a label-ing vocabulary continues to be important, it now assumes secondary significance alongside the now rapid growth of two other basic con-ceptual processes. One involves the growth of rules for transformations and the second the growth of the habit of *evaluation*. It is appropriate to review the chronology of the problem-solving process so that the reader appreciates the mosaic of events involved in a problem-solving episode. Consider a problem in which the child is confronted with some information and acknowledges that there is an answer that he will be able to recognize at the end of a solution phase. In the first phase the child labels or comprehends the initial information. At this point the adequacy and richness of his labeling vocabulary is most critical. Notice, however, that there is a phase of evaluation in which the child should pause to consider the validity of his initial coding. When most adults are reading a newspaper or a book, they seldom make mistakes, and we minimize the role of evaluation in initial coding. For a child learning how to read or mastering basic vocabulary forms, however, the role of evaluation is critical. If the child reads *nickle* for *pickle, 10 cents* for *5 cents, cat* for *bat,* he is not likely to arrive at the correct solution of the problem. The initial decoding or comprehension phase is followed by a proliferation of hypotheses. Now the role of evaluation is most impor-tant, for in many problem situations two or three hypotheses may occur in close succession and each one may appear appropriate. Now the child must evaluate the differential validity of each of these hypotheses. The next stage involves the implementation of the chosen hypothesis, and now the possession of rules is important, whether the rules be formal algorithms, as in the case of arithmetic, or informal mediational nests as in the case of questions such as, "How many ways can you use a news-paper?" Evaluation of the validity of the final response is important for it appears that the children called "high-creative" often do not evaluate the accuracy of their responses and emerge with more "creative" an-swers. In the final phase an answer is reported to an examiner or written on a piece of paper, and once again evaluation of the validity of the response is an important process. In sum, evaluation of the validity of a cognitive act touches the problem-solving process at three places—in the initial coding and comprehension phase, in the selection of a correct hypothesis to implement, and, in the end, in the evaluation of the accuracy of the transformation solution performed. Some children tend to be "fast evaluators" and we have called them impulsive. Many times their evaluations are incorrect and they make frequent errors in problems with high response uncertainty. Children who brood an excessively long time about hypotheses, labels, or answers are called reflective, and they tend to be more accurate. Work over the last 5 years suggests that the disposition to be reflective or impulsive shows high intertask generality and good intra-individual stability (Kagan, 1965a; Kagan, 1965b). Reflection is defined as the tendency to consider alternative solution possibilities, whereas impulsivity is defined as the tendency to make very quick decisions. Data on hundreds of children in the first through the fifth grades indicate that reflection grows with age and that school-age children value reflection and regard it as a positive attribute. Reflective children make fewer errors while they are learning to read (Kagan, 1965c), are less likely to make errors of commission on learning tasks (Kagan, 1966b), and less likely to make errors on inductive reasoning problems (Kagan, Pearson, & Welch, 1966). Oddly enough, if they are boys, reflective children are less likely to be short and broad in their body build, whereas impulsive children are more likely to have a mesomorphic somatotype (Kagan, 1966a).

There is a link, moreover, between reflection–impulsivity at age 10 and behavior during the preschool years. Impulsive 10-year-olds, in contrast to reflective children with similar IQ scores, were extraversive, hyperkinetic, and impulsive at 4 years of age, suggesting that the tendency to be impulsive or reflective begins its growth early in the child's development.

There are broad implications to be taken from these data, for impulsive children are treated differently than reflectives in the school and extraschool environments. If the impulsive child is not verbally facile, he is likely to have trouble in the school milieu. I am pleased to report that a recent investigation with first-grade children indicated that simple direct training techniques can make impulsive youngsters more reflective and that this effect lasts over a period of a month. Although this tendency begins its growth early, it is subject to some modification through direct tuition.

SUBSTANTIVE CONTENT

The preceding section contrasted the growth of formal conceptual structures with specific substantive contents and we shall retain that form. Although the dimensions male–female, good–bad, and potent–impotent continue to grow and crystallize, additional contents are being developed. These include a set of concepts surrounding standards for dependency, aggression, and self-definition concepts dealing with the process of identification. The child now develops evaluative concepts regarding regression, instrumental dependence, and anxiety (the dependency trio), and lying, aggression, and destruction. The child is also learning to apply self-labels to himself, and the central core of this set of self-labels is derived from the fact that he believes he shares similarity with particular models. This belief that he shares similarities with models is called *identification*.

The standard surrounding sex-role appropriateness is also growing at a rapid rate and the child now classifies a variety of activities and events as either appropriately masculine or feminine. Unfortunately, the school and schoolwork fall under the shade of sex-role standards. It is well documented that problems requiring analysis and reasoning, especially spatial reasoning, science and mathematics, are viewed by both sexes as more appropriate for boys than for girls, and girls perform less well on such materials. If problems involving mathematical reasoning are presented with male objects to consider (planets and rockets), girls do poorer than if the reasoning is concerned with cooking or gardening, although the transformation rules are identical. During the early years of school, first- and second-grade boys who have more difficulty than girls in mastering reading and arithmetic perceive the school atmosphere as essentially feminine. A 6-year-old boy is striving to develop a masculine sex-role identification and he resists involvement in feminine acts. The atmosphere of the primary grades is viewed as feminine because the child's introduction to school is mediated by females who initiate the activities of painting, coloring, and singing. Although there are strong semantic associations between the dimensions of masculinity and femininity in specific areas of knowledge for most adult members of Western culture, one would hope that this unfortunate marriage might be neutralized through altering the associational link between the domain of knowledge and the sex roles. This might be brought about through modifications in procedures and atmosphere in the elementary schools.

A SUMMARY STATEMENT

At a most general level it is profitable to view a child's intellectual performance in or out of school as the result of the interaction of five factors—elemental skills, strategies of processing information, motives, standards, and sources of anxiety. The elemental skills involve a primary set of labeling symbols and rules. The child must have a minimal vocabulary level in order to understand speech, comprehend the written word, and report orally the product of his thinking. He must also have learned certain rules that represent combinations of symbols. He should know that $2 \times 3 = 6$, that cities develop where means of transportation are plentiful. Rules and vocabulary are the basic equipment for the production of thought as lathes and drills comprise the necessary equipment for the manufacture of large and complex steel products. Most tests of intellectual ability or achievement simultaneously assess both vocabulary and rules. Since these tests confound both factors, they are not able to determine the specific deficit that led to the mistake. For example, the typical problem in sixth-grade arithmetic books might read, "The circumference of a lake is 200 miles; what is the distance a swimmer must swim from any point on the shore to the exact center of the lake."

The child who fails to obtain the correct answer to this problem may have done so because he did not know the meaning of the word *circumference*. On the other hand, he may have failed because he did not know the rule that the circumference equals $2\pi r$ or because he knew neither the word nor the rule. It is important to diagnose exactly where the cognitive deficit is in order to help the child. As indicated earlier, a second set of processes, usually manifested by age 5, concerns different strategies of labeling the environment and of selecting hypotheses for thought. Here we confront the reflection–impulsivity dimension. Imagine two children, one reflective and one impulsive, who are given the circumference problem described above, and each is not sure whether the formula for the circumference of a circle is $2\pi r$ or πr^2. The impulsive child typically selects one of these formulas quickly without giving the matter much consideration. The odds are 50–50 that he would select the correct rule. The reflective child would pause much longer and evaluate the differential validity of each of these formulas. During the brooding, the reflective child might remember that the area of a square involves the square of a number and conclude that πr^2 must apply to the area of a circle. He would conclude that $2\pi r$ is probably the correct formula for the circumference.

As indicated in the introduction, motives, standards, and sources of anxiety are a trio of processes that exert considerable influence over the quality of the child's cognitive products. Unlike rats in laboratories who learn mazes in order to get pellets of food or avoid painful electric shock, children work at cognitive tasks for a variety of more sophisticated goals. As suggested earlier, the notion of attention as the final route through which motives, standards, and conflicts exert their influence is important, and makes attention essential in all learning and performance. It may turn out to be the basic construct that helps to explain how the motives and conflicts affect the efficiency of learning new skills and ideas. Unfortunately, we do not have attention meters that furnish us with an instant measure of how much attention the child is devoting to a particular task or set of stimuli. It is usually difficult to judge this value from his overt behavior. Day-dreaming is mistaken for thoughtful concentration. Perhaps one day each school desk will be equipped with attention meters and the teacher will monitor from her desk an instrument that informs her of the level of attention of each of her pupils and gives her a rational basis for chiding Johnny for not paying attention to his work.

RELATIONSHIP TO PIAGET'S SCHEME

In the closing parts of this chapter it is appropriate that the points of contact between what has gone on before and the structure that Piaget has given us be considered. At first glance it appears that there is minimal contact between these two systems. Although there are many facets to Piaget and although his effect on work in educational psychology is without parallel, it is instructive to go directly to the heart of his theory. Piaget's scheme can be distilled into four basic principles. (1) Intelligence is defined as the possession of operations or rules of transformation. (2) Development is associated with passage from one stage of operations to another. (3) Passage from one stage to another is a function of both experience and maturation. (4) The operations that define intelligence and which change with age are logical structures that are neither dependent on nor derivative from language. This last assumption reflects the basic conflict between American psychologists and the Geneva intellectual fortress. American theorists argue that mediation and language are at the heart of reasoning. They admit that there are structural changes in the hierarchy in which these mediational units are organized, but mediational structures with content are usually the basic explanations for age, sex, and individual differences in quality and flavor of reasoning and problem-solving products. Piaget's position is in opposition to this view, for Piaget argues that logical structures are independent of language content. In his most recent book with Barbel Inhelder (Inhelder & Piaget, 1964) he argued that structures cannot be explained by nor derived from language. Evaluation of the validity of this argument requires first a definition of logic and logical structures. Piaget evades this definitional issue. Logic must be defined as a set of fixed relationships between symbols. The set of relations, "if a then b, a, then b," is a logical structure which has no necessary reference to content. Let us examine Piaget's contention that logical structures are at the base of conservation of volume, for example, which is a popular Piaget demonstration. A child is shown two vessels with water levels at equal heights. One vessel is then poured into a taller, thinner one and the child is asked which vessel has more water. The child in the stage of intuitive operations says the tall, thin vessel contains more water. The child in the stage of concrete operations does not. Is this age difference explained by differences in logical structures? A set of experiments has suggested that the 4-year-old child does not conserve volume because the word "more" means bigger or taller for him and does not yet possess mathematical meaning. Halbert Robinson (1964) has shown that when the concept of weight is taught to a 3 year old by teaching him the meaning of the word "heavy," the myth about age and the size–weight illusion is lost. The role of language is also relevant for class inclusion problems. Piaget claims that if a child is presented with 16 red blocks and 4 green blocks and asked "Are there more red blocks or more blocks," the child who says "more red blocks" has made a logical error. It may be, however, that a child interprets the question as meaning, "Are there more red blocks or more green blocks?" It is difficult to prove that this error is a logical one rather than a semantic one, and easy to defend the notion that age differences in performance on these problems reflect changes in word and sentence meanings. This attitude is intuitively attractive when one considers the general problem of conservation. If conservations were logical structures, we should be able to talk about the conservation of intelligence or beauty, but experiments on these concepts seem foolish. Intelligence and beauty are not mathematical words and these words do not change their meaning between 4 and 8 years of age. The quantity word *more* does change its meaning during this period as a result of the socialization in mathematical language during the primary grades. The failure to demonstrate a capacity for double classification or class inclusion may involve specific language deficits.

It is not clear that the qualitative differences and the cognitive performance of 3, 6, and 12 year olds derive from different logical structures. We require careful and imaginative empirical studies which would ask whether developmental differences in performance on the Piaget problems are due to different semantic structures, different habits of perceptual analysis, or different logical structures. These investigations might be the most important of this decade.

SUMMARY

Consider an overt cognitive product (a test score, a learning score, or the ease of acquiring early geometry) as the dependent variable, and ask what predictor variables are relevant. We should include (a) the cognitive units of rules and vocabulary resources organized hierarchically, (b) habits for processing information, such as evaluation, analytic versus global perceptual attitudes, and (c) determinants of attentional involvement, including standards, motives, and conflicts. Attentional involvement, habits of processing information, and a reservoir of rules and vocabulary are the basic, overarching variables that interact in determining the quality and variety of intellectual products. We must focus on this whole array, by either including measures of them all or controlling them, if we are to understand the details of conceptual development. There are, indeed, stages of conceptual development, and the stages are characterized by different hierarchical organizations of concepts, rules, habits of processing information, and motives that facilitate or oppose attentional involvement. The task before us is to describe and understand these changing developmental hierarchies.

REFERENCES

Inhelder, B., & Piaget, J. *The early growth of logic in the child.* New York: Harper & Row, 1964.

Kagan, J. Acquisition and significance of sex typing and sex role identity. In M. L. Hoffman & Lois W. Hoffman (Eds.), *Review of child development research.* Vol. 1. New York: Russell Sage, 1964. Pp. 137-167. (a)

Kagan, J. The child's sex role classification of school objects. *Child Develpm.,* 1964, **35**, 1051-1056. (b)

Kagan, J. Individual differences in the resolution of response uncertainty. *J. pers. soc. Psychol.,* 1965, **2**, 154-160. (a)

Kagan, J. Information processing in the child. In P. H. Mussen, J. J. Conger, & J. Kagan (Eds.), *Readings in child development and personality.* New York: Harper & Row, 1965. Pp. 313-323. (b)

Kagan, J. Reflection-impulsivity and reading ability in primary grade children. *Child Develpm.,* 1965, **36**, 609-628. (c)

Kagan, J. Body build and conceptual impulsivity in children. *J. Pers.,* 1966, **34**, 118-128. (a)

Kagan, J. Reflection-impulsivity: The generality and dynamics of conceptual tempo. *J. abnorm. Psychol.,* 1966, **71**, 17-24. (b)

Kagan, J., Henker, B. A., Hen-Tov, A., Levine, J., & Lewis, M. Infants' differential reactions to familiar and distorted faces. *Child Develpm.,* 1966.

Kagan, J., Pearson, L., & Welch, L. Conceptual impulsivity and inductive reasoning. *Child Develpm.,* 1966.

Robinson, H. B. An experimental examination of the size-weight illusion. *Child Develpm.,* 1964, **35**, 91-107.

Schachter, S., & Singer, J. E. Cognitive, social, and physiological determinants of emotional state. *Psychol. Rev.,* 1962, **69**, 379-399.

Thomas, H. Visual-fixation responses of infants to stimuli of varying complexity. *Child Develpm.,* 1965, **36**, 629-638.

CHAPTER 8

LEARNING IN ADULTHOOD: THE ROLE OF INTELLIGENCE

NANCY BAYLEY
UNIVERSITY OF CALIFORNIA
BERKELEY, CALIFORNIA

The task presently before me grows out of the assumption that intelligence is basic to the capacity to learn, and that there is some correlation between level of intelligence and level of ability to learn new and complex concepts.

The specific questions that were posed to me are: "What kinds of intellectual abilities show growth into adulthood? How are these related to concept learning? What are the implications for the teaching of concepts to adults?" The material I am going to report is more relevant to answering the first of these questions. Out of this material may come some suggestions which will be partial answers to the other two questions.

The question of the nature of intellectual function and change in adults has intrigued me ever since I worked with the adult intelligence test scores of Terman's "gifted" subjects. In order to obtain an adequate range of scores on these gifted adults, Terman devised a test which he named the Concept Mastery Test. He defined intelligence as the ability to carry on abstract thinking. It thus appears that he would equate abstract thinking processes with high-level concepts. At the time of the second round of testings in 1951, when Melita Oden and I (Bayley & Oden, 1955) started to compare test-retest scores on the Terman Concept Mastery Test over a 12-year interval, we anticipated lower scores at the second testing. This anticipation was based on previous cross-sectional studies, such as those of Miles (1942) and Jones and Conrad (1933), in which the invariable findings had indicated that most intellectual functions decrease after about 21 years of age.

When, contrary to then-accepted information, these intelligent subjects gained on their retest scores, it became necessary to look for explanations and to consider a new conception of the characteristics of stability and change in mental ability in adults.

A brief review of the findings from the Terman study will serve to form a background for comparison with the new data I wish to present from the Berkeley Growth Study.

Figure 1 presents the mean scores of groups of Terman's gifted subjects and their spouses, all of whom were tested twice, at an interval of 12

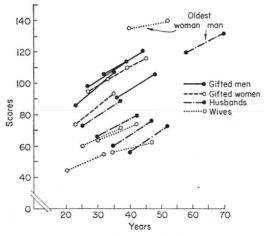

Fig. 1. Curves of changes in scores over a 12-year period for groups of subjects of four age groups, all of whom were tested twice on the Terman Concept Mastery Test. (From Bayley & Oden, 1955.)

years. Subjects are grouped according to the age at first testing, by 5-year age intervals. The overall ages included are generally from 20 to 50 years. Within these age groups the tested population is further divided into gifted subjects, their spouses, males and females. We see that all groups show an increase in scores after 12 years. The increase is present in the oldest as well as the youngest. There is a tendency for the greatest increase to occur in the males, and for the least increase in the older groups of the wives.

The question which immediately arises is whether the results are a function of the highly atypical sample. Terman's original sample had IQs ranging from 140 to 200 on the 1916 Stanford-Binet test. Although their spouses were not selected for IQ, there was obviously some selection exercised by the gifted subjects in the nature of a bias toward choosing relatively intelligent spouses. Terman estimated the spouses' average IQ to be around 125; that is, similar to college undergraduates. Consequently we cannot generalize from such a sample as this to predict intellectual age trends in an average population.

Another problem with the Terman study comes from the nature of the Concept Mastery Test. It has been generally true that scores on tests of verbal comprehension (i.e., information and vocabulary) in comparison with other subtests of a scale are maintained at a relatively high level into later ages. This is true, for example, for the Jones and Conrad (1933) study of a Vermont village sample, and it is true of the normative samples used in standardizing the several Wechsler scales (1939; 1955). The Terman test is highly verbal. The test, however, is composed of two subscales: synonyms–antonyms and analogies. The first of these is probably highly dependent on word knowledge. The second requires proportionately more reasoning. There is some evidence that the increases over the 12-year interval are less in the analogies scale than in the synonyms–antonyms scale. Consequently, it seems clear that we may find a different pattern of age changes in tests which are even less loaded with verbal information.

The findings from the Berkeley Growth Study may yield some partial answers to these questions because it is a less highly selected sample, and because the subjects have now been tested at 5 ages on the Wechsler scales, which contain both verbal and performance (nonverbal) subscales.

Although the subjects of the Berkeley Growth Study (Bayley, 1955; Jones & Bayley, 1941) are not a completely representative sample, they were selected at the time of their birth in 1928–1930 to represent a broad range of full-term healthy babies born in Berkeley, California hospitals. Their fathers' education ranged from third grade to the M.D. and Ph.D. degrees, with a mean of 13.7 years of schooling (S.D. 3.6 years). Attrition has changed the general nature of the sample very little over the 36-year period. It has not been possible to compare the general level of mental ability of these subjects with a random population, because of the unknown practice effects of the repeated testing these people have experienced in their 36 years. For the few who have not missed a single scheduled test, the number of tests taken is 42. The 30-year period starting with the Stanford-Binet at 6 years, includes a total of 16 test ages.

As for the subjects' own achieved education, the distribution is wide, though it is weighted with a high proportion of cases with more than 16 years education (there are 5 M.D.'s among the men tested so far at 36 years and potentially another M.D. and a Ph.D. will be tested). There is, at the other extreme, however, one case who remained in an ungraded class, achieving a barely third-grade level, and there are three others who did not complete high school. The mean education for the total sample of 58 longitudinally followed cases is 15.5 years. By sex the means are for 28 males 15.61, for 30 females 15.41; the S.D.'s are 4.10 and 1.54, respectively.

Most relevant for our present consideration will be an investigation of the scores earned by 52 of these cases tested on the Wechsler scales at

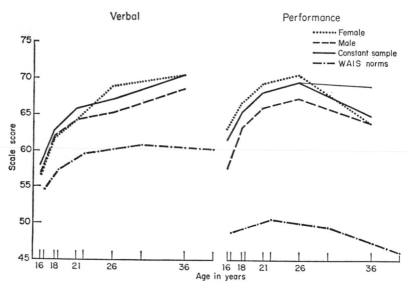

FIG. 2. Age curves of mean scores on the Wechsler Scales of Intelligence, for the Berkeley Growth Study. The Wechsler-Bellevue Test of Adult Intelligence (1939) was given at years 16, 18, 21, and 26; the Wechsler Adult Intelligence Scale (1955) at 36 years. The constant sample is composed of 25 cases of both sexes who were tested at all five ages. The 36-year point on the curve for the constant sample on the performance scale is shown both for the 36-year WAIS scores (heavy line) and for an estimated corrected score (light line). The number of cases at a given age varies for the female sample from 17 to 24, for the male sample from 16 to 22.

some or all of five test ages: 16, 18, 21, 26, and 36 years. At the first four of these ages the test used is Form I of the Wechsler-Bellevue Intelligence Scale; at the 36-year test the Wechsler Adult Intelligence Scale (WAIS) was used. All of the tests were given by the same examiner (Bayley) except for 18 of the 26-year tests, which were given by Dorothy H. Eichorn.

Figure 2 represents the age curves of the means for the verbal and performance scale scores. The three upper lines show the age curves of scores for the males and females separately, and for a core sample, sexes combined, who were tested at all five ages. The means for the males and females are not composed of completely constant samples, as all tested cases were included in each of the appropriate age groups. It is clear from the curve of the constant sample, however, that the age trends in scores are not a function of variations in the composition of the sample. For comparative purposes the WAIS age norms are also represented for a similar range of ages (the lower curve).

Another point necessary to consider here is the degree of equivalence between the Wechsler-Bellevue (W-B) and WAIS scale scores. It was not possible for us to give both forms of the test to our subjects at the same age, and differences between scores over a 10-year interval may be a function of either age changes or nonequivalence in scales, or both. In such published studies (Dana, 1957; Goolishian & Ramsay, 1956; Neuringer, 1963) as we have been able to find on the comparison of the scales at or near these ages, there appears to be no difference in difficulty levels of the verbal scale. On the performance scale, however, repeat tests on the same subjects gave scores averaging 3–5 points lower on the WAIS. We might assume, therefore, that an adjustment upward of 4 points on the performance scale of the WAIS will render the scores on the two forms of the scale approximately equivalent. The curve with such an adjustment at 36 years for the constant sample is indicated on the chart.

If we assume equivalence in difficulty at all five ages on the verbal scale, then we may say that the Berkeley Growth Study subjects clearly show an increase in scores with age over the entire span, though the rate of increase is decelerating. In comparison with the WAIS norms the Berkeley Growth Study increases are greater through 26 years. After this age our sample shows a slight continued increase through 36 years whereas in the normative curve there is a mild decline in scores after 30. Although the males appear to score higher on the verbal scale at 16 through 21 years, there are no sex differences at the later ages, 26 and 36 years.

The performance scale presents a different picture. There are clear increments for the total sample and for both sexes from 16 to 26 years, with the females consistently scoring higher. The curves for males and females make no adjustment for performance score differences on the WAIS. If we were to add 4 points at 36 years to each of these curves, then the males would show no mean change in score between 26 and 36 years, while the females drop an average of $2\frac{1}{2}$ points (about .3 of an S.D.). That is, unlike the Wechsler cross-sectional data, our longitudinal sample shows a tendency for stability in the performance scores with very little falling off in scores after 26 years. Such decline as there is occurs primarily in the females.

In summary, then, the Wechsler scores on our longitudinal sample either increase with age through 36 years on the verbal scale, or remain stable with very little loss of level on the performance scale.

AGE TRENDS IN INDIVIDUAL TESTS

The nature of the age changes in the Wechsler scale mental functions may be investigated more closely by looking at the age trends in the scale scores of the separate tests. These are shown in Fig. 3 for the six verbal subscales. Let us again assume that the two forms of the scale are approximately equivalent. The most consistent and marked increases in score over the 20-year interval are found for both sexes in three highly verbal tests: information, comprehension, and vocabulary. However, another verbal test, similarities, shows a leveling off after 26 years. This test has been changed only very slightly in the WAIS revision, and there may not be enough top in the scale to permit further increments. Alternatively, this kind of ability may have reached its own limits around 26 years.

Both the digit span and arithmetic tests level off after 26 years, with no increase in score at 36. Digit span is the one test which is entirely identical in the two forms of the scale. Although the scale scores for this test are different for the W-B and the WAIS, it has been possible to use raw scores to compare age changes in span. The curves for the raw scores are essentially the same as for the scale scores. Digit span is a test of capacity to retain discrete items in a short span of immediate recall. Immediate recall may be thought of as a basic tool in intellective functions, the capacity to hold in mind several abstract ideas in the associative processes of reasoning. If this is so, then a short span of immediate attention or recall could be a limiting factor in permitting processes of analysis and synthesis in thinking and the consolidation of knowledge in some organized and utilizable form. According to the tables of intercorrelation in the WAIS Manual, digit span correlated most highly with information, vocabulary, and arithmetic. These tests are presented orally, and call for just such a capacity.

Among the verbal subscales, digit span and arithmetic share similar growth curves, except for the fact that the females consistently do less well in arithmetic. This latter finding has been reported in many other studies. Within either sex, however, there is no further growth, but even, perhaps, a slight decline, after 26 years.

In general, it would appear that in the verbal portion of the Wechsler scales the more verbally constituted a test, the more likely it is that these subjects, and intellectually comparable persons, will continue to grow in the capacities tapped in the tests.

The performance subscales again present a somewhat different picture. However, the 36-year portion of these curves must be interpreted with caution. It is in the relative difficulty of these subscales that the WAIS is most different from the Wechsler-Bellevue. All five of the performance

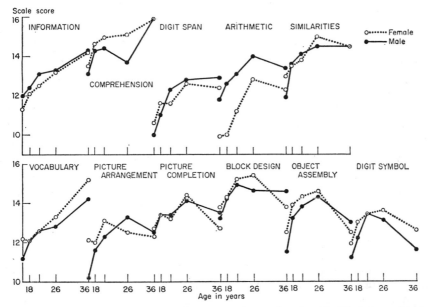

FIG. 3. Curves of mean scores by sex and age for the 11 Wechsler subtests, Berkeley Growth Study.

tests show a drop in score between 26 and 36 years. If, however, by using Neuringer's (1963) comparison of the scales on twice-tested 18 year olds, we make a rough adjustment in order to bring the relative difficulty of the scales into line, the drops for most tests are reduced. Actually, the men's performance on block design would appear to improve at 36 years, whereas picture arrangement, object assembly, and digit symbol would remain stable. Scores on picture completion, however, would drop even further. Using these adjustments, we would be able to conclude that in three of the performance tests the scores level off after 26 years, while in one (block design) scores continue to improve and in one (picture completion) there is a considerable loss.

What is most evident in the performance scale, however, is that at 36 years in four of the five tests the females do relatively poorly. This is in contrast to the earlier ages. For 16 through 26 years the females tended to surpass the males on these tests. The drop for females at 36 years (after scale adjustments not shown here) is most precipitous in picture completion, object assembly, and block design, and least in digit symbol.

To summarize the age trends on the performance scales, we find that, for this total longitudinal sample, growth continues through all five scales through 26 years, but then levels off, with the females showing a drop in scores after 26 years in several of the tests.

If we ask the relevance of these trends for the learning of concepts, we can at this point only reason by analogy to studies of learning and concept formation, which do not seem to have been compared on the basis of level of intelligence. One relevant recent study by Wiersma and Klausmeier (1965) may be cited. They found that of 48 females ranging in age from 20 to 51, the group of women 35 years and older took significantly longer than the younger ones to form the concepts in a task designed to measure speed of learning a concept. This task, which involved classifying cards according to indicated rules, may require types of concepts similar to those in several of the Wechsler scale tasks; namely arithmetic, similarities, picture arrangement, block design, and object assembly. It is interesting to note that four of the five tests are scored partially for speed of response, and that the Berkeley Growth Study women tended to lose ground in three of these five tests, while the men either improved or remained stable in all five.

These findings are by no means conclusive, but they are in line with other studies which show loss of speed in learning with advancing age. A possible age-related sex difference in this form of learning might be well worth exploring.

CONSISTENCY IN MENTAL ABILITIES

So far we have been concerned with general growth trends in increment or decrement in intelligence over the 20-year age span between 16 and 36 years. We may also ask how consistent over time are the scores earned in the several kinds of function as measured in the 11 tests of which the scale is composed.

The correlations between test ages are represented for the six verbal scales in Fig. 4. In this chart the tests are arranged approximately in the order of least to most change in the content of the WAIS Scale from its counterpart in the Wechsler-Bellevue. That is, digit span is placed first because that test was left unchanged, while vocabulary is last because the WAIS uses an entirely new set of words. Within each scale the test–retest correlations are arranged according to the time interval between tests, and to a generally ascending order of age at the later test. Thus, for digit span the first comparison is between 16 and 18 years, then 18 and 21, 16 and 21, 21 and 26, 18 and 26, 16 and 26, 26 and 36, 21 and 36, 18 and 36, and 16 and 36, the last of these being the full 20-year span. The solid dots represent correlations between the two different forms of the scale: the open dots represent correlations between retests on the Wechsler-Bellevue.

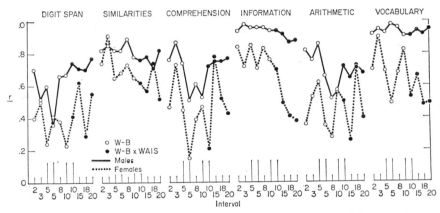

Fig. 4. Berkeley Growth Study test-retest correlations for Wechsler verbal scale scores. The subtests are presented in the order of least to most change in content from the Wechsler-Bellevue to the WAIS. The test–retest intervals are for years 16–18, 18–21, 16–21, 21–26, 18–26, 16–26, 26–36, 21–36, 18–36, and 16–36.

The general size of a correlation (indicated by the height above the zero base line) is in part a measure (in particular for the shorter retest intervals) of the reliability of the test. Consistency over time, or stability in a given function, should be indicated by the extent to which the level of correlation is maintained. That is, if a test is unreliable the rs will be low and often variable. If there are differing individual patterns in rate of growth, for example in vocabulary, we should expect the correlations to become progressively lower as the retest intervals become longer.

It appears, then, that digit span is relatively less reliable than information and vocabulary. It is also, for the males, surprisingly stable over the long intervals, though the shorter interval retest correlations tend to be low between 18 and 26 years. Both reliability and consistency are greater in the males in all six tests. This sex difference is conspicuous for vocabulary and information. The change in form of the test at 36 years does not appear to make any difference in these correlations.

Males are remarkably consistent in vocabulary scores: the r between 16 and 36 years is .95. In contrast, for the same interval the r for the females is only .49. Information has a closely similar pattern of sex differences in correlation.

Several of the lowest rs are at the intermediate ages and retest intervals, in particular for the women. This may very well be a period when there

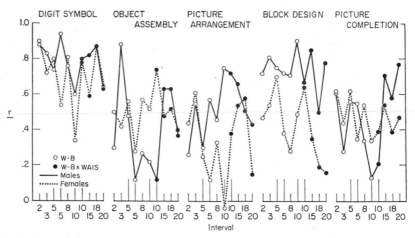

Fig. 5. Berkeley Growth Study test–retest correlations for Wechsler performance scale scores.

are large shifts in the women's motivations and attitudes toward intellectual and educational goals.

The same presentation of correlations is shown in Fig. 5 for the performance tests. Digit symbol (which was changed only by extending its length) appears to be most reliable and stable, with block design second. In general the performance test correlations are lower than in the verbal tests. Block design is the one test in this group that is both more reliable and more consistent for the males. The females show no constancy of scores over the long intervals in block design. Their performance on picture arrangement is erratic. We might say that the males tend to be erratic in the 5–10-year intervals on object assembly and picture completion.

The consistency correlations for the combined scales, as is to be expected, are much more stable than the separate tests. They are also more stable for the males than for the females. The 20-year rs (16 to 36 years) for the males for verbal, performance, and full scale IQs are .94, .88, and .97 whereas for the females, given in the same order, they are .57, .67, and .69. Comparing the verbal and performance scales within a sex, the males appear to be slightly more stable in their verbal scale scores (r of .94 for verbal versus .88 for performance); the females may be relatively more stable in performance (r of .67 for performance versus .57 for verbal).

To summarize these patterns of consistency in test performance, we see greater consistency over this young adult age span in both short- and long-range scores among the males, and for the males most clearly in vocabulary and information, and to a lesser extent in similarities, digit symbol, and block design. These tend also to be the tests (notably vocabulary and information) which show continuing increments in capacity (for both sexes) through 36 years.

COMPARISON WITH LONG-RANGE TRENDS IN
STABILITY OF MENTAL FUNCTIONS

Although over the 16–36-year span, the males, by comparison with the females in this study, are more stable in their test scores, and particularly so in the verbal scale, this is not true at the younger ages. It has been reported previously in several connections (Bayley, 1954; Bayley & Schaefer, 1964) that the mental test scores of boys at about 5–7 months of age are negatively correlated with their scores at school age. The girls' scores in infancy are simply unrelated to their school-age IQs. The differences have recently been brought home more strikingly in an as yet only partially completed analysis (J. Cameron, Nancy Bayley, & N. Livson, 1966) of factorial mental test subscores based on intercorrelations of age at passing the items in the California First-Year and Preschool Scales (Bayley, 1933; Jaffa, 1934), and factorial scores on the Stanford-Binet. In most instances these factors are self-restricted to short age spans, so we find that different functions appear to develop at different periods.

The most striking sex difference occurs for a cluster of items which are found in the 8–14-month age span. This difference is illustrated in the age curves of correlation given in Figs. 6 and 7. Figure 6 presents, as a base for comparison, the correlations of the total test scores at 10 to 12 months (the average of three consecutive test sigma scores) with total test scores at 24 test ages in the span from 1 month to 36 years. The rs with scores at adjacent ages are high but they fall off rapidly and after 4 years of age for the girls, the rs hover around + .20, ranging between 0 and + .34. The curve for the boys is similar, though these rs are generally even closer to 0, the highest r being .20.

Keeping this pair of curves in mind, let us look at Fig. 7. The infancy score used here we have called a Precocity Score for First-Year Factor: Vocalizations. This vocalization precocity score was obtained by adding

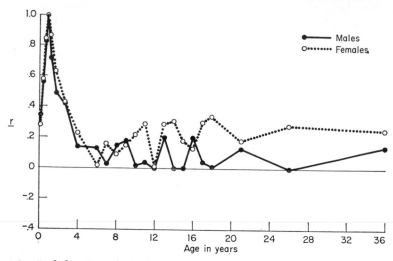

Fig. 6. Berkeley Growth Study. Correlations of the 11-month mental test scores (the mean standard score for ages 10, 11, and 12 months) with IQs at successive ages. For months 1–60 the rs are computed for the mean score of three consecutive ages. For years 6–36, scores for individual tests are compared.

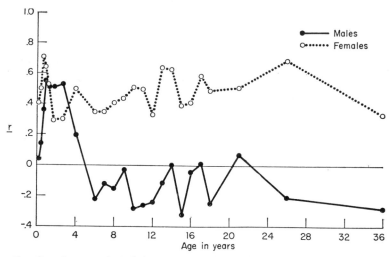

Fig. 7. Correlations of Berkeley Growth Study precocity scores (i.e., age at first passing) on the vocalization factor which occurs around 7 to 15 months, with IQs, as in Fig. 6.

together the age at first passing each of seven test items whose median age placements range from 8 to 13.5 months. The curves in this figure present the age changes in correlation of the vocalization factor with the total test scores for the 36-year span. (The signs of the rs are reversed so that precocity correlates with high IQ.)

In the first 3 years most of the correlations are positive and significant for both sexes. However, after this age the boys' correlations drop precipitously and in most instances thereafter are of negative sign. The girls' correlations, however, remain surprisingly high. They range up to .69 at 26 years and are .50 or higher for 8 of the 17 test ages from 4 to 36 years. For the boys after 4 years of age the rs range between $+ .20$ at 4 years and $- .33$ at 15 years. For 8 (or 47%) of the 17 test ages 4 through 36 years the sex differences in correlation are significant at the .10 level of confidence or better; 16.7% significant at the .05 level.

In a search for an early stable mental factor in the boys, we were able to find one occurring in the preschool period, ranging between 2 and 6 years, which shows significant correlations with later IQ. This factor we had identified as California Preschool Scale Verbal Knowledge. It consists primarily of items labeled "action agent" (what runs, what cries, etc.) and "prepositions" (placing a block in, on, under, behind, etc.). This factor of verbal knowledge reflects, and tends to emphasize, the sex differences in the stability of IQ after 4 years. As a base for comparison, let us again consider the consistency correlations for the full scale. When the standard scores of 4 year olds are correlated with the full-scale scores at all ages, the males, as compared with the females, have lower correlations with their scores in the first 2 years, and higher correlations with their scores after 4 years. In the period 6–15 years the sex differences are small and insignificant but persist. Starting at 16 years, the females show a marked drop in correlation with their 4-year scores, these rs reaching their lowest point of .10 for the 36-year WAIS. By contrast the males' 4-year by 36-year tests correlate .69.

The preschool verbal knowledge factor correlates positively and usually significantly with all of the later IQs for both sexes. These are shown in Fig. 8. Although none of the single paired IQs differ significantly, of these rs, 63% are higher for the boys than for the girls. Also, the boys' verbal knowledge scores correlate significantly with their scores on the Wechsler information test at all five ages, 16 through 36 years. The correlations between the boys' preschool verbal knowledge and the information test range from .49 to .58. By contrast the same variables for the girls correlate only between .09 and .35.

Thus there appear to be different, sex-linked, and differently timed factors of intelligence which show some stable relations with subsequent intellectual performance.

These striking sex differences in early childhood call for a much more complete analysis and study than is appropriate here. It will, hopefully, serve at this time to point up the need to make our analyses of intellectual functioning—including learning—separately for the sexes. The differences are not complete dichotomies, but they are, nevertheless, very considerable. I do not believe they can be explained entirely by cultural expectations or differential environmental experiences and pressures.

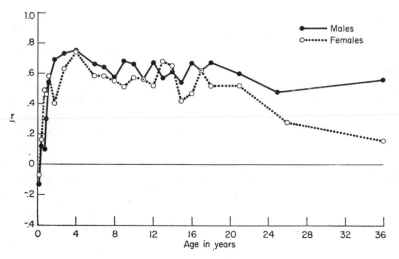

Fig. 8. Correlations of Berkeley Growth Study precocity scores for the preschool verbal knowledge factor (2–6 years) with IQs.

Relevant to this point is the material Bayley and Schaefer (1964) reported recently on behavior correlates of intelligence in this same Berkeley sample. The girls' IQs at 4 years and older were found to be relatively more highly correlated with indicators of their parents' mental abilities, while the boys' IQs for the same ages were correlated more clearly with the way their mothers had treated them as infants as scored on the love–hostility dimension of a rating scale.

We have not yet analyzed statistically the relation of IQ after 18 years to the emotional aspects of behavior, but we do have this relevant correlational material through 18 years. Two of the general findings may be illustrated here, to indicate their nature.

In Fig. 9 is given the pattern of correlations between children's IQs at 5 through 18 years and ratings of the way their mothers behaved toward them during the mental testing sessions in their first 3 years of life. The boys with positively evaluating, equalitarian, affectionate mothers tend to have high IQs. The girls' IQs are, with one exception, unrelated to their mothers' behavior toward them.

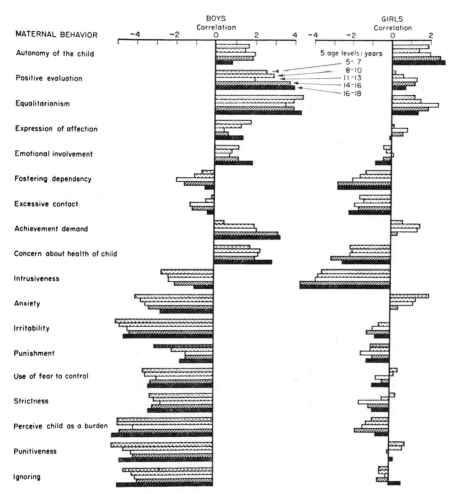

FIG. 9. Correlations between maternal behaviors in the children's first 3 years and their IQs at 5 to 18 years. (From Bayley & Schaefer, 1964.)

There are also characteristic patterns of correlation between several of the children's own behaviors in infancy and their later IQs. Figure 10 shows the relation between ratings of the children's happiness at 10 to 36 months and their IQs at all ages, 1 month through 18 years. Happy boy babies tended to make rather low scores, but as they grew older, especially if they were happy 2–3 year olds, their IQs after 4 years were higher. Happy girl babies made high scores at the time, but the relationship to later IQs became negligible.

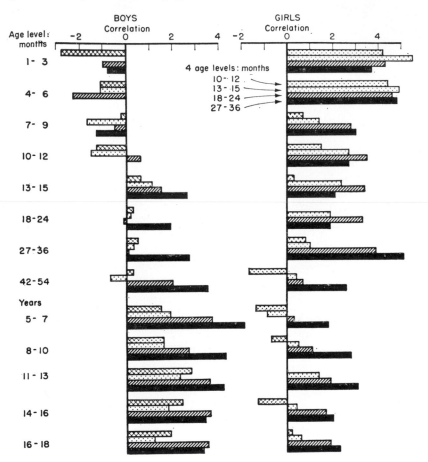

Fɪɢ. 10.   Correlations between ratings of children's happiness at 10 to 36 months with their intelligence scores at 1 month to 18 years. (From Bayley & Schaefer, 1964.)

One hypothesis to draw from these complex patterns of interrelations is that language as a representational–symbolic device for communication is a basic core of intelligence which is present from the second half-year of life. Attitudes of pleasure, eagerness, or annoyance are expressed by the tone and inflection of the voice before words are available. As seen in the first-year vocalization factor, early stabilization in these primitive verbal (or vocal) communications may appear among the girls, who tend to be oriented toward interpersonal relations. There is also evidence at later ages that the girls' intelligence scores are to a greater extent genetically determined, and this genetic control may be established at an earlier age than in the boys. This vocalization factor is not stable in young boys, however, because not only are they slower than girls in maturing, but more importantly their intellectual functioning is more permanently influenced by the emotional climate of their early environment.

The later-established stable mental function in the boys appears to be related to their sex-linked, object-oriented, information-gathering tendencies. Relevant to this point is the study done on these subjects by Bronson (1962), in which he found evidence that for the boys, but not the girls, the period at 10 to 15 months, which was important for establishing orientation toward others and the period at 2 to 3 years, which was important "for development of a sense of personal competence in coping with problems presented by the environment," were predictive of their counterpart behaviors at 10 years. Competence orientation, he found to be correlated with IQ. Responsiveness to persons and IQ were not correlated. The items in the preschool word knowledge factor deal with impersonal things, actions, and spatial relations.

THE RELATION OF INTELLIGENCE TO ACHIEVEMENT

Whatever the early determiners of mental function, by 6 years of age the IQs of both sexes are fairly stable. However, it appears from the correlational data on consistency of scores that the girls' test scores are relatively less stable after 16 years. Perhaps their intellectual functioning at this later time is more likely than the boys' either to be disturbed by emotional factors or influenced by educational experiences. On the face of it, these factors seem to be motivational and interest-directed.

Differences in motivation also seem to play some part in the sex differences found in the correlations between the subjects' IQs and their educational and occupational achievement.

The correlations of mental scores for the first 18 years with parental socioeconomic status are shown in Fig. 11. Though very low in infancy, the correlations are fairly high and stable after 5 years of age. Also, they are higher for the girls than for the boys, and notably so with their parents' education.

Consequently, the nature of the correlations between the girls' IQs

and their own attained education is in striking contrast. For the 16 tests
given from 6 through 36 years the mean of the *rs* is only .26. They range
from .10 at 14 years and .19 at 36 years to .53 at 21 years.

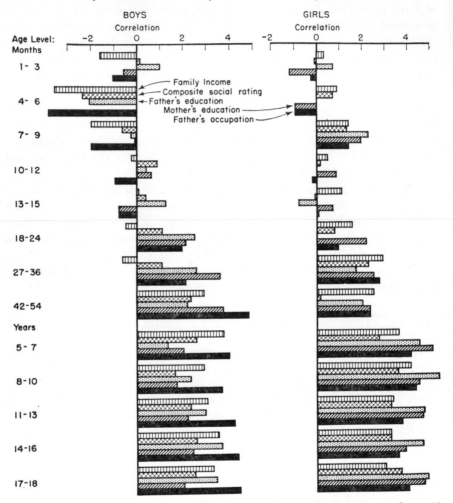

Fɪɢ. 11. Correlations between children's mental test scores, at 1 month to 18
years, and five indicators of parents' socioeconomic status at the time the children
were born. (From Bayley & Schaefer, 1964.)

The correlations between the girls' Wechsler IQs and their Hollingshead occupation ratings are similarly low. For ages 16 through 36 years
the correlations are .38, .46, .33, .46, .21, and .04.

At least a partial explanation of these low correlations is the small variability in educational level. (The S.D. in school grade achieved for the females is 1.54 years. By contrast the S.D. for the males is 4.10 years.) Similarly for occupation: only about one-third of the women had been employed, and those for whom occupational ratings were possible were all classified in the range of only three levels. The males' ratings, on the other hand, were distributed over seven levels.

The boys' correlations over the 6–36-year age span between their own final education and Wechsler IQ are high and in all instances statistically significant, 10 of them at the .01 level of confidence. With the Wechsler full-scale scores the rs are .70, .67, .74, .68, and .79 for the five test ages 16 through 36 years. Their correlations with occupational level on the Hollingshead scale are similarly high; for the same five ages they are .72, .74, .72, .69, and .75.

To the extent that education and occupation represent achievement status of these 36-year-old adults, it appears that the males are achieving pretty much in accord with their mental abilities. The females' achievements, however, as measured on these conventional criteria are very little related to their capacities.

These sex differences in correlation are not unusual. They reflect the difference in educational and occupational goals of males and females. The women, who are, as they often put it, "only housewives," and who apologetically use this phrase to excuse their feelings of inadequacy in the tests, show no more tendency toward any drop in IQ over time than those who are or have been employed as adults. Actually, the women who are classed in our sample as housewives have consistently higher IQs on the average than the women who are or have been employed for pay. It is also true that the woman with the highest and the woman with the lowest IQ in the sample tested at 36 years are both employed.

In both sexes there are individuals whose IQ has dropped at the 36-year testing. But these drops are unrelated to level of IQ, or education, or occupation. In general the trend of scores is up rather than down. The case in the study with the lowest intelligence, a male whose IQs were in the low sixties from the time he was 5 years old, had an IQ of 64 on the Wechsler-Bellevue at 16 years. His subsequent IQs were 70 at 18 years, 72 at 21, 78 at 26, and 80 at 36. He did relatively best on the performance scale, with performance IQs of 79, 78, 83, 89, and 92. However, his verbal IQs also increased: they are 59, 68, 67, 70, and 72. Incidentally, he learned to read after he was 21 years old.

IMPLICATIONS FOR LEARNING

It appears from the foregoing analysis of scores for these Berkeley Growth Study subjects that their intellectual potential for continued learning is unimpaired through 36 years. In the attainment of information and word knowledge their intelligence is continuing to increase. If we relate these results to the findings from other longitudinally studied adult subjects, such as those of Owens (1953), Bayley and Oden (1955), Jones (1959), and others, we may hypothesize that this increase in general verbal capacity may well be maintained through 50 years or longer. There is, however, very little research reported on the relation of intelligence level to learning in adults of various ages.

The extent of our knowledge about learning in adults has been discussed thoroughly by Jones and by Jerome in their chapters in Birren's *Handbook of Aging and the Individual* (1959). There is a surprisingly small amount of established knowledge in this field. I shall summarize it here only briefly.

There is evidence that in older persons loss in speed of mental processes is often compensated for by a greater fund of information and greater skill in its utilization. There is, on the other hand, probably increasing resistance with age toward expending the effort necessary to break old patterns of thought in order to learn new techniques and new ways of organizing knowledge. The extent to which these resistances are overcome may be matters of motivation and opportunity, rather than of intelligence. Jerome (1959) after reviewing studies of learning which predominantly show decline in learning ability after 35 years says, "The data currently available do not provide an adequate basis for deciding whether or not the motivation–speed–indigence–ill-health syndrome can be accepted as a sufficient explanation of the observed age differences in learning performance" (p. 698). Clearly there is an area here for more carefully controlled studies of learning in adults as it relates to both age and intelligence.

The studies on learning in relation to age indicate that although there is usually a decrement with age, learning still does occur, even to a fairly late age (Birren, 1959). It is also possible to develop practice procedures to facilitate learning (e.g., Belbin & Downs, 1965).

As for learning in the fourth decade of life, we may be reminded of a process with which we are all familiar from two examples of highly motivated educational achievements in subjects of the Berkeley study. These are of men who in their thirties resumed their educations, one to get a law degree and one an M.D., after periods of 10 years or so in other employment. At 16 years their IQs were closely similar, and both showed considerable growth through 21 years. After this age, the IQ of one man showed a moderate but consistent drop through 36 years. The other had increases to 26 years and at 36 his IQ remained unchanged. Both, with their advanced degrees, are now starting on new careers, with bright prospects for success.

It would appear that motivation and drive and ample time, rather than small variations in intelligence are the important determiners for much of learning in adults.

REFERENCES

Bayley, Nancy. *The California First-Year Mental Scale.* Berkeley: Univer. of California Press, 1933.

Bayley, Nancy. Some increasing parent-child similarities during the growth of children. *J. educ. Psychol.*, 1954, **45**, 1-21.

Bayley, Nancy. On the growth of intelligence. *Amer. Psychologist*, 1955, **10**, 805-818.

Bayley, Nancy, & Oden, Melita H. The maintenance of intellectual ability in gifted adults. *J. Geront.*, 1955, **10**, 91-107.

Bayley, Nancy, & Schaefer, E. S. Correlations of maternal and child behaviors with the development of mental abilities: Data from the Berkeley Growth Study. *Monogr. Soc. Res. Child Develpm.*, 1964, **29**, No. 6 (Whole No. 97).

Belbin, Eunice, & Downs, Sylvia. Interference effects from new learning: Their relevance to the design of adult training programs. *J. Geront.* 1965, **20**, 154-159.

Birren, J. E. (Ed.) *Handbook of aging and the individual.* Chicago: Univer. of Chicago Press, 1959.

Bronson, G. Critical periods in human development. *Brit. J. med. Psychol.*, 1962, **35**, 127-133.

Cameron, J., Bayley, Nancy, & Livson, N. *The predictability of adult intelligence from early mental and motor factors.* Paper read at Western Psychological Association, April 28, 1966.

Dana, R. H. A comparison of four verbal subtests on the Wechsler-Bellevue, Form I, and the WAIS. *J. clin. Psychol.*, 1957, **13**, 70-71.

Goolishian, H. A., & Ramsay, Rose. The Wechsler-Bellevue Form I and the WAIS: A comparison. *J. clin. Psychol.*, 1956, **12**, 147-151.

Jaffa, Adele S. *The California Pre-School Mental Scale.* Berkeley: Univer. of California Press, 1934.

Jerome, E. A. Age and learning—experimental studies. In J. E. Birren (Ed.), *Handbook of aging and the individual.* Chicago: Univer. of Chicago Press, 1959. Pp. 655-699.

Jones, H. E. Intelligence and problem-solving. In J. E. Birren (Ed.), *Handbook of aging and the individual.* Chicago: Univer. of Chicago Press, 1959. Pp. 700-738.

Jones, H. E., & Bayley, Nancy. The Berkeley growth study. *Child Develpm.*, 1941, **12**, 167-173.

Jones, H. E., & Conrad, H. S. The growth and decline of intelligence: A study of a homogeneous group between the ages of ten and sixty. *Genet. Psychol. Monogr.*, 1933, **13**, 223-298.

Miles, W. R. Psychological aspects of ageing. In E. V. Cowdrey (Ed.), *Problems of ageing: Biological and medical aspects.* (2nd ed.) Baltimore: Williams & Wilkins, 1942. Pp. 756-784.

Neuringer, C. The form equivalence between the Wechsler-Bellevue Intelligence Scale, Form I and the Wechsler Adult Intelligence Scale. *Educ. psychol. Measmt,* 1963, **23,** 755-763.

Owens, W. A. Age and mental abilities: A longitudinal study. *Genet. Psychol. Monogr.,* 1953, **48,** 3-54.

Wechsler, D. *The measurement of adult intelligence.* Baltimore: Williams & Wilkins, 1939.

Wechsler, D. *Manual for the Wechsler Adult Intelligence Scale.* New York: Psychological Corp., 1955.

Wiersma, W., & Klausmeier, H. J. The effect of age upon speed of concept attainment. *J. Gerontol.,* 1965, **20,** 398-400.

CHAPTER 9

INDIVIDUAL DIFFERENCES IN CONCEPT LEARNING

ARTHUR R. JENSEN
UNIVERSITY OF CALIFORNIA
BERKELEY, CALIFORNIA

To contemplate the problems of studying individual differences (IDs) even in relatively "simple" forms of learning, such as conditioning, motor learning, or rote learning, can be an unnerving enterprise. To have to think about IDs in *conceptual* learning is quite overwhelming!

If one of my graduate students were to tell me that he was thinking of doing his dissertation on IDs in concept learning and wondered if I could give him any help in getting started on this topic, my first impulse would be to give him two words of advice: "First, if you want to study concept learning, try to steer as far clear of IDs as possible; second, if you want to study IDs in learning, then steer clear of *conceptual* learning." This might appear to be cowardly counsel. But let me explain. I strongly advocate research on IDs in learning. I deplore the meager state of our knowledge in this area, and I think it is high time that more differential and experimental psychologists launch large-scale, systematic research into this important realm of phenomena. The question I raise concerns the sequencing of our efforts. Practically all of the subject matter of experimental psychology is, of course, eventually going to have to be reworked from the standpoint of IDs. But it also seems reasonable to think that the state of the art in any particular substantive area must attain a suitable stage of ripeness before IDs in this realm can be successfully and fruitfully investigated. We must have some rather clear notions about the main parameters of our phenomena with regard to both the independent and dependent variables. Some degree of theoretical development that can afford a source of testable hypotheses is another sign of the kind of ripeness I have in mind. In so far as concept learning is viewed as being essentially continuous with other simpler forms of learning it shares in the same common body of theoretical development that has grown up around these other forms of learning. If we believe that many of the most basic and pervasive processes of learning are involved in conceptual learning and that some of these processes are the same as those involved in, say, conditioning, or discrimination learning, or verbal rote learning, or short-term memory, then it would seem reasonable to first try to investigate IDs in these more elemental processes in the purest and simplest forms in which they can be found. I believe that a great deal of what we are going to need to know in order to understand IDs in conceptual learning and in order to carry on worthwhile research on this topic will be most easily acquired through intensive investigation of IDs in simpler learning functions. Even here the difficulties are great. But it is my impression that, in general, the difficulties in studying IDs in learning increases disproportionately with the increase in the number of independent, intervening, and dependent variables that are involved in the learning task. Conceptual learning is certainly at the "high" end of this continuum.

Coming back to our hypothetical graduate student, what if he remains undiscouraged by what I have said and refuses to abandon the study of IDs in concept learning for either the usual kind of experimentation on the overall group effects of various independent variables on conceptual behavior or for the study of IDs in comparatively simple learning processes? Is there anything I can give him by way of specific information or general orientation that could be of any value to him in his venture into this forbidding territory? Surely it is wide-open virgin territory, and the student will find little evidence in the literature of previous investigators ever having explored very far into the interior. Nor will he have much company at the present time. He will find perhaps a few rather haphazard footprints around the edges, and perhaps a number of premature and abandoned efforts, but no clear-cut paths or signposts, at least not into the region I would conceive of as the heartland of IDs in learning, conceptual or otherwise.

First of all, let us note some of the possible reasons for wanting to study IDs in learning. There are a number of justifiable aims in this area and these will in some degree determine our approach. It is hoped, of course, that these approaches will increasingly overlap as they are pursued and will converge in a common, systematic body of knowledge and theoretical formulation.

In the first place, we must do something about IDs in learning because, like Mt. Everest, they are there. And they loom large in our research on learning; the more complex the type of learning, the more conspicuous and unavoidable are the IDs. If we are to develop a science of learning, we cannot ignore this vast continent of phenomena involving IDs. It is essential grist for our scientific enterprise, and it deserves higher priority in our investigative efforts than it is now receiving.

If we are primarily interested in prediction and diagnosis of conceptual abilities from a completely applied, practical standpoint, we can probably expect a fair degree of success without having to concern ourselves with many of the kinds of problems that will have to be faced by the investigator who hopes ultimately to achieve a scientific understanding of IDs in learning. Such understanding implies a great deal more than the achievement of a certain degree of actuarial prediction. The ability of psychologists to predict and control behavior has, of course, always been far ahead of their understanding of behavior. Knowing the correlation coefficient between two phenomena can always improve prediction of IDs from one phenomena to the other, but the correlation may or may not add anything to our understanding of these phenomena. If someone tells me that a certain percentage of the "between subjects" variance in a complex reaction time task can be "explained" in terms of IDs in measured IQ, I'm afraid I am left with the dissatisfied feeling that nothing really has been explained, at least not about complex reaction time, though such a finding might afford some glimmer of insight into what might be the nature of "intelligence" or whatever it is that the IQ test measures. I would hope that we can rapidly advance far beyond this level of thinking about IDs in learning.

Even the traditional experimental approach to the study of learning, based on statistical comparisons of experimental and control groups performing under different conditions of particular independent variables, cannot safely proceed very far without paying attention to IDs. The effect of an experimental variable on the performance of *individuals* can often be quite different from the *average* effect on a *group* of individuals. Where there are significant subjects $\times$ independent variable interactions, we should be wary of conclusions concerning the effects of a particular independent variable when these conclusions are based on group mean differences. When these differences are both large and statistically significant, there is less risk than if they are of negligible and insignificant magnitude. I wonder how many of the independent variables that have been relegated as unimportant on the basis of their producing negligible group mean differences in one of the standard experimental paradigms actually produce large and significant interactions with subjects. This "between subjects" variance, of course, is usually just part of the error term in most experimental designs. Perusal of the analyses of variance in the experimental literature on concept learning indicates that some 50–90% of the variance in the dependent variables in these experiments is due to IDs or to some combination of IDs and true experimental or measurement error. Because of IDs in learning-to-learn and because of changes in the factorial composition of IDs influencing learning at various stages of practice, the estimation of measurement error as distinct from variability due to IDs is itself highly problematic at the present time. This is one of the major methodological knots we must contend with in order to make progress in this field. It is troublesome enough in the study of IDs in rote learning. I wouldn't relish facing these problems on the level of concept learning. But they will surely and unavoidably be waiting there, larger than ever, for anyone who wishes to venture in this direction.

The fact of IDs is one of the strongest arguments I know of against the "hollow organism" approach to research on learning. Research on IDs has the effect of making us think more about the inner structure of our "black box" than we are inclined to do when we stick solely to investigating the effects of one independent variable after another. I think that this increased concern with the black box, which will result from paying more attention to IDs in learning, will have a beneficial effect on the development of our theories of learning. Knowledge of IDs in learning provides both a source of hypotheses about the nature of learning processes and a means of testing certain deductions from theoretical formulations. For example, a theory might postulate a single process as being involved in two phenotypically different concept learning tasks; and a computer simulation involving this single process could be made closely to approximate the performance of a human subject on both of these tasks. But what if we give these two tasks to a large number of persons and discover that the subjects show a reliably different rank order of ability on one task than on the other? Obviously our uniprocess model would have to be revised. In short, our models must be formulated and tested, not only with respect to group mean effects of independent variables or with respect to the performance of an individual subject (in which case IDs would never enter the picture), but with respect to the subjects × independent variable interaction. This class of data affords a rich and valuable source of constraints on our theories or models of any particular kind of learning. I dare say we will find out more about the nature of learning from the systematic study of the subjects × independent variable interactions than from the group mean differences resulting from the manipulation of independent variables. Both approaches are, of course, necessary for a comprehensive account of learning. And it is mainly through the manipulation of independent variables that we can discover and further investigate IDs in our dependent variables.

THE TAXONOMY OF CONCEPTUAL LEARNING

In order to make our subject matter amenable to research at all, it will have to be subdivided in some systematic fashion. Conceptual behavior comprises a very broad class and no one can set out to study IDs in conceptual behavior per se. Preliminary to any serious attempt to do research on IDs in concept learning, some kind of taxonomic analysis should be made of the whole field. For example, there are a number of fairly obvious broad classes of phenomena with which we are dealing here. Unless proper distinctions are made among these classes of phenomena, whatever results we may find in our study of IDs are apt to be quite blurred, possibly contradictory, and probably highly unsuitable for theoretical assimilation. We want to avoid, if possible, merely adding to the already overstocked store of uninterpretable psychological facts.

One basic distinction would seem to be that between concept *formation* and concept *attainment*. Underwood (1952) had some such distinction in mind when he distinguished between the initial *learning* of the elements that are involved in the concept and the *recognition* of elements comprising the concept. In the former case, the subject learns the concept almost from scratch, since at the beginning the relevant dimensions of the concept are not yet salient; the subject has not yet learned to discriminate the dimensions of the stimuli and has no readily available labels for whatever components of the stimuli he may be able to discern. Under these conditions we can speak of concept *formation*. In concept attainment, on the other hand, the subject comes to the task having already learned to distinguish and label all the stimulus elements; he simply has to discover in the concept attainment task which dimensions the experimenter has selected to be relevant for the attainment of the concept. It seems a safe guess that different processes and abilities are involved in these two forms of concept learning and they will, therefore, have to be kept clearly separated when it comes to studying them in relation to IDs.

Three other broad distinctions should also be kept in mind. First, there is concept learning on the basis of primary stimulus generalization. Whether or not stimulus generalization should be regarded as conceptual behavior may in some cases be a rather arbitrary distinction. This does not matter so long as we are aware of the extent to which primary stimulus generalization as distinguished from other processes, such as semantic generalization, may play a part in our concept-learning tasks. The breadth and form of the gradient of primary stimulus generalization could, and probably does, involve IDs. This source of IDs would be important in concept learning only to the extent that the concept-learning task depended upon stimulus generalization.

A second kind of concept learning depends largely upon discrimination learning. Hull's experiment with Chinese pictograms is an example (Hull, 1920). Here different complex figures are presented, each of which does or does not contain some particular element. Throughout the learning trials only this single element of the complex stimulus is differentially reinforced until eventually it is discriminated by the subject, at least to the extent that it can serve as the cue for his identification of the complex figure as being a positive or negative instance of the concept to be acquired. This type of concept learning is closely akin to simple discrimination learning, so we might expect to find some of the same ID factors operating in both these forms of learning. Some of these factors would probably be much easier to discover in relatively simple discrimination learning tasks. Once found, their effects could then be sought in more complex concept-learning tasks of this variety.

The third main type of concept learning involves transfer of learning on the basis of symbolic mediating responses. The first two types of concept learning I mentioned—those based upon primary stimulus generalization and those based on discrimination—can also involve mediational processes. But they do not necessarily depend upon mediation. In this third category, however, I would include only those tasks in which the concept could not conceivably be attained except by means of symbolically mediated learning. This usually means verbal mediation. An example would be a sorting task in which such dissimilar objects as a watermelon, a potato chip, and a glass of milk were exemplars of the concept. The concept could never be attained by the processes of primary generalization or by discrimination alone, but would depend upon the stimuli eliciting a common verbal mediating response, in this case the word "food." This type of concept learning introduces a host of sources of ID variance that are not apt to play a prominent role in simpler types of learning. Mediated concept learning will be affected to a large extent by transfer of learning from the subject's past experience. The subject's verbal repertoire, the structure of his verbal associative network, the strength of the subject's tendency to make verbal responses to nonverbal stimuli, and other such processes which are a mixture of nature and nurture will figure among the main determinants of IDs in concept learning of the mediated variety.

Finally we must distinguish between tasks that involve only concept identification, without any learning whatever being tapped by the task, and tasks that involve learning parameters. The Columbia Mental Maturity Scale (Burgmeister, Blum, & Lorge, 1959) is a good example of a test of concept identification; it tests whether or not the subject has acquired a given concept at some time prior to the test. No learning is involved in the test itself. For example, the experimenter shows the subject a series of pictures—a locomotive, a ship, an automobile, a house, and an airplane—and the subject is asked to pick out the one that is "different." Such a test taps past learning and recall rather than current learning. It is useful as a measure of status but not of process. It is, of course, generally easier to measure IDs in status than to measure IDs in processes, but it is the latter with which I am mainly concerned.

Beyond these broad categories concept-learning tasks can be analyzed and classified in many other ways in terms of the degree of control over the various independent variables involved in the learning situation and the nature of the responses the subject is supposed to acquire. The innumerable independent variables that play a part in experimentation on concept learning should be classified in such a way that the investigator of IDs in any one type of concept learning or in any one experimental paradigm will be able to have some notion of the extent to which his findings can be generalized to other sets of conditions. For this purpose an index of similarity between concept-learning tasks would be useful; such an index could also help us in understanding relationships between specially contrived laboratory learning tasks and paradigms and their possible counterparts in "real life" learning situations, such as in the classroom. One way of developing a taxonomy of concept tasks would be by the Q-sort method. Just as persons can be compared and classified by means of a Q-sort, so could experiments on concept learning. In surveying the literature of this field one would note all the elemental characteristics of a large number of learning tasks and experimental arrangements. These would be put on cards to form the Q-sort. Trained judges could then perform Q-sorts on all kinds of concept-learning situations. We could, then, better answer such questions as "Are tasks A and B more alike than tasks A and C?" Here are just a few of the kinds of variables that could be entered in our Q-sort deck: the form of the task, such as card sorting, and successive or simultaneous presentation of stimuli; the number of dimensions in the stimuli and the number of values on each dimension; the number of relevant and irrelevant dimensions; the type of concept to be acquired—simple or unidimensional or involving two or more dimensions and whether these are conjunctive, disjunctive, or relational; the sequencing of positive and negative instances and whether these are subject-ordered or experimenter ordered; subject-paced versus experimenter-paced stimulus presentation; whether the subject gets feedback information after each stimulus or after scanning a succession of stimuli; the length of the feedback and postfeedback intervals; whether the stimuli are repeated in identical form throughout the learning trials or are never the same except for the relevant dimension; the length of exposure of each stimulus; the extent to which the experimenter makes available the information gained on past trials; the "concept size"—that is, the ratio of the number of relevant dimensions to the total number of dimensions in the stimuli; and so on. This may seem wearisome, but unless some kind of taxonomy is worked out in this field and is worked out in a way that could permit quantitative comparisons among concept-learning tasks, research findings on IDs in relation to concept learning are apt to present a highly confusing picture. If ability X or trait Y correlates with speed of concept attainment in situation A but not in situation B, we can hardly draw any reasonable conclusion unless we know a good deal about how situations A and B differ. I decided in reviewing this literature that some kind of Q-sort method would help to cut through a good deal of the confusion that already exists. What are we to make of it when one investigator reports that, say, anxiety correlates $+.40$ with speed of concept attainment and another investigator, using a different concept attainment task, reports a correlation of $-.40$. Let us not settle for a box score or an average of the findings of a host of various experimental findings. This would be the ultimate in non-science.

CATEGORIES OF INDIVIDUAL DIFFERENCES

A useful distinction is that between intrinsic and extrinsic sources of IDs in learning. When we think of IDs in learning, we are usually thinking of extrinsic IDs. Age, sex, intelligence, motivation, and personality are examples of extrinsic IDs that are sometimes correlated with performance in learning tasks. Extrinsic IDs are those which merely represent correlations with some measureable trait which does not bear any direct resemblance to learning or its inferred processes. Intrinsic IDs, on the other hand, are those which exist in the processes of learning. In other words, not all variance due to IDs is extrinsic in the sense that the totality of the "between subject's" variance in a learning task can be accounted for in terms of variability in subject characteristics that lie outside the learning domain. Most of the variance in learning is not going to be accountable in terms of psychometric test scores, personality inventories, age, sex, and other extrinsic personal characteristics. Therefore we need to study IDs in the intrinsic processes of learning. This means working out the dimensionality—the factorial structure—of the IDs in learning which arise from all the various subjects $\times$ independent variable interactions.

This is a big order, and the order gets bigger as the number of possible independent variables that govern the learning process increases. In this sense conceptual learning is highly complex and is bound to present considerable difficulty to the investigator who chooses to study intrinsic IDs in this domain. There would be no problem, of course, if subjects maintained the same rank order of ability in performance on every kind of concept-learning task. Then all we would have to do would be to determine the extrinsic correlates of this unitary concept-learning ability. We would "explain" some of it in terms of measured intelligence, some of it in terms of personality traits, and so on. But unfortunately things are not that simple. We know that subjects do not maintain the same rank order of ability from one learning task to another, or even within the same task under variations of the independent variables. I am not speaking of unreliability of measurement, but of reliable changes in subjects' rank order of performance on learning tasks under variations in the conditions of learning. This source of variability seems not to be tapped to any appreciable extent by psychometric tests. The process variables involved in a learning task are very different from those involved in performing on a paper and pencil test. When the learning depends on transfer from specific previously acquired knowledge or skills, and when these forms of knowledge can be assessed by psychometric tests, then we can expect to account for some of the variability in our learning measures in terms of our psychometric measures. Even under the best of conditions of this type considerably less than half the true ID variance in learning can be accounted for by extrinsic factors. In fact, until we gain some understanding of the dimensionality of IDs in intrinsic processes in learning, I doubt if there is much to be gained from determining correlations between single learning measures and extrinsic factors. The results are too uninterpretable, since some change in the conditions of learning can completely alter the pattern of correlations between learning measures and extrinsic measures. My greatest hope is that some of the main intrinsic factors that might be discovered in the realm of simpler forms of learning might be able to account for much of the variability we find in conceptual-learning tasks. These basic dimensions of learning ability, I would imagine, can be more easily discovered in less complex forms of behavior than conceptual learning. At present, for example, I am studying IDs in learning at the level of short-term memory. Since short-term memory plays an important role in concept attainment (Dominowski, 1965), I would expect that the factors discovered in short-term memory tasks will also account for some of the ID variance in concept attainment tasks. This will, of course, depend upon the particular memory requirements of the concept attainment task.

THE NEED OF A THEORY OF INDIVIDUAL DIFFERENCES

Since there is such an enormous number of independent variables which in various combinations could interact with subject variables in concept learning, it would be practically hopeless to attempt to explore this realm without some theoretical conceptions about IDs in learning to guide our search. At present we have very little theory along these lines. We do not yet know the main dimensions of IDs in simple forms of learning. As these are delineated by our research we will have more basis for theorizing about the dimensions of IDs in concept learning.

It is my belief, which I have spelled out in greater detail elsewhere (Jensen, 1965), that the tremendous variety of IDs in phenotypically different types of learning has a limited number of genotypic sources. A subject's performance on any given task will be a product of his standing on these basic dimensions of learning and the degree to which the learning task involves these factors. Our job is to discover what these basic factors are and to devise means of reliably measuring them. Some of these basic factors might have labels such as rate of buildup of habit strength, susceptibility to various kinds of interference effects, such as proactive and retroactive inhibition, speed of formation and dissipation of reactive inhibition, breadth of generalization gradient, rate of consolidation of memory traces and so on. The most economical way to proceed at present seems to be to hypothesize some process that seems basic to a number of phenotypically different learning tasks, to measure IDs in performance on these tasks, and to determine by means of some appropriate form of multivariate analysis whether the various tasks are loaded on the hypothesized factor in the way one would predict. For example, I have factor analyzed a number of simple learning tasks that were made up to differ in terms of the degree to which interference effects, such as proactive and retroactive inhibition, were thought to play a part in determining the subject's performance (Jensen, 1965). Tasks did, indeed, line up on certain factors in accord with the hypotheses. On the factor identified as susceptibility to interference, for example, the tasks hypothesized to involve a large degree of interference had larger factor loadings than did tasks hypothesized as being less influenced by interference. Actually three different kinds of interference factors were identified: one involving principally retroactive inhibition, one involving proactive inhibition, and one involving interference due to response competition. Dominowski (1965) has claimed that the memory effects in concept attainment can be regarded as involving both proactive and retroactive inhibition of short-term memory. So our proactive and retroactive inhibition factors might well be important basic sources of IDs in concept attainment. Subjects who score either high or low on our reference tests of these factors could be compared on concept attainment tasks that differ in their memory requirements. Predictions would be made concerning the effects of IDs in proactive and retroactive inhibition on speed of concept attainment on these various tasks. A fundamental question would be whether or not the factors we have identified in short-term memory are referable to the same genotype as those we find in concept attainment.

There are a number of features of concept learning, however, such as strategies, which are not shared to any appreciable degree by simpler types of learning. These independent variables which seem more or less peculiar to concept learning also probably interact with subjects and will have to be investigated in their own right on the level of concept learning. I would make every effort, however, to analyze any type of concept learning down to its lowest possible denominator before studying it from the standpoint of IDs.

THE CURRENT STATE OF OUR KNOWLEDGE

I have saved a report on the current state of our knowledge till near the end, since it is a disappointing picture. As I have already indicated, we know next to nothing about IDs in simple forms of learning, much less concept learning. Only extrinsic IDs have been studied, principally age and intelligence and manifest anxiety. Findings are usually reported in the form of correlation coefficients, and I must say I derive little satisfaction from reading about these or from reporting them. The fact of the matter seems to be that you can obtain just about any kind of correlation you wish between concept-learning scores and scores on tests of intelligence or anxiety. The correlations in the literature spread over a range from about —.60 to +.60. Averaging the correlations would result in something close to zero for the correlation between "concept learning" and intelligence or anxiety.

To find out how these ID variables interact with concept learning requires a highly analytical, experimental approach. Correlation coefficients alone cannot do the job.

The clinical literature provides most of what little we know about IDs in conceptual behavior. Since it has been believed that various forms of psychopathology affect conceptual behavior, we have a number of clinical tests of conceptual ability, such as the Goldstein-Scheerer tests, the Vigotsky or Hanfmann-Kasanin test, and the Wisconsin Card Sorting Test. Poor conceptual ability, as assessed by these tests, has been referred to by clinicians as "concreteness" and is generally associated with mental deficiency and organic brain conditions. Payne (1961) has reported that five independent clinical measures of concreteness, when factor analyzed along with tests of intelligence, had loadings ranging from .57 to .83 on g or the general intelligence factor. A seemingly opposite condition referred to as "overinclusiveness," in which concept boundaries are extended far beyond their conventional limits, is characteristic of schizophrenic performance. Payne (1961) has thoroughly reviewed the literature on the clinical study of conceptual behavior. Most of these findings and the clinical tests on which they are based are not sufficiently analytical to elucidate the workings of IDs in the realm of conceptual behavior. Many dimensions of conceptual learning are involved simultaneously in these various clinical tests, and we have no way of knowing the precise locus of the effects of brain damage, of measured IQ, of anxiety, and so forth, on the processes involved in these complex tasks. Whatever their value in clinical diagnosis may be—and it is reportedly meager—the scientific value of these tests as they are used in the clinic is practically nil.

INTELLIGENCE AND CONCEPT LEARNING

There can be little doubt that knowledge of everyday concepts and the spontaneous tendency to verbalize them, overtly or covertly, is highly correlated with measured intelligence. In fact, the Columbia Mental Maturity Scale, a test of general intelligence which was specifically made to correlate highly with the Stanford-Binet intelligence test, is based almost entirely on the subject's ability to recognize common concepts and classes of things in the natural environment.

When it comes to speed of concept learning the picture is much less clear. A study by Baggaley (1955) is rather typical of the psychometric approach to this problem. He correlated a composite measure of response time and number of errors in a concept attainment task involving five bilevel dimensions with Thurstone's tests of Primary Mental Abilities. He found that level of concept learning had low but significant correlations with inductive and deductive reasoning ability (as measured by the figure analogies test) and with speed of perceptual closure (as measured by the embedded figures test). His conclusions were that level of concept attainment on a card-sorting task was positively correlated with inductive and deductive thinking, with strength and speed of perceptual closure, and with ability to concentrate on one aspect of a complex stimulus at a time. Here it seems to me we are attempting to explain one poorly understood complex process (concept attainment) in terms of a number of even more complex and less well understood processes. I believe that ultimately IDs in psychometric tests are going to have to be understood in terms of processes discovered in the learning laboratory rather than vice versa.

The type of analytical, experimental approach that is needed to make headway in this area is exemplified by two excellent studies by Sonia Osler (Osler & Fivel, 1961; Osler & Trautman, 1961). In these studies children at several age levels and of either average or superior IQ were compared on concept tasks that differed in the complexity of the stimuli and the number of potential hypotheses the stimuli were capable of eliciting. It was found that more intelligent subjects attained concepts by hypothesis testing based on verbal mediation of the concept. Their learning curves showed sudden rises as compared with the more gradual slope of the learning curves of less intelligent subjects. But here is the really interesting point. It was hypothesized that "If hypothesis testing is more frequent among superior than normal Ss, it should be possible to influence the performance of the superior group by varying the number of irrelevant dimensions, on which hypotheses can be based, in concept exemplars. For Ss of normal intelligence, who tend to achieve solution by the gradually building up of an S-R association, no systematic relation between the number of stimulus dimensions and speed of solution is anticipated" (Osler & Trautman, 1961, p. 9). It actually turned out that the high IQ subjects were slowed down, as compared with the average subjects, in attaining concepts when the stimuli were complex. The complexity of the stimuli made no difference in speed of concept attainment for the average IQ subjects. The superior subjects had to extinguish more erroneous hypotheses in order to attain the concept than did the average subjects. Thus it is possible experimentally to manipulate the correlation between IQ and concept-attainment ability. If the hypotheses or mediators needed to attain the concept were subtle or complex, the high IQ subjects would have shown up as markedly superior to the average subjects. The particular independent variables involved in any concept-learning task will strongly determine the nature of the interaction between performance on the task and the ID variables. For this reason it is impossible to draw any overall conclusion about the correlation between an ID variable and performance in concept-learning tasks in general.

MANIFEST ANXIETY AND CONCEPT LEARNING

The same thing seems to hold true for personality variables. The only personality measure that has been studied to any extent in relation to concept learning is anxiety, usually as measured by the Taylor Manifest Anxiety Scale. Some studies have shown a positive correlation between manifest anxiety and speed of concept attainment (e.g., Wesley, 1953), whereas others have shown an equally large negative correlation between anxiety and concept attainment (e.g., Beier, 1951). Again it appears that one can produce almost any correlation one desires between anxiety and speed of concept attainment by manipulating the conditions of the learning task. Concept attainment seems to be facilitated by high drive or anxiety when the relevant dimensions for the attainment of the concept are high in the subject's hierarchy of hypotheses or mediators. When the relevant dimensions are low in the subject's hierarchy of mediating responses, anxiety or high drive hinder concept attainment. This generalization is, of course, in accord with the Spence-Taylor hypothesis concerning the interaction of drive with performance on tasks that involve response competition. The evidence in the field of concept attainment is consistent with this formulation but is still too sketchy for it to be considered a settled issue.

IDS IN SPONTANEOUS VERBAL MEDIATION

In concluding, I wish to draw attention to one aspect of IDs in conceptual behavior which has extremely important implications for education but which has not been subjected to thorough study. I refer to the tendency for nonsocial, nonverbal stimulus situations to elicit verbal mediational behavior in subjects. Howard and Tracy Kendler (1962) have touched on this problem in their study of the mediational response in reversal and nonreversal shift learning. The tendency for concept learning to be verbally mediated increases with age. But at any age there seem to be IDs in subject's spontaneous tendencies to mediate verbally in learning and problem-solving situations. Not only must concepts be learned, they must also be capable of being evoked by stimuli when the subject is not explicitly encouraged to look for or to verbalize the concept. Some pilot studies carried out in our Berkeley laboratory and in Martin Deutsch's Institute of Developmental Studies at New York Medical College indicate that there are large IDs in the tendency to use the concepts one has acquired. What are the determinants of this source of IDs in conceptual behavior? Here is a simple example of IDs in the tendency to make use of a well-learned concept. A group of children is given practice to the point of overlearning in responding with the words "same" or "different" to a large number of pairs of stimulus figures in which the two parts of each pair are either identical or are different. The children thoroughly learn the concepts of *same* and *different* and eventually never falter in giving the correct verbal label to the pairs of stimuli. The children are then put into a different experimental situation in which equivalent pairs of stimuli are presented but no overt verbal responses are called for. The subject is rewarded for pushing button A when the stimuli in the pair are identical and is rewarded for pushing button B when the stimuli are different. Though all the children have learned to verbalize the concepts *same* and *different,* some of them do so in this nonverbal task and some of them do not. Those who verbalize learn the task immediately and are consistently rewarded. Those who do not verbalize learn very slowly, achieving consistently rewarded responses only after many trials. Apparently almost no use is made by these subjects of the previously acquired concepts of *same* and *different*. Age, intelligence, and social class seem to be correlated with this phenomenon, which might be referred to as IDs in the threshold of verbal mediation in nominally nonverbal situations.

Finally, as I previously indicated, the subject of IDs in concept learning, indeed in any kind of learning, is virgin territory waiting to be explored by researchers with ingenuity and fortitude. At first the going will be rough and the initial hard-won advances may seem inelegant and meager. But this is inevitable in pioneering. And since there are bound to be mishaps and casualties along the way, I think it important that many investigators commit their research efforts to this field if we are to see any substantial progress.

REFERENCES

Baggaley, A. R. Concept formation and its relation to cognitive variables. *J. gen. Psychol.*, 1955, **52**, 297-306.

Beier, E. G. The effect of induced anxiety on flexibility of intellectual functioning. *Psychol. Monogr.*, 1951, **65**, No. 9 (Whole No. 326).

Burgmeister, Bessie B., Blum, Lucille H., & Lorge, I. *Columbia Mental Maturity Scale.* (Rev. ed.) New York: Harcourt, Brace & World, 1959.

Dominowski, R. L. Role of memory in concept learning. *Psychol. Bull.*, 1965, **63**, 271-280.

Hull, C. L. Quantitative aspects of the evolution of concepts. *Psychol. Monogr.*, 1920, **28**, No. 1 (Whole No. 123).

Jensen, A. R. *Individual differences in learning: Interference factor.* U.S. Office of Education Cooperative Research Project No. 1867. Berkeley: Univer. of California, 1965.

Kendler, H. H., & Kendler, Tracy S. Vertical and horizontal processes in problem solving. *Psychol. Rev.*, 1962, **69**, 1-16.

Osler, Sonia F., & Fivel, Myrna W. Concept attainment: I. The role of age and intelligence in concept attainment by induction. *J. exp. Psychol.*, 1961, **62**, 1-8.

Osler, Sonia F., & Trautman, Grace E. Concept attainment: II. Effect of stimulus complexity upon concept attainment at two levels of intelligence. *J. exp. Psychol.*, 1961, **62**, 9-13.

Payne, R. W. Cognitive abnormalities. In H. J. Eysenck (Ed.), *Handbook of abnormal psychology.* New York: Basic Books, 1961. Pp. 193-261.

Underwood, B. J. An orientation for research on thinking. *Psychol. Rev.*, 1952, **59**, 209-220.

Wesley, Elizabeth L. Perseverative behavior in a concept-formation task as a function of manifest anxiety and rigidity. *J. abnorm. soc. Psychol.*, 1953, **48**, 129-134.

PART III

LEARNING—TEACHING PROCESSES

CHAPTER 10

MEANINGFUL RECEPTION LEARNING AND THE ACQUISITION OF CONCEPTS

DAVID P. AUSUBEL
UNIVERSITY OF ILLINOIS
URBANA, ILLINOIS

I have been asked to explain what is meant by meaningful reception learning and to indicate how principles of meaningful reception learning apply to the learning and teaching of concepts. To carry out this assignment in a meaningful way, it seems to me that I should at least attempt to answer certain minimal questions. First, it will be necessary briefly to distinguish between reception and discovery learning, on the one hand, and between meaningful and rote learning, on the other. This should give us a reasonably clear picture of the nature of meaningful reception learning and of its relative role and importance in the total enterprise of classroom learning.

Second, it will be necessary to consider, in greater detail, meaningful learning as a *process*, and the relationship of the meaningful learning process to the nature of its *product*, namely, to the nature of meaning itself.

Third, once it is clear what I think meaning is, we shall be ready to carry the argument one step further, and to consider *generic* meanings or concepts and how they are acquired. Here the principal problem will be that of differentiating between concept formation as an example of meaningful discovery learning and concept assimilation as an example of meaningful reception learning. Fourth, it will also be desirable to consider some of the changes in cognitive development that affect the nature and relative importance of concept formation and concept assimilation at different stages in the life cycle.

Last, I shall want to discuss, by way of illustration, one of the problems involved in the optimal organization of subject-matter material that would apply to the meaningful reception learning of concepts.

RECEPTION VERSUS DISCOVERY LEARNING

The distinction between reception and discovery learning is not difficult to understand. In *reception* learning the principal content of what is to be learned is presented to the learner in more or less final form. The learning does not involve any discovery on his part. He is only required to internalize or incorporate the material (e.g., a list of nonsense syllables or paired adjectives, a poem or a geometrical theorem) that is presented to him so that it is available for reproduction or other use at some future date. The essential feature of *discovery* learning, on the other hand, is that the principal content of what is to be learned is not given but must be discovered by the learner before he can internalize it. The distinctive and prior learning task, in other words, is to discover something—which of two maze alleys leads to the goal, the precise nature of a relationship between two variables, the common attributes of a number of diverse instances, etc. After this phase is completed, the discovered content is internalized just as in reception learning.

ROTE VERSUS MEANINGFUL LEARNING

Now this distinction between reception and discovery learning is so self-evident that it would be entirely unnecessary to belabor the point if it were not for the widespread but unwarranted belief that reception learning is invariably rote and that discovery learning is invariably meaningful. Actually, each distinction constitutes, in my opinion, an entirely independent dimension of learning. Hence, both reception and discovery learning can each be rote or meaningful depending on the conditions under which learning occurs. In *both* instances, meaningful learning takes place if the learning task is related in a nonarbitrary and nonverbatim fashion to the learner's existing structure of knowledge. This presupposes (a) that the learner manifests a *meaningful learning set,* that is, a set to relate the new learning task nonarbitrarily and substantively to what he already knows, and (b) that the learning task itself is *potentially meaningful* to him, namely, relatable to his structure of knowledge on a nonarbitrary and nonverbatim basis. Thus, irrespective of how much potential meaning may inhere in a given proposition, if the learner's intention is to internalize it as an arbitrary and verbatim series of words, both the learning process and the learning outcome must be rote or meaningless. And, conversely, no matter how meaningful the learner's set may be, neither the process nor outcome of learning can be meaningful if the learning task itself consists of purely arbitrary, verbatim associations as in paired-associate or rote serial learning.

It is only when we understand that meaningful learning presupposes only these two basic criteria, and that the rote–meaningful and reception–discovery dimensions of learning are entirely separate, that we can appreciate the important role of meaningful reception learning in classroom learning. Although, for various reasons, rote reception learning of subject matter is all too common at all academic levels, this need not be the case if expository teaching is properly conducted. We are gradually beginning to realize that not only can good expository teaching lead to meaningful reception learning, but also that discovery learning or problem solving is no panacea for meaningful learning. Problem solving in the classroom can be just as rote a process as the procedure whereby Thorndike's cats learned to escape from their problem boxes. This is obviously the case, for example, when students simply memorize rotely the sequence of steps involved in solving each of the "type problems" in a course such as algebra, without having the faintest idea of what they are doing and why, and then apply these steps mechanically to the solution of a given practice or examination problem, after using various rotely memorized cues to identify it as an exemplar of the problem type in question. They get the right answers and undoubtedly engage in discovery learning. But is this learning any more meaningful than the rote memorization of a geometrical theorem as an arbitrary series of connected words?

THE NATURE OF MEANINGFUL LEARNING

By meaningful learning, therefore, I am referring primarily to a distinctive kind of learning process and to the outcome of this process, namely, the acquisition of new meanings. I have characterized this process as one of relating a learning task in nonarbitrary and nonverbatim fashion to relevant aspects of what the learner already knows, and have also specified that this presupposes both (a) that the learning task is potentially meaningful, or that it can be related nonarbitrarily and substantively to the learner's structure of knowledge, and (b) that the learner manifest a corresponding set to do so.

Whether new material is potentially meaningful or nonarbitrarily and substantively relatable to a given learner's structure of knowledge is a somewhat more complex matter than meaningful learning set. It obviously depends on the two factors involved in establishing this kind of relationship—that is, on the nature of the material to be learned and on the availability of relevant content in the *particular* learner's cognitive structure. Turning first to the nature of the material, its properties must be such that it could be related on a nonarbitrary and substantive basis to *any* hypothetical cognitive structure exhibiting the necessary ideational background and intellectual maturity.

But meaningful learning or the acquisition of meanings, as has already been emphasized, takes place in *particular* human beings. Hence, for meaningful learning to occur, in fact, it is not sufficient that the new material simply be relatable to relevant ideas in the abstract or general sense of the term. It is also necessary that the cognitive structure of the *particular* learner include the relevant ideational content and the requisite intellectual abilities. Inevitably, of course, this latter content and these intellectual abilities are *idiosyncratic* in nature. Thus the potential meaningfulness of learning material necessarily varies with such factors as age, IQ, occupation, subject-matter sophistication, and social class and cultural membership.

What precisely do we mean by saying that in order to be potentially meaningful, the nature of the material must be such as to be nonarbitrarily and substantively relatable to relevant ideas in the abstract sense of the term? The first criterion, *nonarbitrariness*, implies some plausible or reasonable basis for establishing the relationship between the new material and the relevant ideas in question. This may be a simple relationship of equivalence, as when a synonym is equated to an already meaningful word or idea. In more complex instances, as when new concepts are learned, they may be related to existing ideas in cognitive structure as examples, derivatives, subcategories, special cases, extensions or qualifications; or they may consist entirely of *new* combinations, superordinate, or otherwise, of the new material and existing ideas. The second criterion, *substantiveness* (or nonverbatimness), implies that an *equivalent* symbol or group of symbols could be similarly related to the same relevant ideas without any resulting change in meaning. In other words, the potential meaningfulness of the material is never dependent on the *exclusive* use of particular words and no others; the same concept or proposition expressed in synonymous language would induce substantially the same meaning.

LOGICAL VERSUS PSYCHOLOGICAL MEANING

At this point it might be helpful to distinguish between logical and psychological meaning. Psychological meaning is the actual or phenomenological product of a meaningful learning process. It refers to the idiosyncratic cognitive content that results when a particular learner, employing a meaningful learning set, relates potentially meaningful material to relevant ideas in *his* cognitive structure. Logical meaning, on the other hand, refers only to the potential meaning inherent in symbolic material, that is, whether it is relatable on a nonarbitrary and substantive basis to relevant ideas in any appropriately mature *hypothetical* cognitive structure. When an individual meaningfully learns logically meaningful concepts and propositions, therefore, he does not assimilate their logical meanings, but the invariably idiosyncratic psychological meanings that such learning induces in his particular cognitive structure. The idiosyncratic nature of psychological meaning, however, does not preclude the possibility of social or shared meanings. This possibility of shared meanings reflects both the same logical meaning inherent in concepts and propositions that are potentially meaningful to many persons, as well as many common aspects of ideational background in the cognitive structures of different individuals.

SIGNIFICANCE OF MEANINGFUL LEARNING PROCESS FOR CLASSROOM LEARNING

The significance of meaningful learning for acquiring and retaining large bodies of subject matter becomes strikingly evident when we consider that human beings, unlike computers, can incorporate only very limited amounts of discrete and verbatim material, and, can also retain such material only over very short intervals of time unless it is greatly overlearned and frequently reproduced. Hence, the tremendous efficiency of meaningful learning as an information-processing and storing mechanism can be largely attributed to the two properties that make learning material potentially meaningful. First, by *nonarbitrarily* relating potentially meaningful material to established ideas in his cognitive structure, the learner can effectively exploit his existing knowledge as an ideational and organizational matrix for the incorporation of new knowledge. Nonarbitrary incorporation of a learning task into relevant portions of cognitive structure, so that new meanings are acquired, implies that the new learning material becomes an organic part of an existing, hierarchically organized ideational system. Thus, as a result of this type of anchorage to cognitive structure, the newly learned material is no longer dependent for its incorporation and retention on the frail human capacity for assimilating and retaining arbitrary associations. This anchoring process also protects the newly incorporated information from the interfering effects of previously learned and subsequently encountered similar materials that are so damaging in rote learning. The temporal span of retention is, therefore, greatly extended. Second, the *substantive* or nonverbatim nature of thus relating new material to and incorporating it within cognitive structure, circumvents the drastic limitations imposed by the short item and time spans of verbatim learning on the processing and storing of information. Much more can obviously be apprehended and retained if the learner is required to assimilate only the *substance* of ideas rather than the verbatim language used in expressing them.

How valid is the contention that much classroom learning must necessarily be rote in character? Admittedly, such representational learning, as mastering the letter symbols in reading, the names of various concepts, and foreign language vocabulary, *does* approach the rote level. This is so because most symbols obviously represent their referents on an arbitrary and verbatim basis. Such rote-like learning, however, tends to form a very small part of the curriculum, especially beyond the primary grades once pupils have mastered the basic letter and number symbols. Furthermore, it is much *less* arbitrary to equate, for example, a particular new foreign-language word to its known native-language counterpart, than to establish, on a completely random basis, a connection between the two *already* meaningful members of a given paired associate. In the former instance, since a new, previously meaningless word becomes meaningful, we evidently have an example of meaningful learning at a very primitive level.

In meaningful classroom learning, the balance between reception and discovery learning tends, for several reasons, to be weighted on the reception side. First, because of its inordinate time-cost, discovery learning is unfeasible as a primary means of acquiring large bodies of subject matter. The very fact that the accumulated discoveries of millennia can be transmitted to each new generation in the course of childhood and youth is possible only because it is so much less time-consuming for teachers to communicate and explain an idea meaningfully to pupils than to have them rediscover it by themselves. Second, discovery learning, on developmental grounds, is pedagogically sound for the meaningful acquisition of subject matter only in the case of more difficult and unfamiliar material, and more frequently during the elementary school than in subsequent periods. Finally, although the development of problem-solving ability as an end in itself is a legitimate objective of education, it is less central an objective, in my opinion, than is the learning of subject matter. The ability to solve problems calls for such traits as flexibility, resourcefulness, originality, and problem sensitivity, that are not only less generously distributed in the population of learners than is the ability to understand and retain verbally presented ideas, but are also less teachable. Thus, relatively few good problem-solvers can be trained in comparison with the number of persons who can acquire a meaningful grasp of various subject-matter fields.

THE NATURE OF WORD MEANING

Our discussion of meaningful learning thus far leads to the conclusion that *meaning itself* refers to the differentiated conscious experience, mental content, or idea evoked in a given learner by a particular symbol or group of symbols after meaningful learning has taken place. The acquisition of meanings is thus coextensive with the process whereby new symbols come to represent for a particular learner, objects, situations, events, ideas, and other symbols in the external world. At the simplest level of representation, as in learning the names of familiar objects in the environment, new symbols become meaningful when they gradually become capable of evoking approximately the same cognitive content as their significates, after being repeatedly and contiguously associated with them. "Naming" thus involves the establishment in cognitive structure of a relationship of representational equivalence between first-order symbols and concrete images. Other, second-order symbols or groups of symbols can then acquire meaning by being related in various ways to previously acquired meanings in cognitive structure (as synonyms, antonyms, derivatives, elaborations, superordinates, qualifiers, and new combinatorial products), without requiring that the learner have any direct, current contact with their significates. Thus, in contrast to the views of the mediational theorists and verbal associationists, the acquisition of simple meanings, as in naming, is not regarded as a manifestation of conditioning or rote verbal learning, but rather as a meaningful cognitive process involving the establishment of new representational equivalents.

GENERIC MEANING

As yet, no distinction has been drawn between simple signs referring to particular objects (or situations) and generic signs referring to classes of objects. Actually, of course, most of the words used in ordinary language, except for proper nouns and such, and with the exception of words used by very intellectually immature children, are primarily generic signs. Such words, therefore, are also clearly defined concepts with distinctive criterial attributes of their own. How then can we explain the generic meanings elicited by the conceptual use of terms in contradistinction to the characteristic kinds of meanings elicited by terms referring to particular objects? Obviously, since the type of meaning experience that emerges depends on the type of cognitive content that is evoked by the eliciting symbol, the difference between the meaning experiences elicited, respectively, by particular and conceptual terms must be sought in the type of cognitive content each category of term evokes.

Thus, paralleling the difference in the use of the terms themselves, the cognitive content corresponding to a conceptual term is generic rather than particularistic in nature. Instead of consisting of a concrete image of a particular object, it consists either (a) of a modal or idealized image of a first-order, relatively concrete concept such as *chair* or *dog,* or (b) of various combinations of first-order conceptual meanings in ways that constitute the criterial attributes of more abstract, higher-order concepts, such as *chief of state* or *chief executive of a republic* in the case of *president.*

The generic nature of the cognitive content of conceptual terms naturally reflects the prior occurrence and effects of the distinctive cognitive processes involved in concept formation. When a child, through hypothesis testing, abstracts, for example, the criterial attributes of *dog* from diverse examples of dogs, differentiates them from those which are not criterial (or which are criterial of other concepts), and then generalizes the criterial properties to all members of the class, it is evident that the resulting cognitive content *has* to be generic in nature. The last step in the process of concept formation is establishing representational equivalence between the generic symbol and the generic cognitive content it evokes.

CONCEPT ASSIMILATION VERSUS CONCEPT FORMATION

It is true, of course, that in most instances of concept attainment after early childhood, particularly in the school environment, the criterial attributes of concepts are *not* discovered inductively through a process of concept *formation,* but are either presented to learners as a matter of definition or are implicit in the context in which they are used. Concept attainment, therefore, largely becomes a matter of concept *assimilation.* And since, as far as the formal education of the individual is concerned, the educational agency largely transmits ready-made concepts, it is unwarranted and somewhat dangerous, I feel, to extrapolate findings from typical laboratory studies of concept formation to the attainment of concepts in a classroom setting.

Since the older learner of school age and beyond does not typically acquire a given concept through such processes as abstraction, differentiation, and generalization, where does the potential generic meaning expressed in its presented criterial attributes come from? Evidently when an individual acquires a conceptual term as a consequence of didactic exposition, its corresponding generic cognitive content *implicitly* reflects the previous occurrence of these latter processes in the historical evolution of the language. That is, since his cultural forebears did the abstracting, differentiating, and generalizing for him in evolving the concept, its symbolic term subsequently elicits generic cognitive content after he currently assimilates the presented criterial attributes in question.

Thus in concept assimilation, just as in concept formation, the learner's representational equation of a particular arbitrary term with its corresponding generic meaning for him, is merely the *final* step in the concept attainment process. The more crucial preliminary step, whereby the learner acquires the new conceptual meaning by reception learning, involves the assimilation of the new generic content itself. The most significant aspect of the concept assimilation process, in other words, involves relating, in nonarbitrary, substantive fashion, the potentially meaningful generic content contained in the term's definition or contextual cues, to relevant established ideas in the learner's cognitive structure. The precise relationship of the new potential generic meaning to existing ideas in cognitive structure, e.g., derivative, elaborative, qualifying, superordinate, which results in the phenomenological emergence of the new generic meaning in the learner, is stipulated by the criterial attributes contained in the new term's definition or contextual cues.

The choice of a particular arbitrary symbol to represent a new concept is not the *only* role of language in concept attainment, nor is it the *first* time that it is used in this process. Verbalization does more than just attach a symbolic handle to a concept so that one can record, verify, classify, and communicate it more readily. It constitutes, rather an integral part of the very process of concept attainment itself; its generic properties and unique manipulability and transformability influence both the nature and product of the cognitive processes involved in acquiring concepts. Thus, when an individual uses language to acquire a concept, he is not merely labeling a newly learned generic idea; he is also using it in the *process* of concept attainment to acquire a concept that transcends by far—in clarity, precision, abstraction, and generality—the level of concept acquisition that can be achieved without the use of language.

DEVELOPMENTAL CONSIDERATIONS

The role of language in concept attainment provides an important clue to the problem of why concept *assimilation* presupposes certain *minimal* levels of verbal ability and cognitive functioning, whereas concept *formation* can take place at almost any level of cognitive functioning once symbolic representation becomes possible, but, generally speaking, is most characteristic of the preoperational or preschool stage of cognitive development.

Concept assimilation, by definition, requires the ability to incorporate verbally presented relationships between ideas, that is, the criterial attributes of concepts, into existing cognitive structure. But the pre-operational child, although capable of understanding and using verbal symbols, cannot manipulate, *internally*, new logical *relationships* between the ideas they represent, either in reception or discovery learning; he can only manipulate *overtly* the relationships between the objects or situations represented by the symbols. Thus, the only alternative open to him in acquiring concepts is to *discover* their criterial attributes by overtly manipulating diverse instances of objects or events, using sub-verbally the necessary conceptualizing operations of abstraction, hypothesis testing, differentiation, and generalization. Because of its sub-verbal nature, however, the difficulty level of such concept formation is obviously limited.

During the elementary-school years (or Piaget's stage of concrete logical operations) the learner *is* able internally to manipulate new relationships between verbally expressed ideas, and hence can *assimilate* concepts, providing that he has some recently prior or concurrent concrete exposure to particular exemplars of the concept in question. Thus, although he does not have to perform the conceptualizing operations, or actually discover by himself the criterial attributes of *most* concepts, in order to acquire them, his understanding of them is only semiabstract and intuitive; it lacks the true abstractness, generality, and precision of the final (i.e., formal) stage of concept development when relationships between highly abstract and general ideas can be assimilated (or discovered) without any dependence whatsoever on concrete and particularized experience. Thus, during the concrete stage of cognitive development, when the conceptual learning task happens to be particularly unfamiliar or difficult, the process of discovery, or of actually performing the necessary conceptualizing operations, probably enhances the intuitive meaningfulness of the new concepts as a result of bringing the learner into more intimate contact with the concreteness and specificity of the experience upon which such meaningfulness depends. To a lesser degree, the same situation holds true for adolescents and adults when initially exposed to new concepts in an entirely unfamiliar discipline, since such learning also tends to be somewhat semi-abstract and semi-intuitive in nature—despite genuinely abstract cognitive functioning in other, more familiar subject-matter areas.

It thus appears that progressive development of the ability to *assimilate* concepts depends on the following three aspects of language development: (a) gradual acquisition of an adequate working body of higher-order abstractions that provide the component elements of the relationships constituting the criterial attributes of more difficult concepts; (b) gradual acquisition of "transactional" terms, that is, of substantive words such as *state, condition, basis, property, quality,* and *relationship,* and of such functional or syntactical terms as conditional conjunctives and qualifying expressions, that are necessary for bringing abstractions into relationship with each other in ways characteristic of the dictionary definition of new concepts; and (c) gradual acquisition of the cognitive *capacity* itself that makes it possible to relate abstract ideas to each other and cognitive structure on a completely internal basis—eliminating, first, dependence on overt manipulation of the referents themselves, and, then, dependence on recently prior or concurrent exposure to concrete and specific exemplars of such referents. Concept *formation,* on the other hand, like other forms of discovery learning, also takes place at lower levels of language ability. It can and does occur, of course, at higher levels also, but not typically in classroom learning—both because it requires so much more ability and effort than concept *assimilation* at these higher levels, and because it is much too time-consuming to constitute an efficient primary means of acquiring large bodies of subject-matter knowledge.

PEDAGOGIC IMPLICATIONS OF MEANINGFUL
RECEPTION LEARNING

I would like to suggest some pedagogic implications of the nature of meaningful reception learning for concept assimilation or the type of concept acquisition that is characteristic of classroom learning. I shall refer more to general logical implications than to specific evidence, both for reasons of time, and because little research evidence of a definitive nature is available.

Since meaningful reception learning depends on the relatability of potentially meaningful material, such as new concepts, to a particular learner's cognitive structure, it follows that *cognitive structure itself*, that is, the substantive content of the learner's knowledge in a particular subject-matter area or subarea at any given time, and its organization, stability, and clarity, should be the major factor influencing meaningful reception learning and retention, and hence concept assimilation as well, in this same area or subarea. Inasmuch as potentially meaningful concepts are always assimilated in relation to an existing background of relevant concepts, principles, and information, which provide a basis for their incorporation, and make possible the emergence of new generic meanings, the content, stability, clarity, and organizational properties of this background should crucially affect both the accuracy and clarity of these emerging new meanings and their immediate and long-term retrievability. If cognitive structure is clear, stable, suitably organized, and contains appropriately relevant ideas, accurate and unambiguous generic meanings should emerge and tend to retain their separate identity or availability. If, on the other hand, cognitive structure is unstable, unclear, disorganized, and contains no suitably relevant ideas, it should tend to inhibit meaningful learning and retention. Thus, according to this reasoning, it is largely by strengthening salient aspects of cognitive structure that meaningful new learning and retention can be facilitated. When we deliberately attempt to influence existing cognitive structure so as to maximize meaningful reception learning and retention, we come to the heart of the educative process.

Hence, the learner's acquisition of a clear, stable, and organized body of knowledge would constitute more than just the major, long-term objective of classroom learning activity, or the principal *dependent* variable (or criterion) to be used in evaluating the impact of all factors impinging on meaningful learning and retention. This same knowledge, at every stage of its acquisition, would also be, in its own right, the most significant *independent* variable influencing the learner's capability of acquiring more new knowledge in the same field. The importance of cognitive structure variables, however, has been generally underestimated in the past because preoccupation with short-term, fragmentary, non-cognitive, and rote kinds of learning has tended to focus attention on such situational and intrapersonal factors as practice, drive, incentive, and reinforcement variables.

The major implication of all this for teaching concepts is that inasmuch as existing cognitive structure reflects the outcome of all previous meaningful learning, control over the accuracy, clarity, longevity in memory, and transferability of the concepts to be assimilated can be exercised most effectively by attempting to influence the crucial variables of cognitive structure. In principle, such deliberate manipulation of the relevant attributes of cognitive structure for pedagogic purposes should not meet with undue difficulty. It could be accomplished (a) *substantively,* by using for organizational and integrative purposes those unifying concepts and propositions in a given discipline that have the widest explanatory power, inclusiveness, generalizability, and relatability to the subject-matter content of that discipline, and (b) *programmatically,* by employing suitable principles of ordering the sequence of subject matter, constructing its internal logic and organization, and arranging practice trials. Hence, transfer in the classroom acquisition of new concepts would depend on so shaping the learner's cognitive structure, by manipulating the content and arrangement of his *antecedent* learning experience in a particular subject matter, that the subsequent assimilation of these concepts would be maximally facilitated.

Both for research and practical pedagogic purposes it is important to identify those manipulable dimensions or variables of existing cognitive structure that influence the meaningful reception learning of subject-matter knowledge of which concept assimilation naturally forms such a prominent part. On logical grounds, three such variables seem self-evidently significant for the transfer functions of cognitive structure in meaningful reception learning. These variables are (a) the *availability* in the learner's cognitive structure of relevant ideas to which the new learning material can be nonarbitrarily and substantively related, so as to provide the kind of anchorage necessary for the incorporation and long-term maintenance of the availability of subject matter, (b) the extent to which these relevant ideas are *discriminable* from the new ideas to be learned, so that the latter can be incorporated and retained as separate entities in their own right, and (c) the *stability* and *clarity* of the relevant cognitive structure ideas, which affect both the strength of the anchorage they provide for the new learning material, as well as the discriminability between the established and the new ideas. Each of these variables, in turn, suggests certain pedagogic principles of programming subject-matter material. I shall have time to discuss only one such hypothesized principle that is related to the second of these variables, namely, the discriminability between new learning material and existing ideas in cognitive structure.

THE ROLE OF DISCRIMINABILITY IN MEANINGFUL RECEPTION LEARNING

The discriminability of new learning material from previously learned ideas has been proposed as a major cognitive structure variable in meaningful reception learning. In the effort to simplify the task of interpreting

the environment and its representation in cognitive structure, new learning material often tends to be apprehended as identical to previously
acquired knowledge, despite the fact that objective identity does not
exist. Existing knowledge, in other words, tends to preempt the cognitive
field and to superimpose itself, if at all possible, on similar potential
meanings. Under these circumstances, the resulting meanings obviously
cannot conform to the objective content of the learning material. In other
instances, the learner may be cognizant of the fact that new concepts
differ somehow from established concepts in cognitive structure but
cannot specify the nature of the difference. When this latter situation
prevails, ambiguous meanings emerge, permeated by doubt, confusion,
and alternative or competing meanings. In either case, however, the
newly learned meanings presumably enjoy relatively little separate
identifiability from relevant existing concepts at the very *onset* of their
incorporation into cognitive structure.

In addition, because of the presumed natural tendency for even clearly
discriminable meanings to undergo memorial reduction to established
ideas in cognitive structure, nondiscriminable meanings quite under-
standably manifest even less longevity. If new meanings cannot be
readily distinguished from established meanings, they can certainly be
adequately represented by them for memorial purposes. This would be
especially true for longer retention periods. Over short retention intervals, nondiscriminable material could be retained on a purely rote basis.

The discriminability of a new learning task is, apparently, in large
measure a function of the clarity and stability of existing concepts in the
learner's cognitive structure to which it is relatable. In learning an unfamiliar passage about Buddhism, for example, subjects with greater
knowledge of Christianity make significantly higher scores on the
Buddhism test than do subjects with less knowledge of Christianity
(Ausubel & Blake, 1958; Ausubel & Fitzgerald, 1961). This significantly
positive relationship between Christianity and Buddhism test scores holds
up even when the effect of verbal ability is eliminated (Ausubel &
Fitzgerald, 1961). Thus, much of the effect of overlearning—both on
retaining a given unit of material and on learning related new material—
is probably a reflection of enhanced discriminability, which can be accomplished by increasing the clarity and stability of either the learning
material itself, or preferably of the ideas in cognitive structure to which
it is related.

INTEGRATIVE RECONCILIATION

The proposed principle of integrative reconciliation in programming
instructional material stems directly from consideration of the role of

discriminability in meaningful reception learning. It may be best de-scribed as antithetical in spirit and approach to the ubiquitous practice among textbook writers of compartmentalizing and segregating particular ideas or topics within their respective chapters or subchapters. Implicit in this latter practice is the assumption (perhaps logically valid, but hardly tenable psychologically) that pedagogic considerations are ade-quately served if overlapping topics are handled in self-contained fashion, so that each topic is presented in only *one* of the several possible places where treatment is relevant and warranted. That is, the assumption is customarily made that all necessary cross-referencing of related ideas can be satisfactorily performed, and customarily is, by students. Hence, little serious effort is made *explicitly* to explore relationships between these ideas, to point out significant similarities and differences, and to reconcile real or apparent inconsistencies.

This latter approach gives rise to many undesirable consequences. First, multiple terms are used to represent concepts that are intrinsically equivalent except for contextual reference, thereby generating incalcul-able cognitive strain and confusion, as well as encouraging rote learning. Second, artificial barriers are erected between related concepts, obscur-ing important common features, and thus rendering impossible the acqui-sition of insights dependent upon recognition of these commonalities. Third, adequate use is not made of relevant, previously learned ideas as a basis for incorporating related new information. Finally, since significant differences between apparently similar concepts are not made clear and explicit, these concepts are often perceived and retained as identical.

The programming principle of integrative reconciliation also applies when subject matter is organized along parallel lines, that is, when re-lated materials are presented in serial fashion but there is no *intrinsic* sequential dependence from one topic to the next. Unlike the case in sequentially organized subject matter, successive learning tasks are in-herently independent of each other in the sense that understanding of part II material does not presuppose understanding of part I material. Each set of materials is logically self-contained and can be adequately learned by itself without any reference to the other; order of presenta-tion is, therefore, immaterial. This situation, for example, prevails in presenting alternative theoretical positions in ethics, religion, and episte-mology; opposing theories of biological evolution; and different systems of learning and personality theory.

Nevertheless, although successive learning tasks of parallelly organized material are not intrinsically dependent on each other, much cognitive interaction obviously occurs between them. Earlier learned elements of a parallel sequence serve an orienting and subsuming role in relation to later-presented elements. The latter are comprehended and interpreted in relation to existing understandings and paradigms provided by analogous, familiar, previously learned, and already established ideas in cognitive structure. Hence, for learning of the unfamiliar new ideas to take place, they must be adequately discriminable from the established familiar ideas; otherwise the new meanings are so thoroughly laden with ambiguities, misconceptions, and confusions as to be partially or completely nonexistent in their own right. If, for example, the learner cannot discriminate between new idea A' and old idea A, A' does not really exist for him; it is phenomenologically the same as A. Furthermore, even if the learner can discriminate between A and A' at the moment of learning, unless the discrimination is sharp and free from ambiguity and confusion, there will be a tendency for A' to be remembered as A as the two ideas interact during the retention interval.

In some instances of meaningful learning and retention, the principal difficulty is not one of discriminability, but of apparent contradiction between established ideas in cognitive structure and new concepts in the learning material. Under these conditions, the learner may summarily dismiss the new concepts as invalid, may try to compartmentalize them as isolated entities apart from previously learned knowledge, or, hopefully, may attempt integrative reconciliation under a more inclusive concept. Compartmentalization, under these circumstances, could be considered a commonly employed but unadaptive form of defense against forgetting, particularly in learners with a low tolerance for ambiguity. By arbitrarily isolating concepts that seemingly conflict with relevant, established ideas in cognitive structure, one forestalls their confusing interaction with and, hence, rapid assimilation by the latter. But this, of course, is merely a special case of rote learning. Through much overlearning, relatively stable rote incorporation may be achieved, at least for examination purposes. But, on the whole, the fabric of knowledge learned in this fashion remains unintegrated and full of contradictions, and is, therefore, not very viable on a long-term basis.

One of the strategies that can be employed for deliberately enhancing the positive effects of cognitive structure variables generally in meaningful reception learning, and hence for promoting integrative reconciliation as well, involves the use of appropriately relevant introductory materials or "organizers" which, in their own right, are maximally clear and stable. These organizers are introduced in *advance* of the learning material itself, and are also presented at a higher level of abstraction, generality, and inclusiveness; and since the substantive content of a given organizer or series of organizers is selected on the basis of their appropriateness for explaining and integrating the material they precede, this strategy simultaneously satisfies the substantive as well as the programming criteria for enhancing the positive transfer value of existing cognitive structure on new meaningful reception learning. Summaries and simple overviews, on the other hand, are ordinarily presented at the same level of abstraction, generality, and inclusiveness as the learning material itself. They simply emphasize the salient points of the material by omitting less important information, and largely achieve their effect by repetition and simplification.

The hypothesized function of the organizer is to provide ideational scaffolding for the stable incorporation and retention of the more detailed and differentiated material that follows in the learning task, and, in certain instances, to increase discriminability between the latter material and apparently similar ideas in cognitive structure. In the case of completely unfamiliar learning material, it would be necessary to furnish only an *expository* organizer consisting of more inclusive or superordinate ideas that could subsume or provide ideational anchorage for the new material in terms that are already familiar to the learner. But in the case of relatively familiar learning material, or material organized along parallel lines, a *comparative* organizer would be used, both to integrate ostensibly new concepts with basically similar existing concepts in cognitive structure, as well as to increase discriminability between new and existing ideas which are essentially different but confusably similar.

Comparative organizers, therefore, are expressly designed to further the principle of integrative reconciliation. They do this by explicitly pointing out in what ways previously learned, related ideas in cognitive structure are either basically similar to or essentially different from new concepts in the learning task. Hence, for one thing, such organizers explicitly draw upon and mobilize all available, similar concepts in cognitive structure that are relevant for and can play a subsuming and integrative role in relation to the new learning material. If successful, this maneuver could effect great economy of learning effort, avoid the isolation of essentially similar concepts in separate compartments that are noncommunicable with each other, and discourage the confusing proliferation of multiple terms to represent ostensibly different but essentially equivalent concepts. In addition, it appears logical to hypothesize that this type of organizer would increase the discriminability of genuine differences between the new learning material and seemingly analogous ideas in the learner's cognitive structure. This second way in which comparative organizers purportedly promote integrative reconciliation is predicated upon the assumption that if the distinguishing features of new concepts are not originally salient or readily discriminable from established ideas in cognitive structure, they can be adequately represented by the latter for memorial purposes, and hence would not persist as separately identifiable memories in their own right. It is assumed, in other words, that only discriminable variants of previously learned concepts have long-term retention potentialities.

Thus, if an organizer can first delineate clearly, precisely, and explicitly the principal similarities and differences between the ideas in a new learning passage, on the one hand, and existing related concepts in cognitive structure, on the other, it seems reasonable to postulate that the more detailed ideas and information in the learning task would be grasped with fewer ambiguities, fewer competing meanings, and fewer misconceptions suggested by the learner's prior knowledge of the related concepts; and that as these clearer, less confused new meanings interact with analogous established meanings during the retention interval, they would be more likely to retain their identity. Comparative organizers, for example, have been successfully used in facilitating the meaningful learning and retention of an unfamiliar passage dealing with Buddhism (Ausubel & Fitzgerald, 1961; Ausubel & Youssef, 1963).

CONCLUDING STATEMENT

Perhaps the principal import of what I have tried to suggest in this paper—more by way of implication and illustration than explicitly—is that principles of concept *formation*, based on laboratory studies, may not necessarily be coextensive with or even analogous to principles of concept assimilation in mastering subject-matter material. In the first place, the kinds of variables influencing the processes involved in conceptualization, and thus underlying the discovery of the criterial attributes of concepts, may be quite different from the kinds of variables influencing the meaningful reception learning of the same criterial attributes. Second, it presumably should make some difference whether the learning task involves merely the short-term acquisition of single, somewhat contrived concepts in a laboratory setting or whether it involves the long-term acquisition of the complex network of interrelated concepts characterizing an organized body of knowledge.

I appreciate that in our current neobehavioristic age, many of my notions may appear hopelessly old-fashioned, mentalistic, and philosophical: the distinctions between discovery and reception learning, and between logical, potential, and psychological meaning; the identification of meaning in terms of mental content and as the product of a meaningful learning process; the identification of a concept with a generic mental content rather than with a common response to stimuli sharing certain attributes in common; the insistence that the acquisition of concepts or generic meanings requires certain antecedent conceptualizing or cognitive processes; and the distinction between concept formation and concept assimilation.

These are obviously not the only ways of conceptualizing meaning or concept learning. But I feel that they have a certain heuristic value and a special relevance for classroom or subject-matter learning, which, in my opinion, largely consists of the reception learning of new meanings from potentially meaningful verbal materials. In this type of learning, new meanings are typically acquired in relation to hierarchically organized, existing bodies of knowledge in the learner. Thus, it is useful, I believe, to define potentially meaningful learning material in terms of nonarbitrary and substantive relatability to the learner's cognitive structure, and to think of the principal determinants of subject-matter learning in terms of various salient properties of the learner's existing body of knowledge as they are relevant to the learning task.

REFERENCES

Ausubel, D. P., & Blake, E., Jr. Proactive inhibition in the forgetting of meaningful school material. *J. educ. Res.*, 1958, **52**, 145-149.

Ausubel, D. P., & Fitzgerald, D. The role of discriminability in meaningful verbal learning and retention. *J. educ. Psychol.*, 1961, **52**, 266-274.

Ausubel, D. P., & Youssef, M. Role of discriminability in meaningful parallel learning. *J. educ. Psychol.*, 1963, **54**, 331-336.

CHAPTER 11

A MODEL FOR THE ANALYSIS OF INQUIRY

J. RICHARD SUCHMAN
UNIVERSITY OF ILLINOIS
URBANA, ILLINOIS

Inquiry has been variously described as an attitude, a state of mind, a way of learning, a process of investigation, an uncovering, and a search for the truth. Such descriptions serve to characterize phenomena only as they appear on the surface. To understand inquiry requires a look, however speculative, beneath the surface at the elements of the human condition and human functioning that play a role in the course of inquiry.

The purpose of this chapter is to present a model to provide a theoretical framework for the analysis of the behavior of inquirers. The model evolved through 7 years of research into the inquiry process as it is manifested by intermediate-grade children. This work was done at the University of Illinois with the outside support of the U.S. Office of Education. The initial purpose was to identify the necessary and sufficient conditions for stimulating and supporting inquiry in the elementary classroom and to develop methods and materials for creating these conditions. In time, the center of focus shifted toward the nature of the inquiry process itself, particularly the major psychological dimensions related to the processes of perception, motivation, storage and retrieval, overt action and the family of intervening functions loosely categorized as "thinking" or "information processing."

The process of inquiry can be made observable in the classroom setting by allowing children to formulate theories and gather data to test them in a group setting. Having seen discrepant physical events, they are challenged to formulate and test their own theories to account for the events. They have access to data through question-asking and can at any time verbalize their explanatory or theoretical formulations. Since no attempt is made by the teacher to either explain the events to the children or to render judgments about their theories, the children quickly learn that they have to judge the power of their own or each others theories and that this can be done through verbally mediated empirical tests or experiments.

Because of these specific conditions, the transactions between teacher and pupil represent true and open inquiry where the responsibility for initiative and control in the learning situation rests squarely and consistently on the shoulders of the inquirers, the children. These transactions under these conditions are available for tape recording and analysis. It is thus possible to manipulate various personal and environmental independent variables to test relationships with a number of dependent inquiry process variables.

The model to be discussed in this paper grew out of and was to some extent verified through the observation and analysis of the inquiry process as it emerged in these studies. It should be understood that the population was restricted to fifth and sixth grade boys and girls and that the inquiries were verbal and focused largely on physical events presented on motion picture film.

We begin with a working definition: Inquiry is the *pursuit of meaning*. By this I mean that it is motivated by the desire to obtain a new level of relatedness between and among separate aspects of one's consciousness. Obviously, I am making the assumption that there is a consciousness, and that it plays a significant role in human behavior. I shall not argue the merits of that assumption at this time. It is also assumed that human beings do seek to make their encounters with reality more meaningful and that increments in meaning are satisfying. Inquiry, then, is a form of human behavior in which a person acts to increase the meaningfulness of his knowledge and experience. For example, a person who sees a strange object and examines it more closely is inquiring in that he is conducting his intensive examination in hopes of obtaining more data and thus finding a way to reduce the strangeness of the object. This may be achieved through increased familiarity and by finding ways to relate it to what he already knows or is familiar with. If the object turns out to be "like a rock," he then has available all that he knows about rocks to add to the meaningfulness of the object.

Consider for a moment the process by which we assign meaning to experience. Existence consists of an almost continuous series of *encounters* with the environment. Not all encounters, however, are equally meaningful. Indeed, a large proportion of daily encounters are totally ignored, let alone interpreted. In order to obtain meaning one must employ some form of *organizer* that serves to select out and pattern certain aspects of an encounter. We can reduce to symbolic form the statement that encounters, when processed through organizers, yield meaning (Fig. 1).

Fɪɢ. 1.   Encounters when processed through organizers yield meaning.

But what exactly *is* an organizer? It is *any* idea, image, recollection, abstraction—any available pattern that can add to the meaningfulness of an encounter. A child's *second* encounter with a hot dog can be more meaningful to him in the light of his recollection of the first such encounter. Prior encounters as retrieved from storage can serve as organizers. A previously formed generalization or conclusion can also be an organizer. The belief that snakes can be harmful is in itself a meaningful notion and adds meaning to any encounter with a snake. Even a concept such as "balance" or "honesty" can enable a person to extract additional meaning from certain kinds of encounters. The former might have broad application to art, music, physics, mathematics, etc., whereas the latter is only appropriate in adding a new dimension of meaning to encounters with people.

The analysis of the generation of meaning in terms of encounters and organizers, has certain advantages. The examination of the teaching–learning process is considerably enhanced as we try to identify the kinds of encounters, organizers, and meanings available to the pupil. Does the teacher attempt to feed meanings to the children directly through verbal and other symbolic means or are meanings allowed to emerge as children apply organizers to analyze encounters? Where do the children obtain new organizers? Are they allowed to invent and test their own or are certain conceptual systems engineered into the children's thinking as the "proper" ways of interpreting encounters.

One can construct a simple taxonomy of teacher–pupil interaction from this model (Fig. 2). The vertical arrows feeding down into the

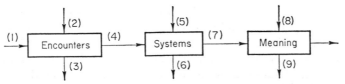

Fɪɢ. 2.   A simple taxonomy of teacher–pupil interaction. See text for explanation.

boxes represent symbolic (verbal) teacher inputs. A teacher can generate a vicarious encounter (arrow 2) by description or by simply giving out raw data (e.g., "Bill had 10 marbles and lost 2"). He can didactically provide new *systems* (arrow 5), new ways of handling data (e.g., subtraction is a system). The teacher can also offer new meanings (arrow 8; conclusions, generalizations, or "truths") to the pupils (e.g., 10 minus 2 is 8).

By the same token, the teacher can elicit the same three kinds of knowledge from the pupil (arrows 3, 6, and 9). He can request a child to retrieve and report a previously stored encounter (arrow 3), a system (arrow 6), or a meaning (arrow 9). Much traditional teaching consists of feeding knowledge units in at one or more of these levels and later eliciting responses from the children *at the same level.*

The horizontal arrows represent transformations from one level of knowledge to the next. Encounters can lead to the generation of new systems by the learner himself (arrow 4), and systems can be applied to encounters to yield new meanings (arrow 7). Teachers can generate more pupil involvement by maximizing encounters (arrow 1) and allowing pupils to try out various systems or invent new ones. The value of a system is related to the amount of new meaning it can generate. Meanings can lead to action (arrow 10).

Described in terms of this model, inquiry is the active quest for increased meaning through (a) the generation of encounters, and (b) the selection and synthesis of systems for the purpose of analyzing, classifying, and interpreting encounters. Encounters, systems, and meanings can all serve as organizers. Since meanings result from an interaction of encounters and organizers, the inquirer avails himself of both elements and then tries to combine them in a way that is productive of new meaning. Strategies vary enormously, all the way from data gathering through a succession of almost random encounters to a series of experiments (highly controlled encounters) expressly designed to test a particular meaning (e.g., a generalization, theory, or conclusion).

To get on with the process of explicating the model, I shall start with a function called *storage.* Here we find the residue of experience, and the reservoir of organizers. These include encounters, systems, and meanings that have been given to the learner or synthesized by him. Any or all of these may be available to serve as organizers, to give meaning to new encounters. The storage function is represented in Fig. 3.

The relationships among stored units greatly affect the retrievability and utilization of these units for inquiry or any other kind of cognitive operation. The Bloom taxonomy (1956) makes a careful distinction be-

tween knowledge and comprehension. The former consists in the retrievability of discrete informational units whereas the latter is the
capacity to move meaningfully and deliberately among the parts of a
lattice of related information with an understanding of the transformations that link the parts together. One can *know* that water boils at 212°F
at sea level by simply applying two systems, temperature and altitude,
to a few encounters with boiling water. The *comprehension* of the phe-

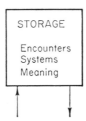

FIG. 3.   The storage function.

nomenon of boiling requires the ability to relate temperature to vapor
pressure through the concept of molecular motion and to relate altitude
to atmospheric pressure through the concept of gravitation. Finally, boiling is accounted for in terms of the relationship between vapor pressure
and atmospheric pressure.

Stored generalizations or conclusions have much greater power, flexibility and utility when they are well articulated with encounters and
relevant systems. Such articulation is best achieved when generalizations
are generated by the learner himself from encounters which he analyzes
with systems he has selected or synthesized on his own. One comprehends best that which he has struggled to understand in his own terms.

Here we can see how the process of inquiry can affect the character of
learning. If inquiry is the pursuit of meaning *through* the generation of
encounters and the development of systems to interpret them, it would
seem almost inevitable that an increase of comprehension would accom-
pany an increase in inquiry. The intake function is represented in Fig. 4.

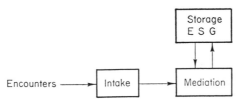

FIG. 4.   The intake function.

Encounters simply make new information available, but the meaning and significance derived from an encounter depends upon the organizers that are applied to it. A person encountering a tree may perceive a source of shade, a hiding place, an object of beauty, or perhaps all three. There will be differences from person to person and, within one person, differences from instance to instance. The model must, therefore, reflect the fact that there is no one-to-one relationship between a given encounter and the meaning derived from it. There is selection and control that regulates the retrieval of organizers from storage and the use of these gives form and meaning to intake. In Fig. 4 the regulatory function is represented by the box labeled "Mediation." The two arrows between mediation and storage represent the dual processes of storage and re-

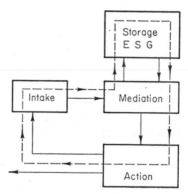

FIG. 5.   The action function completes the *inquiry cycle* (dotted lines).

trieval. The model does not show how the mediation function regulates the generation of meaning, it shows only that it *does* stand in a crucial pivotal position between storage and intake, the respective loci of stored organizers and new encounters.

The next function to be accounted for is overt action. The human can modify his environment and his relation to it. Actions take many forms and have at least two principal purposes: one is to produce new or altered environmental conditions; the other is to generate new data. A person may break a piece of chalk in two because he wants it broken—he prefers to have two pieces rather than one or because he wants to learn more about the properties of chalk, its strength or brittleness.

Figure 5 shows an arrow from mediation to action indicating that action is influenced by the same control system that regulates intake, storage, and retrieval. The action function has two efferent arrows, one directed back toward the external environment, representing action to change the environment and one directed toward the intake function, representing action for the purpose of generating new encounters.

Notice now that the arrows connecting the four functions constitute a closed loop which I have designated as the *inquiry cycle* (dotted lines). It corresponds to the sequence of behaviors that can be observed in children as they pursue meaning through inquiry.

Consider the example of a child who has witnessed a discrepant event, a demonstration of a blade that behaves in strange ways as it is held over a flame. First it bends downward as it is heated (Fig. 6). Then it straightens as it is cooled in a tank of water. The second time heat is applied it bends upward!

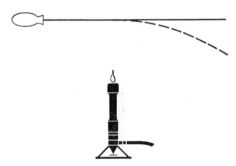

FIG. 6. The bimetallic strip bends downward the first time it is heated; melting is generally thought to be the cause.

The first part of the event is assimilated by the child because he has two available organizers in storage, the concepts of melting and gravity. When combined they provide a satisfactory model to account for the behavior of the blade. As the demonstration continues, the blade is held in a tank of water whereupon it straightens out. It is then inverted and held over the flame again. This time it bends upward, *away from the flame* (Fig. 7)!

The child is surprised and puzzled. The event is clearly discrepant. He has no single stored encounter, no system, no meaning, in short, no organizer that will enable him to assimilate *in toto* this encounter.

His subsequent behavior can be translated in the terms of the model.

1. Encounter with blade bending upward.
2. Mediation function scans storage for organizer to match encounter.
3. No such organizer is available.
4. At this point the child usually wants to pick up the blade and examine it more carefully, flex it in his hands, perhaps hold it in the

flame again, in short, learn more about the properties of the blade. In terms of the model, he is taking action to generate new encounters, taking in the data and scanning storage for organizers that will make the encounter more meaningful.

5. Without success he takes more action and generates more encounters.

In time he will find some organizers that permit him to assimilate at least part of the encounter. He will surely associate heat (a system) with the bending and suspect that the expansion and contraction (two more systems) of the metal are relevant. He might test this theory through

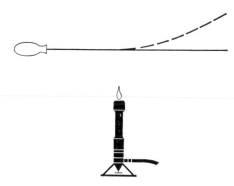

Fig. 7. The second time the bimetallic strip is heated, the blade bends upward—a discrepant event for most children.

various measurements (controlled encounters). In time new data will bring new organizers into play and these will in turn suggest what new encounters are needed.

At all times, the decision as to what operation comes next is made through the mediating function. In other words, the process of inquiry is internally regulated and serves to bring encounters and theories together for matching so that each builds on the other. Whenever a match is made between a theory and an encounter, to a degree the theory is supported and the encounter assimilated.

Only an autonomous mediation function can operate in response to the shifting data-gathering and theory-modifying requirements of inquiry. Any attempt to intervene, such as programming data input or instructing the inquirer to utilize certain organizers tends to convert the process from pure inquiry into some form of externally manipulated learning. It is not my purpose here to argue the relative pedagogical merits of different proportions of inquiry as opposed to didactics. Suffice it to say that there are gains accrued from both and that an optimal educational program would probably vary widely between the two extremes.

In order to complete the inquiry model, one more function must be incorporated: *motivation*. It is necessary to account for the fact that the inquiry cycle does not swing into high gear with every phenomenon or problem posed to a person. People are selective and behave in accordance with a system of values which dictates the directions of inquiry and the degree of urgency with which it is undertaken. The urgency factor is particularly important since the behavior of the mediating function seems to change in relation to the amount of pressure it is under. High pressure reduces the tendency to accommodate, to modify,

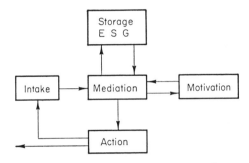

Fɪɢ. 8.   Model including the motivation function.

and regroup organizers. Urgency tends to prompt either total inaction or rigid action based on habitual organizers. Low pressure allows the luxury of reflection and playfulness with ideas. Under these conditions the mediating function can retrieve a greater range of organizers from storage and generate more encounters, as well.

Figure 8 presents the completed model with the motivation function linked to mediation by two arrows. The inward arrow represents the effects of motivation on the mediating process, effects that influence both direction *and* style of inquiry. The outward arrow represents the feedback, the fact that motivation is itself altered by the inquiry process and the intellectual products that it produces. For example, there is a marked effect on the motivation to inquire, once a sense of closure is gained. Furthermore, involvement in the process of inquiry accentuates another kind of motivation that seems to relate to the excitement of the act of inquiry, itself. When the mediation function is autonomous and in high gear the motivation to continue seems to become less and less related to the productiveness or closure generated by the activity and more and more by something even more intrinsic. There is a sense of power and competence that grows out of the manipulation of data and the construction of workable theories. On the other hand, there is for some a sense of wonder and excitement in exploring unfamiliar domains. In any case, motivation is clearly interactive with inquiry and should be linked to mediation through a feedback loop.

One criterion for the value of a model is its validity, the degree to which it matches observable phenomena, and provides a basis for accurate prediction and/or control of behavior. For the present, my claim for validity is based mostly upon objective but unquantified evidence, the kinds of observational data that led to the construction of the model in the first place. Quantified data are more difficult to obtain but by no means impossible. For example, if the motivational and mediational characteristics of a learner could be controlled one might be able to predict inquiry productivity from the number and quality of encounters and organizers available.

A second criterion is generality. Is this simply a model for question-asking in physics or does it reflect the more general interrelation of functions that characterize the human intellective system regardless of the mode of activity? I believe I can make a case for the latter. This case is based upon the facility with which the model serves as an organizer for didactic teaching, the very antithesis of inquiry.

Suppose a teacher wants to provide his pupil with a new set of organizers that will enable him to comprehend the essential structure and functions vital to electronic tubes. He might begin by showing his pupil an actual tube or a cut-away model. This would be an encounter made available through direct sensory intake. He might then say, "A tube is something like a valve." In doing this he is instructing the pupil to retrieve from storage a particular organizer (in this case a system or concept) and bring it down into the arena of thought for further consideration. By bringing in the "valve" concept the teacher is also suggesting the model of a "flow being regulated," since that is what valves are for.

He continues, "But instead of a valve to regulate liquids, a tube regulates the flow of electrons, a kind of electric current." Some new organizers have been brought into the picture to modify the earlier one.

"Notice this object here," says the teacher pointing (and thus generating a new encounter). "Electrons flow from this anode to this plate." The encounter is extended verbally as more data are thrown in. "Between the anode and the plate is something which acts like a venetian blind, to admit varying amounts of current." Once again a model or system is retrieved from storage as an organizer. Past encounters plus a concept of a venetian blind make the grid of the tube immediately more meaningful.

Of course, the skillful teacher will check all along the way to be sure that he knows what organizers are actually being employed by the learner and what meanings for the learner they are generating when applied to the encounters.

The main distinction between this process and inquiry is in the role of the mediating function. It is, in this case, being carefully manipulated by the teacher. Each retrieval from storage, each new encounter taken in is the result of the teacher's decision, not the learner's. As a result the process and the resulting cognitive gains should match more closely the teacher's goals than the pupil's, providing the teacher is skillful. There is an enormous amount of conceptual growth that can be brought about by skillful teachers who can provide an optimal combination and sequencing of encounters and organizers. But he must have maximum feedback from the pupil in order to employ his skill as diagnostician and practitioner in deciding what next step is best for a given learner at a given time. Of course, anything less than a one-to-one teacher–pupil ratio reduces the effectiveness of the diagnostic didactic tutor.

What is missing here is the freedom of choice afforded the inquiring learner and hence the opportunity to develop learner autonomy, but education has many goals and must have an equal number of approaches to achieve them.

To summarize, this paper proposes, explicates, and illustrates a model for the inquiry process that is an attempt to relate the functions of storage, retrieval, perception, overt action, and motivation through a central, ego-like mediating function. Didactic teaching as well as inquiry were described in terms of the model.

REFERENCES

Bloom, B. S. (Ed.) *Taxonomy of educational objectives.* Handbook I. *Cognitive domain.* New York: McKay, 1956.

CHAPTER 12

LEARNING IN THE DISADVANTAGED

CYNTHIA P. DEUTSCH
NEW YORK MEDICAL COLLEGE
NEW YORK, NEW YORK

In some respects, a title such as "Learning in the Disadvantaged" is reminiscent of the "Honeybunch" series of children's books: the differing titles such as "Honeybunch in the Country" and "Honeybunch in New York" served only to identify different locales in which the saccharine little girl had the same experiences with the same kinds of people. Honeybunch herself always exhibited the same reactions and never changed. In the title suggested for this paper, "learning" could be similarly regarded as a stable given, and the samples or populations or topics referred to as variable factors, having no intrinsic influence on the process itself. In that sense, the particular social category of the learner is quite irrelevant to understanding and discussion of the process. There is historical precedent for considering learning in this way, in that it has been extensively studied in simple situations, such as maze running, with the aim of abstracting principles to be applied to other organisms, situations, and levels of complexity. In other words, learning can be seen as a property of the organism—or, more accurately, of its nervous system—and a property which can be reduced to neurophysiological essentials. Therefore a title such as "Learning in the Disadvantaged," like "Honeybunch in the Country," could be simply a device for altering minimally the arena of discussion rather than designating a particular content.

Learning, however, can be viewed in a manner which includes particular attributes of the learner, the context, and the content of the material to be learned. Despite the fact that the S-O-R paradigm offered a basis for it, the experimental psychologists who specialized in learning theory 20 and 30 years ago eschewed such emphasis; as a result the findings from the multitude of learning studies yielded very little of relevance to human learning in a realistic social context. A variable such as the meaningfulness of what was being learned, in fact, was something that got in the way, so nonsense syllables were the content of choice for many experiments. The learning curves derived from such material find little application in the study of school learning, or in evaluating the differences in learning among differing populations.

With the current emphasis on education, and on the search for more effective teaching methods, learning theory has found its way through the maze and into the classroom. This process has brought about a focus on the learner and his specific characteristics—and in that context, a title such as "Learning in the Disadvantaged" takes on a rather specific meaning. It is in this sense that this paper has been prepared. It includes, therefore, some discussion of the characteristics of the disadvantaged with respect to some of the skills underlying learning, and some treatment of the stimulus organization consistent with the learner's characteristics, and the stimuli represented by the materials to be learned.

There are different kinds of learning and different kinds of disadvantage. For the population referred to in this paper, "disadvantaged" is only the latest in a series of euphemisms, which have included "slum dwellers" and just plain, "poor people." These last two terms are concretely descriptive of the economic situation of these people, but by using the term "disadvantaged" the intention is also to convey a categorization involving social or psychological variables. But there can be disadvantage only in a relative sense, and, therefore, the term needs somewhat further explication. For purposes of this discussion, the designation is used relative to the demands of the school and, later, the job market; the population being referred to are disadvantaged with respect to what is demanded for educational attainment and occupational mobility and advancement. The conditions of life at home for the children in this population are not continuous with the milieu of the school and do not prepare them well for the demands placed on them by the school and by the broader society.

There are three major assumptions on which the discussion which follows will be based.

First is the assumption that the social milieu in which the child grows up is highly influential in determining the kind and degree of his experience. This is rather obvious on the macroscopic level: the slum child has a different milieu and therefore a different set of experiences from the middle-class child. In current studies at the Institute for Developmental Studies (IDS), however, we are finding this true on a more microscopic level as well. An instrument known as the Deprivation Index, when applied to households of ostensibly the same socioeconomic status (SES) level yields differences between families in social experience such as trips away from the neighborhood, interaction between parent and child, organization of the home and of the family schedule, and so on. These differences are also found to be associated with scores on verbal and IQ measures given to the children. These data have been initially reported (Whiteman, Brown, & Deutsch, 1966), and more extensive discussion and analyses will be forthcoming.

Second is the assumption that the ease of acquisition of new knowledge and skills—learning—is based in large part on the prior experience and knowledge of the organism. Ample documentation for this position is to be found in Hunt's *Intelligence and Experience* (1961), which includes much work from many sources.

Third is the assumption that the nature of the stimulus—its organization, speed and manner of presentation, and the like—is influential in acquiring new knowledge. The relationship established between the experiential background of the organism and the nature of stimulus presentation is what Hunt refers to as the "match."

The discussion which follows concerns verbal, perceptual, and attentional characteristics of children who come from disadvantaged circumstances, and how these characteristics are related to their learning.

Let us begin with the verbal area.

A large cross-sectional language study done at IDS has indicated that children from disadvantaged backgrounds enter school with a somewhat different language system than do middle-class children. These differences obtain particularly in the grammatical structure of the language used, and in language used to relate one thing to another, as contrasted with the more simple descriptive uses (Deutsch, 1965; Deutsch, Maliver, Brown, & Cherry, 1964). These differential language findings are consistent with the reports of Bernstein (1961, 1962), and with data reported by Jensen (1963). In general, the language used by the disadvantaged children may be described as simpler in syntax, and less rich in descriptive terms and modifiers than is the language of the middle-class child.

These differences come about apparently because the homes from which the children come are far less verbal than the average middle-class home. Verbal interaction between parent and child tends to be in brief sentences and commands rather than in extensive interchange, and a great deal of communication in the very low-income home is gestural. Labeling of objects and actions in the environment is not emphasized. There are few if any books or magazines in the home, and the child gets little exposure to the printed word as a source of information or of communication.

These differences in linguistic background between the disadvantaged and the more privileged home are too well known to belabor further here. The point to be made about them is that the verbal and linguistic experience of the child influences his learning. Not only does the child who has an impoverished verbal background have a more restricted vocabulary and especially, as indicated earlier, a narrower and simpler syntax for purposes of communicating with others, but in all probability he has what Jensen calls a "higher threshold" for verbal mediation (Jensen, 1965). This would mean that the child, as a result of his experiential background, is less able to solve problems by verbal mediation than would be true of the child with greater language experience. The potential importance of this for learning cannot be overestimated, in view of the fact that problems whose solutions are facilitated by verbal mediation are not limited to verbal problems, or even to problems verbally stated. In many so-called nonverbal tasks, verbalization plays an integral role, and many nonverbal problems are solved with the use of verbal mediation. Jensen (1965) points out the crucial role of verbal mediation in the solution to the problems posed by the Raven Progressive Matrices. Other examples may be found in such a test as the WISC. The picture completion subtest, for example, presents the subject with a series of pictures in which something is missing. This is, of course, a visual stimulus—but the response called for is a verbal one: a label. Another example would be the object assembly subtest on the same scale. There is considerable evidence to show that having labels for unfamiliar objects facilitates learning about them. If this applies to tasks such as those in the object assembly, then it may well be that the child who thinks in verbal terms—and is, therefore, more likely to label the incomplete object as he is working with it—will perform better even on such highly spatial tasks.

The exact nature of the verbal skills which underlie verbal mediational processes is still obscure. Whether simple exposure to a highly verbal environment lowers the threshold for the use of verbal mediation or whether what is important is extensive practice with verbal-type problems is not really known yet. Although it will take extensive longitudinal studies on large samples to make such determination, a promising tool has been formulated in the last several years: the Illinois Test of Psycholinguistic Abilities (ITPA). This test is composed of nine subtests, and is organized according to Osgood's theory of language. It is a diagnostic test, in the sense that what emerges for each subject is a profile of scores along several linguistic dimensions, such as auditory decoding, visual–motor association, vocal encoding, and so on. In this way, as with any constructed scale, the components of a given overall score can be analyzed in terms of patterning of strengths and weaknesses.

In an effort to learn more about the linguistic organization and growth of young children, especially those from disadvantaged backgrounds, we have been applying this test to the children in our preschool enrichment groups and to a control group. Although all the data are not yet fully analyzed, the preliminary results are that the experimental group performs at a higher level on the test than does the control, but that the subtest patterning of the two groups is almost identical. Apparently, the language experiences which the experimental group had during the enrichment year raised their overall level, but did not alter the patterning of language skills. Our same two groups of children were also tested on the Kendler concept-formation paradigm (Kendler, 1963), but there was no significant difference between the experimental group and the controls in the number of subjects who could be designated "mediators" according to Kendler's system. Further investigation and retesting, it is hoped, will determine if further language training does alter the ITPA pattern, and if such patterning can be predictive of mediational behavior on the reversal shift technique. The level of performance of the experimental group on the ITPA was below the average—though on some subtests the difference was not significant—so it may also be that the overall ITPA score could predict mediation. If so, the implication would be that a language-enriched curriculum could foster the growth of verbal mediational processes in disadvantaged children, even without giving them any specific training in the use of verbal mediation.

Language was selected as one of the three areas of emphasis in this paper because it is obviously crucial to reading and to other academic performance. In the cross-sectional study previously referred to, one finding was that there were greater differences between the lower-class and middle-class children at the fifth-grade level than at the first grade (Deutsch, 1965). Although the data do not come from a longitudinal study, it still seems warranted to note that the disadvantaged children seem to become more so, at least in the language area, as they go through school. What this indicates about the effects of the school on development is, for the moment, irrelevant. The point is that ground can be lost, relative to the development of the more privileged group. To the extent that language influences other learning, this developmental decline can be especially serious.

In evaluating possible remedies for poor progress in language development, cautious optimism seems the appropriate attitude. The ITPA results quoted above, as well as the test–retest gain of experimental enrichment groups on the Peabody Picture Vocabulary Test, indicate that such scores can increase following an experimental compensatory education program. But it is not yet known if such increase will be maintained over long periods of time, with or without a continuing enrichment program, nor if language growth carries as a necessary corollary the growth in learning skills per se. As indicated above, one aspect of this question is being addressed in the ITPA study. Our longitudinal study— carrying the same groups of children through a special curriculum from the nursery year through the third grade, and continuing extensive evaluation of them through the sixth grade—will also yield some information on this question, but it will still be several years before those results are obtained.

In the meantime, Bernstein's work (1961, 1962), the work of Bereiter and his group, that of Gray and her group, the Baltimore language study, and others, as well as our own, are all contributing information and hypotheses in this area, language enrichment, which seems to be quite universally recognized as critical in the learning—and the teaching—of disadvantaged children.

In the perceptual area there is somewhat less widespread interest and work at the present, but its importance justifies a greater emphasis. Historically, theorists and researchers in this area have been concerned with the mechanisms of perception, and the influence that the organization of the stimulus field—particularly the visual field—exercises on what is perceived. The work on social influences on perception [with the exception of the well-known early study by Bruner and Goodman (1947) and a few scattered cross-cultural studies] has been concerned almost exclusively with the short-term influences of particular experimentally imposed or manipulated experiences. Unlike language, which is so obviously determined by social experience, perception has traditionally been regarded as a function quite independent of one's overall social milieu. This is an assumption which is open to serious question.

The fundamental contradiction to the assumption would be based on the proposition that experience and practice are influential in perceptual development. This does not seem an unusual assumption when one considers the visual deprivation experiments as examples, and it is certainly not unreasonable to view deprivation as a continuum. When it is, it becomes logical to assume that deprivation of varying degrees can be associated with perceptual disabilities of varying degrees. For example, as shown in the studies reported by von Senden (1932), people deprived of visual form experience for varying periods of time will show varying degrees of impairment in form discrimination. Might it not be true also that people deprived *in varying degrees* of visual form experience would show lesser, and perhaps more subtle, deficiency in form perception?

Slum homes provide few toys or other playthings for a child; neither are there picture books. Furthermore, there is usually a paucity of household objects. Might it not be that restrictions such as these in the visual field inhibit the development of form perception? How can a child learn to differentiate the forms of a square and a triangle if the differences are not explicitly pointed out to him, even if his visual–sensory apparatus is intact? What is the role of familiarity in accurate perception? Is it possible that new forms will be more easily differentiated if their components are more familiar, or if the child had a wider range of familiar forms against which to compare the novel? Fantz's work (1965) indicates that preference develops in accord with early exposure. Why shouldn't accuracy and ease of discrimination similarly relate to experience?

These questions have no definite answers at the present time. Posing them in this way places perceptual discrimination in a developmental and a social context which is open to intensive experimentation, and, hopefully, removes the issue from the now sterile "nativism–empiricism" controversy.

The suggested questions for investigation have related to visual perception primarily, but the implication should not be drawn that they are applicable only to vision. For further explication, let me briefly restate the hypothesis about auditory discrimination which I have discussed elsewhere at some length (Deutsch, 1964). That is that the noisy background and the weak signal conditions under which slum children live predispose them to learn well and early to tune out auditory stimuli. Both the signal-to-noise ratio itself and the inattention which it promotes operate to reduce the amount of auditory discrimination experience to which the child is exposed, and this eventuates in his later poorer performance on auditory discrimination tasks. Although we do not as yet have sufficient data either to confirm or disconfirm this hypothesis definitively, so far our investigations in the area have supported the assumptions.

It is pertinent here to mention some recent specific analyses of auditory discrimination data which relate both to perceptual and to linguistic development. One of the primary tests used to evaluate auditory discrimination is the Wepman (1958). This test uses 40 pairs of words, of which 30 differ from each other in one phoneme. This one differing phoneme can be at the beginning, the middle, or the end of a word.

Item analysis of Wepman protocols done by my colleagues has shown that the most frequent items missed are those pairs which differ in the final phoneme, and that whenever in our samples groups of children with learning disabilities are compared with control groups, there are significant differences in final phoneme discrimination whether or not the differences in initial phoneme discrimination are significant. Although analyses of all the Wepman data for all the children to whom we have administered the test are not yet complete, the findings for the several hundred protocols already analyzed are quite consistent. It seems fairly certain that the differences in performance by placement of phoneme are real ones. The implications for grammar and syntax are obvious, since most grammatical inflections in English are carried at the end of the word. There are also conceptual implications, in that accurate definition of number and tense can be very important in both stating and solving problems. Here it is relevant to note that in the ITPA study, the subtest patterns show, for both the experimental and the control groups, the poorest performance in those which involve auditory stimuli and call for knowledge of grammar and of function. Perhaps even more interesting is the fact that these are also the two subtests on which the experimental group is farthest above the control group. Unfortunately, data on the Wepman for these groups are not yet analyzed.

That discrimination can be successfully taught to young children can be implied from the experimental–control group differences in the ITPA data. Whether it can be trained in older children, especially those who already show considerable deficiency, is less clear. A study recently concluded at the IDS involved the testing and training of auditory discrimination in a group of third-grade reading retardates. The purpose of the study was to determine if training in auditory discrimination would enable retarded readers (who, we have found, are deficient in this skill, with respect to average or good readers) better to profit from reading instruction. Four groups were defined: one which received regular auditory discrimination training and also remedial reading, one which received only auditory training, one which received only remedial reading, and a control group which received neither. The second two groups also had a play period (during which the activities were neither auditory nor book-or-reading-related) in order to equalize the time spent with the tutor. A battery of eleven auditory discrimination tests was administered before, immediately after, and twice more at spaced intervals after the training period, which was one school semester's length for each group. The special work given the children was in addition to their regular schoolwork. Over-all analyses indicate no differential auditory discrimination improvement for those children who had specific auditory training. The more microscopic analyses are still underway, and it is not yet known whether some differential performance or patterning of performance will be defined.

Attentional processes are, in essential respects, a part of both perceptual and linguistic development. They are being considered separately here for convenience. It is obvious that experience will mean little unless the input channels are sufficiently open and attuned to the stimuli being presented. Both the state of the organism and the organization of the stimuli and the field in which they are presented influence attention. The state of the organism can be considered to include both the neural state and the motivational state. While the former may not be too directly influenced by the social environment (though the possibility of a somewhat indirect influence must not be negated), certainly the latter is. And here the social environment quite directly influences the selection of stimuli which are perceived.

The educators of the thirties were quick to point out that if children lose interest, they do not attend and, therefore, do not learn. As a result much effort was expended to attract the children's attention. Unfortunately, almost all this effort was directed toward making the stimuli compelling, and practically none toward insuring the kinds of experience which would influence the motivational state of the child. A child who feels lost in school because its demands and materials are unfamiliar and discontinuous with what he previously experienced at home will not attend properly to the stimuli presented. A child who has not previously been exposed to as much as 10 minutes of uninterrupted speech will have great difficulty in listening all the way through so long a statement, and a child who has not previously learned to respond to rather elaborate spoken directions will not be able even to attend to all the directions, let alone follow them. Difficulties such as these have strong negative effects on motivation and as a result negatively affect the child's attentiveness and, therefore, his learning. Once the attentiveness has been, as it were, tuned out on the inside, it is difficult to reinstate it, no matter how attractively and seemingly effectively attention has been engineered by organization of the stimulus field. Furthermore, the stimulus organization, to be effective, must relate to the child's background of experience.

Very early, a child learns to be selective in what he perceives: this is a prime necessity, inasmuch as one is always assailed by many more stimuli than it is possible to respond to. Hierarchies of attentional and response systems are established, apparently on a neural as well as an experiential level, related to sensory modality preference and efficiency as well as the "compellingness" of individual stimuli. A stimulus field organization, to be effective in channeling a child's attention to the aspects most relevant to the learning task, should be consistent with a child's already learned hierarchies. What these are for different children at different ages are far from clear, and many an experimenter as well as many a teacher has found a child relating to what was conceived of as a nonessential part of the stimulus material. It is probable that a child's background yields not only particular amounts and kinds of stimuli, but also some *channeling* of his attention to particular aspects of the stimuli present. Here it may well be that the middle-class background gives a child not only a great amount and variability of stimuli, but also an attentional channeling which is consistent with his response to aspects of stimuli which are most relevant for his school performance.

Apart from these built-in hierarchies and proclivities, however, one must address the question of the manner in which attention is engineered by stimulus field manipulation, and how often the original purpose is outstandingly defeated. The best example of this is the modern primer. Because color attracts attention, it is used quite lavishly. Because children like pictures—or are thought to like pictures—they are included multitudinously. But by these measures, the children's attention, of course, is attracted to the colored pictures, rather than to the print, which is the stimulus to be learned. The child is confronted with the task of attending to a relatively small black and white stimulus in the face of a strong competing large colored one. It is good to note that some of the new experimental reading series have abandoned this format, whether or not for conscious reasons of better visual and attentional coordination. Another example of self-defeating stimulus organization may be found in many elementary school classrooms. They are often a riot of color: posters all over the walls, pictures the entire length of the room, and so on—all distractions from the teacher's voice and from whatever content is placed on the blackboard or the bulletin board, or in the pupil's notebook in front of him. These comments do not reflect support for a movement back to the austere, dull, and undecorated classroom, but simply for a movement toward a judicious use of attention-getting aids. A stimulus analysis of the classroom and the learning materials presented would yield considerable information about the objects to which attention is really being called. Then, a redesigning of the placement of the stimuli and of the stimuli themselves should enable the creation of attractive classrooms and materials without the danger of engineering the child's attention to the nonessential stimuli.

With regard to other correlates of attention, I would like to cite a series of studies at IDS involving the use of our modification of the Continuous Performance Test (CPT). This is a technique, originally developed by Rosvold and Mirsky and their associates at the National Institute of Mental Health, using letters as stimuli (Rosvold, Mirsky, Sarason, Bransome, & Beck, 1956). Our version uses colored dots, inasmuch as the subjects for whom it was adapted were young children and retarded readers. Briefly, the task is a vigilance one, which involves attending continuously to a series of stimuli and pressing a button when the one previously designated as correct is presented. The visual form of our test uses a memory drum, on which colored dots are presented at the rate of one per second. Each dot appears in the aperture for .6 second, and there is .4 second between stimuli. This is subjectively rather a rapid rate, and it is necessary to pay close attention in order not to miss a stimulus. Subjects are told to press the button every time the red dot appears. An auditory analog uses the naming of the colors in the same order and at the same rate, with the same stimulus (red) being the correct one. In all our studies using this device, the clinical-type sample has always done more poorly than its control group. For example, retarded readers perform more poorly than good readers (Katz & Deutsch, 1963). The original scoring of the technique involved a simple tabulation of incorrect and correct presses, and missed presses (i.e., when the correct stimulus appeared and the button was not depressed). More recently, however, we have connected the device to an electronic clock, so it is possible to record the elapsed time between stimulus presentation and button press. When these results are analyzed, what is found is that many of the responses labeled incorrect by the old scoring method are really simply late responses to the correct stimulus. That is, the retarded readers, for instance, are responding correctly to the stimuli, but their responses are made too late to be recorded as correct. (They occur too soon to be real responses to the stimulus following the correct one, so it is obvious that they are slow but correct.) Since the Rosvold et al. (1956) and Kornetsky and Orzack (1964) studies with the CPT indicate that what it is sensitive to are central changes in arousal or attention, it seems most reasonable to view the children with learning disabilities as having faulty or slow attentional processes.

Recent drug studies by Kornetsky and Orzack (1964) and their colleagues indicate that there are differential effects of various substances, depending on whether the timing of a task such as the CPT is experimenter- or subject-controlled. Although the drug studies as drug studies are irrelevant for this discussion, the fact that the two types of stimulus presentation control can be differentiated is highly relevant—and relevant to understanding the role of attention in performance.

Even before the implications of all these CPT findings for children's learning have been investigated experimentally, their relevance for the classroom seems obvious. What is needed is a well-engineered stimulus field and a speed of presentation adjusted to the children's actual rate of response. This latter may be harder to accomplish than it looks. Some classroom observational data collected by some of my colleagues show that, without being at all aware of it, many if not most teachers tend to give less response time to the child whom they see as a poorer student than they give to the child whom they are more sure knows the answer. This practice results in less time being given to the child who in reality takes longer to respond, than is given to the child who actually needs less time. This kind of teacher behavior also influences directly the number of success experiences of the slower responding child, and also influences his performance indirectly, by conveying subtly that the teacher does not expect him to know the answer. For the children are aware of the differential time allotment and of its implications even though the teachers in the sample are not.

What are the implications for "Learning in the Disadvantaged" from these brief discussions of the verbal, perceptual, and attentional processes? Many of the studies referred to drew samples from lower-class and middle-class groups in order to make direct comparisons between them. Other data, gathered for other purposes, also yielded information on such comparisons. For example, in the studies of retarded versus normal readers, we are dealing with populations which are biased on SES lines. That is, the prevalence of reading retardation is much higher —estimates range from 4 to 10 times higher—in disadvantaged groups than in middle-class groups. Hence, whatever characteristics are found in retarded readers will be found in a larger proportion of disadvantaged children than in middle-class children.

The burden of the data and the hypotheses presented is that disadvantaged children suffer in the three areas mentioned and that these areas represent crucial underlying skills in school learning. Furthermore, the implication is that these children are deficient in these skills as a result of the deficits they experience in their home backgrounds. Data are adduced to show that skills in these areas can improve, though there is not yet concrete evidence to indicate that such improvement will result in over-all academic or conceptual improvement. There are no data to the contrary—it is simply that the whole approach to the specific areas is too new to have permitted as yet the gathering of definitive data.

Another fairly clear point is that children from more privileged backgrounds are superior in most of these skills and that groups of such children show a lower rate of reading and other learning disabilities. Therefore, it does seem reasonable to conclude that improvement in these skills could result in better progress in school learning, and a lower rate of learning disabilities.

Evidence that this is very likely the case may be adduced from the fact that many of the disadvantaged children who have difficulty with school learning learn many other things most adequately, when their experiential background is appropriate for such learning. For example, large numbers of 5-year-old children are quite capable caretakers for their infant and toddler siblings. They can be quite independent in personal care from a very early age, dressing themselves and then helping younger siblings to dress at ages when middle-class children do not do so. More examples could be cited, but the point is made: these children do not show the same disabilities in learning when the behavior called for is consistent with their experience. Perhaps this is an instance in which the old concept of cultural relativism is appropriate: the middle-class children learn well those tasks which are consistent with their training and experiences, and so do the lower-class slum children. The problem is that it is the school-type learning which is related to the values of the broader society—and to the later job needs of the children—and this is the type for which the middle-class child's background best equips him. The implication is, therefore, that it is not the learning ability per se of the slum child which is deficient, but only his background of experiences. It is on this basis that compensatory education programs have been established by us at the IDS, and by various other groups around the country. As both our measuring instruments and our curricula are sharpened, the answers to many of the questions posed in this paper should be forthcoming.

Two words of caution are in order before concluding.

One is that, despite the cultural relativism hypothesis put forth above, it must be recognized that the deficiencies which seem to exist in the slum child have to do in part with cognitive and concept-formation behavior, and these are skills which underlie many problem-solving abilities, even in nonverbal areas. If, as is hypothesized, it is impoverishment of experience which negatively affects the development of these skills, then that impoverishment is associated with a debilitation at the center of the growth of basic learning skills, and not with more superficial, and presumably more easily compensated, skills.

The second word of caution applies especially to the area of training and curriculum. It is highly likely that experience alone is not enough to enable the disadvantaged child to overcome the poverty of his background. That is, what is probably necessary is experience that is engineered, labeled, verbalized, and repeated in such a way that it is made relevant both to the child's previous experience and to his later activities. In other words, simply a trip to the zoo will not make up for the child's lack of previous trips, acquaintance with animals, with the use of transportation to get there, and the like. What is necessary is the organizing of the trip in such a way that it reinforces knowledge the child already has, and imparts specific labels and procedures that he can make use of in the future. For example, a trip to the zoo can contribute to an understanding of the concepts "larger" and "smaller" by making obvious for the child the sizes of the various animals and comparing one to the other in the words of the concept: the elephant is *larger* than the monkey; the ostrich is *smaller* than the horse. Simply taking the child to the zoo and expecting him to acquire this concept himself is unrealistic.

That this is true can be seen in unplanned real life examples as well as in pedagogical theorizing and evaluation of enrichment curriculum experiences. I recently had occasion to meet a number of children of migrant workers. These children are disadvantaged not only by their impoverished home backgrounds, but by their irregular school attendance as a result of the family's travel from one crop harvest to another. But the children, in contrast to city slum children, are not disadvantaged by a geographical narrowness: by the age of 10, those to whom I spoke had traveled thousands of miles, usually in cars or small trucks. When some of the children from city slums who have never been more than 10 blocks in any direction from their homes show little concept of distance, geography, or mileage, it is easy to attribute their deficit to simple lack of experience. But when migrant children show the same type of deficit, it becomes apparent that experience alone is not enough. The migrant children, who were interviewed informally and with no sampling procedure, had a very poor concept of distance and time. They gave for the width of the continent estimates which varied from 10 to 100 miles, even though they themselves had traveled from Oregon to Texas and back several times, with a trip or two from Texas to Florida in between. It seems clear that their deficient knowledge and unrealistic estimates were due to the lack of any attempt to specify and make meaningful their extensive geographical experience. Apparently, a child can travel thousands of miles, but if the time, the mileage, and the geography are not pointed out to him in some meaningful manner, little specific learning about distance is gained.

Curricula which simply present a cafeteria of experience, and experiences which do not include some direction, cannot be expected to succeed—or to accomplish as much—in ameliorating the school learning disabilities manifested by the disadvantaged child. Therefore, the evaluation of the specific skills and deficits of children from varying backgrounds should continue, and the attempt should be made to devise curricula and experience which will be consistent with the current skills of the child and which will be effectively directed toward his growth in the areas of deficit.

REFERENCES

Bernstein, B. Social structure, language and learning. *Educ. Res.*, 1961, 54, 163-176.

Bernstein, B. Social class, linguistic codes and grammatical elements. *Lang. and Speech*, 1962, 5, 221-240.

Bruner, J. S., & Goodman, Cecile C. Value and need as organizing factors in perception. *J. abnorm. soc. Psychol.*, 1947, 42, 33-44.

Deutsch, Cynthia P. Auditory discrimination and learning: Social factors. *Merrill-Palmer Quarterly*, 1964, 10, 277-296.

Deutsch, M. The role of social class in language development and cognition. *Amer. J. Orthopsychiat.*, 1965, 35, 78-88.

Deutsch, M., Maliver, Alma, Brown, B. R., & Cherry, Estelle. *Communication of information in the elementary school classroom*. U.S. Office of Education Cooperative Research Project No. 908. New York: N.Y. Medical College, 1964.

Fantz, R. L. The origin of form perception. In P. H. Mussen, J. J. Conger, & J. Kagan (Eds.), *Readings in child development and personality*. New York: Harper & Row, 1965. Pp. 72-84.

Hunt, J. M. *Intelligence and experience*. New York: Ronald, 1961.

Jensen, A. R. Learning in the pre-school years. *J. nursery Educ.*, 1963, 18, 133-138.

Jensen, A. R. Verbal mediation and educational potential. Unpublished manuscript, 1965.

Katz, Phyllis, & Deutsch, M. *Visual and auditory efficiency and its relationship to reading in children*. U.S. Office of Education Cooperative Research Project No. 1099. New York: N.Y. Medical College, 1963.

Kendler, Tracy S. Development of mediating responses in children. In S. C. Wright, & J. Kagan (Eds.), Basic cognitive processes in children. *Monogr. Soc. Res. Child Develpm.*, 1963, 28, No. 2 (Whole No. 86), 33-48.

Kornetsky, C., & Orzack, Maressa Hecht. A research note on some of the critical factors on the dissimilar effects of chlorpromazine and secobarbital on the digit symbol substitution and continuous performance tests. *Psychopharmacologia*, 1964, 6, 79-86.

Rosvold, H. E., Mirsky, A. F., Sarason, I., Bransome, E. D., Jr., & Beck, L. H. A continuous performance test of brain damage. *J. consult. Psychol.*, 1956, 20, 343-350.

von Senden, M. *Raum-und Gestaltauffassung bei operierten Blindgeborener vor und nach der Operation*. Leipzig: Barth, 1932. Cited by D. O. Hebb, *The organization of behavior*. New York: Wiley, 1949. Pp. 28-31.

Wepman, J. M. *Manual of directions: Auditory Discrimination Test*. Chicago: Author, 1958.

Whiteman, M., Brown, B. R., & Deutsch, M. Some effects of social class and race on children's language and intellectual abilities. In V. Haubrich (Ed.), *Studies in deprivation*. Washington, D.C.: Equal Educ. Opportunities Program, 1966, in press.

PART IV

CONCEPTS IN VARIOUS SUBJECT MATTER FIELDS

CHAPTER 13

CONCEPTS IN MATHEMATICS

KENNETH LOVELL

UNIVERSITY OF LEEDS

LEEDS, ENGLAND

In this chapter I was asked to speak of three points. First, what is the nature of mathematical concepts? Second, what are the main points of view regarding the learning of mathematical concepts? Third, how valuable is the work of Piaget from the point of view of understanding the nature and learning of mathematical concepts?

It is necessary to begin with a few remarks about both concepts and mathematics, in order that what follows may be seen in broad perspective. As I have to give some recognition to the work of Piaget, I am going to propose my own definition which is more in keeping with his formulations. By concept we mean any term that can be recognized as a recurrent feature in an individual's thinking, provided the individual can go back over the mental actions from which the term was derived and anchor it in his experience of first-hand reality. Thus, a piece of verbal behavior, such as the use of a specific word, does not necessarily qualify it for the status of a concept. Later, it will be indicated that different kinds of mathematical concepts are elaborated at different levels of thought.

The precise ways in which concepts arise remain unknown, for we have little exact knowledge as yet regarding the ways in which the child imposes some sort of order upon the chaos of the environment. As he develops, however, the flow of ideas directed toward some end or purpose, i.e., thought, becomes more aware of itself and more directed and deliberate. Sometimes such directed thinking can have its validity assessed by the criteria of formal logic, and sometimes it cannot. In the former case we may, following Kneebone (1963), call the thinking *manipulative;* in the latter it can be called *dialectical.* Now in logical thought, concepts behave very much as things do, for they have definitions, are treated as constant entities, and have their names manipulated. In dialectical thought, however, concepts act as foci of organization in the continuous change or flow of thought. The child's thinking in the second case will be influenced by his total experience, by what he knows and believes, by his presuppositions, and by the usual responses he makes to particular situations, as well as by the immediate stimulus input from the environment. In manipulative thought, thinking is more abstract and dissociated from its immediate concrete context even if it is directed to matters of concrete experience, whereas dialectical thought is inseparable from intuitive awareness. Although in manipulative thought we use what may be termed definable concepts, when concepts are experienced in dialectical thought they can no longer be precisely defined but become intuitive, for they are the foci of organization in our total awareness of the situation. So it seems that dialectical thought brings about new concepts or gives greater width and meaning to existing ones. And with the growth of concepts there is an increase of rational organization in the flow of our total awareness, and this, in turn, makes it easier for the individual to recognize further features of the situation by intuition. With time, concepts are thus conceived in a more comprehensive way, and those only vaguely discerned at first come to be understood. Hence concepts appear to evolve dialectically by the absorption of what was first discerned intuitively, and by both the growth and shape that they transmit to the cultural tradition.

When we turn to mathematics we can do no better than follow Bourbaki's interpretation of mathematics, given in the *Eléments du mathématique* (1939-63) as the study of structures or systematic pattern of relations. For Bourbaki there exist today the three great families of structures—"the mother structures"—that dominate the whole of mathematics, namely, the algebraic, topological, and ordinal structures. New kinds of structures, at present outside the bounds of our imagination, may, however, be of significance in the future.

Looking now at mathematics from the sixth decade of the twentieth century there appear to be two broad ways of looking at the study (Kneebone, 1963). It can be regarded as a totality of deductive "theories" all of which are grounded in pure logic, or as an autonomous activity of the individual the ultimate source of which is the primordial faculty of intuition. However, the former viewpoint does not appear to be in favor in many quarters since the metamathematical theorem of Godel implies that formal logic is incapable of ever containing the whole of intuitive mathematics. Although formal logic is indispensable to mathematics it does not appear to be able to provide the ultimate criterion of the validity of mathematical assertions. Or, as Courant and Robbins (1941) pointed out in their distinguished book *What is Mathematics?*, constructive invention and intuition are at the heart of mathematical achievement and provide the driving force, although a neat logical deductive system may well be a goal, as well as giving us a better understanding of mathematical facts and their relationships, and of the essence of the concepts involved.

The simplest intuitions of all seem to arise from the awareness of our own mental states which succeed one another in time. And as far as the intuitionists' view of mathematics is concerned, the child's mental development reaches some stage where the idea of the natural numbers is implicit in the stream of consciousness, and arithmetic is seen as arising directly from first-hand experience with the environment. But once the natural numbers and their properties have been isolated, as it were, by more abstract thinking which is able to reflect on the results of intuition, mathematics at once becomes a more conceptualized construction.

Mathematics seems to have had its origin in the activities of early man as when, for example, flints were handed around until there was a one-to-one correspondence between flints and men; or a pebble was put aside to check the presence of each animal. But even the use of tallying was limited. Early man's concept of fiveness would be in terms of the number of fingers on the hand, not the abstract five. It was a big step, intellectually, to move from sign signifiers that stood for small model groups to sign signifiers that stood for abstract numbers. For natural numbers are derived essentially as the result of an abstraction or a dissociation; they are properties of sets of entities, not of the entities themselves. Exactly how this happened we do not know. There had to be in early man as in every child today, an intellectual jump to the idea of "twoness" or "threeness." Mathematical concepts thus originate in the mind of man. True, the abstract notion of twoness—the primordial intuition of mathematics—on which is built the natural numbers, the real numbers, and so the whole of mathematics, almost certainly requires a certain level of cultural and neurophysiological development. But it is the primordial intuition that facilitates conceptual growth—that growth which reflects something of the very essence of man, for under all circumstances he tries to make order out of the chaos in his environment and thus make the universe of things and events as significant to himself as possible.

WHAT IS THE NATURE OF MATHEMATICAL CONCEPTS?

Let us now turn to the question "What is the nature of mathematical concepts?" It can be suggested that they are one class of concept; they are terms that exist in thought indicating generalizations about systematic patterns of relations. It is sometimes useful to classify mathematical concepts in three ways.

(1) Pure mathematical concepts. These deal with number and the relationships between numbers and are independent of the notation used to express the number.

(2) Notional concepts. These deal with properties that arise because of the way in which we express numbers, as in the case of "place value" in the Hindu–Arabic notational system.

(3) Concepts of length, weight, time, and the like. Although pure mathematicians may object to these, I have deliberately included them for two reasons. First, they cannot be neglected from a developmental point of view. Second, it is extremely interesting to see how the physicist and mathematician, starting from the same observations, elaborate two different conceptual frameworks with which they solve their problems. We cannot say which of the two frameworks is the better one. Each does the job for which it was intended.

Not all mathematical concepts are at the same level of abstraction. Some concepts such as number and length appear to arise out of the child's first-hand experience of reality. These are mainly the concepts of arithmetic. Later, concepts develop through reflection on these first-order concepts, and an entirely new concept such as proportionality or functionality becomes available to the pupil. Moreover, mathematical concepts, like other concepts, do not usually develop suddenly into their final form. They widen and deepen with experience and are often only available in specific situations at first. The process of concept formation thus differs from the learning of facts and of isolated details.

WHAT ARE THE MAJOR POINTS OF VIEW IN THE LEARNING OF MATHEMATICAL CONCEPTS?

We are now in a somewhat better position to discuss some of the major points of view concerning the learning of mathematical concepts. Indeed, I suggest the viewpoints may be classified along two main dimensions. First, intuition and constructive thinking compared with analytic thinking; second, the behaviorist or neobehaviorist approach compared with that of ontogenetic studies. Each of these is now discussed in turn.

Bruner (1960) pointed out some of the differences between intuitive and analytic thought. In the former, thinking tends to involve mental maneuvers which appear to be based upon implicit perception of the total problem, the thinker being unaware of the process by which he obtained his answer. Usually, intuitive thinking depends upon considerable familiarity with the field of knowledge involved and with its structure. Analytic thinking, on the other hand, usually requires considerable awareness of the information used and the operations involved. It is a careful step-by-step process, and the process can be communicated to others. Moreover, concepts are formulated and defined before they are used. In his early work on concept formation and personality, Dienes (1959) suggested that the child first gets an intuitive perception of something not fully understood, and this vague perception urges him on to constructive or creative effort to confirm the intuition by logical argument. In his view, constructive thinking takes place before analytic thinking although both are required for mathematical and scientific studies. In a later book, *An Experimental Study of Mathematics Learning,* Dienes (1963) again extolled the value of play, and points out that even in simple manipulative play involving varied discrete objects, the young child will construct the concept of, say, three. The natural numbers seem to arise, at a given level of development, to indicate the relative sizes of groups of objects. Dienes pointed out, of course, that this may not satisfy Piaget, for in the latter's view, unless the child grasps both the cardinal and ordinal aspects of number together, the concept of number is not truly understood. It is obvious, however, that before long, analytic thinking will have to be applied to the idea of the natural numbers derived intuitively through perception and action. While two, three, and four have their origins in action and group impression, and are the symbols we give to certain properties of these groups—using the term "group" in the everyday sense—the higher cardinal numbers are a substitute, in a conceptual way, for properties of groups of objects that cannot be known by action or by a simultaneous apprehension of the constituent objects.

On this general view the child first builds mathematical concepts by intuitive processes, and without being aware of the relationships between these and other concepts. Moreover, it seems that a particular concept is more likely to develop if the child receives many different perceptual impressions of the concept—visual, tactile, kinesthetic—all embodied in a number of different materials and in situations which the child can construct for himself, but in situations which, nevertheless, all exemplify the same underlying structure. The considerable amount of experimental work carried out by Dienes is in line with this general thesis. His views are given in a number of books ranging from *Building Up*

Mathematics (1960) to *Modern Mathematics for Young Children* (1965), and they cover a very wide range of concepts. Note the emphasis on the children acting on materials, and building and discovering the concept.

Before we leave this general approach a word must be said both about the role of language, and the use of so-called discovery, or as I prefer "finding out," methods in learning. All would agree that once the infant can use language, thought is extended over an immensely increased range. He now has a more flexible and less transient model of the outside world, for he is no longer dependent upon immediate perception for thought. But at this point I must make my own attitude clear. I know of no evidence to refute the view of Piaget that, although language aids the formation and stabilization of a system of communication constituted by concepts, it is not in itself sufficient to bring about the mental operations which are the essence of systematic thought, and which make possible the elaboration of mathematical concepts. The level of understanding seems to modify the language that is used rather than vice versa; or language serves to translate that which is already understood (Ripple & Rockcastle, 1964). But having said that, let it also be made plain that language plays a role in concept formation at that level of abstraction which the level of the child's thinking makes possible.

Again, since stress has been placed on the need of the child to be placed in a situation where he has the chance to build his own mathematical concepts, I must also state my agreement with Ausubel (1964) when he spoke to the Annual Meeting of the Association of Mathematics Teachers of New York State in 1963. He stated that discovery methods are no panacea, and that expository and problem-solving approaches can be rote or meaningful according to the conditions under which they operate. Furthermore, I would add that, although the adolescent who has reached the stage of Piaget's formal operational thought still needs to act on his environment, nevertheless, verbally presented abstract arguments and concepts also become an important kind of learning experience for him for he now has the capacity to appreciate the form of an argument. The future may well show that it is a question of adjusting the mixture of discovery and verbal presentation as the child progresses.

I next turn to the other main dimension along which the viewpoints concerning the formation of mathematical concepts can be classified. It was essential to choose this dimension, but in doing so I realized that I might be heading for trouble. First, I am not well acquainted with all the very many facets of behavior theory. Second, I realize that if we contrast aspects of behavior theory with the ontogenetic approach we may often be saying the same thing using different terminologies. For example,

Suppes (1965) has pointed out that he does not look on as different, cognitive formulations that are isomorphic to stimulus sampling theory, so that, say, a strategy corresponds to a state of conditioning. Likewise Berlyne (1965) pointed out that when Piaget uses the term "interiorized actions" he means what other psychologists mean by incipient or implicit responses, or when he uses "schema" we may translate that as "complex tendency."

Unfortunately, few behaviorists have written specifically about the growth of mathematical concepts. Staats and Staats (1963) pointed out that although the learning of mathematics seems to be a fairly straightforward extension of behavioral analysis of language, there is little laboratory evidence to draw on. Nevertheless, these writers, in a spirit of caution, do go on to suggest how one may explain counting behavior, addition, multiplication, division, and even simple instances of originality in mathematics in terms of S-R theory, although they are also careful to point out (p. 242) that it is not intended to suggest that complex examples of mathematical originality are capable of explanation in terms of learning principles at the present time. Of course, even those who are not greatly in sympathy with a behavioral approach may not deny that certain aspects of the language of mathematics, and certain techniques, might be learned in the way suggested by Staats and Staats providing the pupil has the requisite cognitive structures.

When we discuss the work of Suppes (1965), so firmly based on behaviorism, we are in particular difficulty. He pointed out that the notion of "understanding" is a vague and ill-defined term, and later declines to offer any serious characterization of what it means to understand a concept. Nevertheless we dare not pass by his seemingly fundamental contribution even if we do not see at the moment quite where it is taking us. Suppes (1965) described a series of experiments—some of which had been published earlier—underpinned by a variant of stimulus-sampling theory first formulated by Estes. I confess that I am not as familiar with the work of Estes as I ought to be, but perhaps this does not matter, since the experiments themselves must be taken seriously even if their theoretical foundations have to be relaid in the future. The tentative suggestions of Suppes, based on six experiments involving kindergarten and first-grade pupils seem to run like this. The learning of very simple mathematical concepts is an approximately all-or-one process although there are significant deviations from this; learning is enhanced by contiguity of response, stimulus, and reinforcement; learning is more efficient if the child who makes an error is required to make an overt correction response in the presence of the stimulus; and that in learning related mathematical concepts the amount of overall transfer from one concept to another is small.

It does not appear to me to be profitable to speculate about the future value of a behavioral approach to the learning of more complex mathematical concepts, for the work reported, as far as I know it, deals only with rudimentary notions. Even Suppes admitted that the correct response to what has been the British Sixth Form mathematics examination cannot be explained by any simple principle of stimulus-response association. I suppose he means, although he does not add, "at present."

Perhaps at this point I can say just a few words more about language before I discuss the ontogenetic approach to mathematical concept formation. Language seems to provide the means of pinning down and clarifying concepts once the cognitive structures are approaching the stage where the concepts can be elaborated. Thus Tough (1963) in a small but valuable study showed that the use of appropriate language at the same time as the experience helped 5 year olds to perform seriation and ordinal correspondence. Again, Wohlwill (1960) was explicit that mastery of the verbal labels "one," "two," etc. plays an important role in helping the child to pass from the stage where number is responded to wholly on a perceptual basis to the stage where number is responded to conceptually in the sense that four green circles can be matched with four red triangles. For the schools this suggests the need for active concrete experience and the stimulation of discussion to go along together.

Standing now at the other end of this second dimension is the ontogenetic approach of Piaget, who stresses the active role that the subject plays in organizing his experience. He also uses terms such as awareness and comprehension. In these respects he differs from the behaviorist. It is necessary to stress that for Piaget, what we know as intelligence increases as the child's *actions* assume an inward form as thought, and as the latter becomes less and less dependent upon perception, and exerts more and more influence on perception and action. We are at a loss to know how the transition from action to thought via the image comes about. Bruner has expressed the view that in adults the achievement of an image to represent a sequence of actions seems based on practice and the overlearning of the action sequence, although in children we know very little about the conditions necessary for the growth of imagery. It seems feasible, at least to me, that it is through the child's proprioceptive sense that the manual action becomes internalized. The child finds himself with a stock of images, visual and other, but through his actions he acquires a stock of "maneuverable" or "operational" images—i.e., thoughts.

Using the Piagetian formulations in respect of cognitive development one may distinguish three levels of abstraction and two levels of mathematical concept.

(1) The lowest level of abstraction determines the dissociation or abstraction of objects and their properties on the basis of their behavior characteristics, e.g., duck, pen, hot.

(2) The second level is attained when the child can dissociate or abstract the part played by himself in ordering his experience rather than on the characteristic of that experience. The ordinary child, by 7 to 8 years of age, can, as it were "turn round on his schemas." Because he can identify the criteria by which he builds his categorizations, he is *aware* of the sequences of his mental actions, and so for any action in his mind he can often see that there are other sequences that give the same result. That is, he can see equivalences for he can coordinate actions in his mind. Thought is now systematized, and the operational structures available correspond to structures which Piaget calls elementary groupings. The basic concepts of mathematics may now be elaborated. It is possible for the child to understand the logical operations of adding, subtracting, multiplying, dividing, setting terms in correspondence, etc., and to perform what Piaget calls infralogical operations which involve quantity, measurement, time, and space. But the mathematical concepts that are elaborated are only those that can be derived from contact with reality. They are first-order operational concepts.

(3) A third level of abstraction begins to be reached at about 11 to 12 years of age in very able children and at 13 to 14 in ordinary pupils. Here there is a coordination of actions upon relations that are themselves the result of the coordinations of actions. The properties of formal operational thought are, in Piaget's view, isomorphic with those of the group and lattice. Examples of concepts elaborated at this level are *proportion* in mathematics and *heat* in physics. If we take 4 is to 5 as 12 is to 15, the adolescent has to build a certain relationship between 4 and 5; a certain relationship between 12 and 15; and establish that there is an identity relationship between the two earlier established relationships. Although 9 and 10 year olds can work arithmetic progressions, they are unable to work geometric progressions unless they can be solved by straightforward multiplication or division by positive whole numbers. For example, in a recent intensive study of 50 children in this age range, all of whom had WISC verbal IQs over 140, only five pupils could complete the statement: "3 is to 7 as 9 is to . . . ." In the case of *heat,* the concept depends on the earlier elaboration of the concepts of mass and temperature. The latter are developed as first-order operational concepts since each is a coordination of some intuitive aspect of reality, but their product is not.

Concepts developed at this level may be termed second-order operational concepts. They depend on the first-order operational concepts being completely detached from their concrete contexts and manipulated as "pure" concepts. It should be noted that although the levels of abstraction seem to be three, the *order* of abstraction is unlimited, since two or more concepts of a lower order can be taken to make one of a higher order.

Thus, for Piaget the kind of mathematical concept that can be elaborated is linked to the quality of the child's thought, and is dependent ultimately on the latter's actions especially at the level of first-order operational schemas. For Piaget, mathematical concepts cannot be brought about by using the symbol of mathematics, rote learning, or verbalizations. They are arrived at by manipulating things; not from the things themselves but from an awareness of the significance of actions performed with them. For example, it is the actions actually performed on objects or figures that will enable the child to construct and transform spatial figures and thus conceive a coherent system of spatial relationships. In short, geometrical thought is in essence a system of interiorized operations.

TO WHAT EXTENT IS PIAGET'S DEVELOPMENTAL PSYCHOLOGY USEFUL IN DETERMINING THE NATURE AND LEARNING OF MATHEMATICAL CONCEPTS?

Piaget's vast collection of data, and his conceptualization of the process of cognitive development, throw light on some of the problems that confront us in the field of concept formation in mathematics, but they are at a loss to explain others. For the sake of clarity let us consider a number of points in turn, starting with those on the credit side, but bearing in mind that those on the debit side will modify, somewhat, the picture first presented.

(1) The Geneva school has shown how complex a business is the growth of mathematical concepts. By providing such a great amount of data relating to the growth of these concepts, it has done more than any other source to show educationists the difficulties and pitfalls that beset the child in this field of knowledge. Almost all my students are experienced teachers, and I can recall none who has claimed that a study of Piaget's developmental psychology has failed to illuminate his task in respect of the teaching of mathematics, science, and in other subject areas.

(2) Piaget's formulations suggest the kind of education that might be helpful in aiding a child to develop mathematical concepts. It is

perfectly true that we do not know in any exact sense the best kind of experiences to give our pupils, but we can say that his views support an approach in which the young child is essentially active in contrived situations which involve some conceptual conflict. Piaget's observations with young children led him to believe that it is schemas in the process of organization that children tend to repeat playfully and with seeming pleasure. When such schemas become organized the apparent pleasure disappears and the schemas cease to be repeated unless they are combined to form new schemas or serve as a means to an end. When the schemas required for the solution to some problem are not too far removed in complexity from those available to the child, the inadequacy of existing schemas will force him to accommodate to the conditions of the problem. Hence the child restructures his own schemas toward greater cognitive adaptation to his environment. Not only does the child solve the problem but he extends his capacity for further learning. On this view, the function of the teacher is to provide the right gap, as it were, between the schemas available to the child and those demanded by the mathematical concept. Yet in spite of all the help that Piaget has given us in coming to grips with the child's level of understanding, what is involved in arranging the "gap" remains vague and has to be left to the teacher's professional insights.

At the level of second-order operational schema, Piaget's conceptualization suggests that verbal learning can play a vital role, although even at this stage school pupils or college students still need frequent opportunities to act on their environment and verify their findings. In short, Piaget's developmental psychology suggests that mathematical concept formation is more likely to be brought about by the child actively operating on his environment and restructuring his own thinking, than by repeatedly carrying out the instructions of, and being reinforced by, the teacher, in a teacher-directed situation. At the same time, however, we must not ignore the fact that a store of mechanical routines may be a precondition for, or actually accelerate, operational systematization of thought and, hence, of concept formation. For example, the combination of addition and subtraction, with the same numbers in close succession and in practical contexts may help forward the growth of elementary numerical relationships. Only research can clarify these issues. I shall, however, return to this general point again at the end of my paper.

(3) It is possible to think of mathematical concepts in terms of levels of abstraction. This has already been dealt with and I shall not add much more. Teachers are offered an explanation as to why the elementary school child attains the relational concept of "equal to" but not the rela-

tional concept of "function of," or the operational concept of "addition" but not the operational concept of "differentiation." Moreover, Piaget's conceptualization suggests to teachers what children at various age levels can, and cannot, get out of particular exercises devised to illustrate specific mathematical concepts when such concepts are embodied in, say, physical material or in a game. If teachers are to foster mathematical understanding it is necessary for them to examine critically the concepts they are using and the nature of the thinking involved.

(4) Piaget's system suggests that the climate of opinion in which the child is reared, the *Zeitgeist,* or the demands of the culture pattern for certain kinds of cognitive strategies, will affect the facility with which operational schemas, and in particular second-order operational schemas, are elaborated. Bruner's views on cognitive growth would stress this more. Such cross-cultural studies as are available tend to confirm the effect of culture, whereas a longitudinal study of adolescent thinking at Leeds suggests, but does not prove, that years of rather formal, teacher-directed education in a "downtown" area may hold back the onset of formal thought. The formation of mathematical concepts is bound to be affected by these factors.

(5) The developmental psychology of the Geneva school can illuminate the problem of transfer of training in relation to mathematics or other subject area. Transfer may occur at any level of thought, but the quality of the transfer depends upon the quality and flexibility of the schemas. Indeed, there is the possibility of transfer of training of any schema to "similar" objects or situations, for objects and situations are similar if they lend themselves to the same schemas. The simpler schemas in humans or animals may be able to handle perceptual equivalences only. First-order operational schemas allow the child to recognize, say, different number bases as having a certain similarity, whereas second-order operational schemas allow the adolescent to see the applicability of vectors to forces and velocities.

(6) The teacher is given a greater appreciation of the difficulties of English, educationally subnormal, special school children, or American, school educable, retarded pupils. Our work and that of others has indicated that first-order operational schemas are available to only a proportion of such pupils at 15 years of age. The majority of these pupils, like preschool children, learn a linear sequence of actions at which it does not seem possible to elaborate a set of equivalences. They learn much, but understand little. It will, therefore, be beyond the capacity of most of these pupils to understand that $4 + 4 = 5 + 3 = 9 - 1$; to measure the same distance in feet and inches and understand that dif-

ferent figures mean the same thing; or decompose 32 into 3 tens and 2 units with understanding. If we are to attempt a radical improvement in the thinking of these pupils it is my belief that we must begin very early in life.

So much for the credit side. It will be appreciated that many of the points that I have made are related to one another. Now for the debit side.

(1) There is the general point, frequently made, that Piaget's own interest in logic and mathematics, has led him to see more systematization and structure in children's thinking than there actually is. It is extremely neat to use the models of the elementary groupings and of the group-lattice, and to suggest that the mother structures of the Bourbaki group correspond to the natural, spontaneous development of the child's thought. But the overall result is that Piaget's system is too rigid, and this affects its value in respect of the growth of mathematical concepts. The system will have to be modified in the future to take into account all the known facts. As yet we do not appear to have the techniques to approach, experimentally, the problem of intellectual structure, for as Smedslund (1964) reminds us at the end of his monograph, it seems necessary to study concrete inference patterns using only a single set of percepts and a single goal object.

(2) A serious matter is the frequent finding that correlations between performances on different tasks, said to involve the same cognitive structure, are often low. The relevant literature is extensive and only a few points can be made here. Dodwell (1960; 1961) showed that there was only a moderate correlation between tests which, in Piaget's view, involved the same level of thinking and which all involved integral aspects of the number concept. He also showed (Dodwell, 1962) that while the concepts of class and number develop within the same age range, there was no clear indication either that any one arose before the other or that they both arose together. Likewise Dodwell (1963) found, as we have found at Leeds, that a pupil could be at different stages of thought in three tests dealing with the concept of axes of reference. Further, Piaget himself (1960) has admitted that operations are only gradually applied to larger and larger numerical sets, and he has always made it clear that it takes a child 2 years to generalize concrete operations involved in appreciating conservation of quantity before they can be applied to conservation of weight although from the point of view of cognitive structure the operations are the same. Even when the concept involved remains the same, we have found that a child's level of thought may vary according to the apparatus (cf. Lovell & Slater, 1960).

We must, of course, be fair and point out that the Geneva school has made provision for some of these eventualities. Inhelder and Piaget (1958) pointed out that concrete operations consist of the direct organization of immediately given data and they cannot be generalized to all situations at once. For example, length is conserved before weight. This, in the view of Inhelder and Piaget, is because it is more difficult to serialize, equalize, etc., objects of which the properties are less easy to dissociate from one's actions, e.g., weight, than to apply concrete operations to properties that can be rendered more objective, e.g., length. Piaget (1956) also speaks of the notion of "horizontal differentials." This suggests that the same or similar concepts, when derived from different materials or situations, develop in staggered sequence rather than simultaneously. But this notion does not fit well into his general theory.

At the level of formal thought we find much the same. In studies not yet published we find that the ability to complete a series involving proportion correlates to the extent of about .6–.7 moderately with performance on Inhelder and Piaget's "balance" and "rings" experiments. Furthermore, the proportionality concept is not available in simple problems involving, say, money, speeds, area, and so forth at the same time, although our Principal Components Analysis does show a large general factor. Mathematical schemas are only available at first in specific situations, even when they depend on second-order operational schema. Lack of specific experience, information, vocabulary, or individual differences in intellectual functioning which are unknown, most probably all play some part.

(3) It is by no means certain that the idea that the child's conception of space begins with topological concepts which are transformed concurrently into concepts of projective and Euclidean space, is correct. This thesis has been called in question by Lovell (1959), Lunzer (1960), and Fisher (1965).

(4) Little help is obtained in explaining why girls seem less apt than boys in developing mathematical concepts at secondary (high school) level. The relative failure of the girl may be a culture pattern effect, but we are at a complete loss to understand exactly how the natural interests of the girl, or the expectations of the culture pattern for her, affect her thinking in relation to mathematics. Studies of formal thought in areas other than mathematics have not shown any sex differences as far as I am aware.

(5) We are still at a loss to understand why some pupils who have clearly developed first- and second-order operational schemas find great difficulty in forming mathematical concepts. Far from all pupils who are

backward in mathematics are intellectually dull, emotionally disturbed, or have had a paucity of relevant experience.

In conclusion I would like to comment on a point that I have already raised from a slightly different viewpoint. Whatever shortcomings Piaget's equilibration model has, Flavell (1963) reminds us that apart from having brought about much interesting research, it has specifically posited the internal reorganization of cognitive structures. Certainly the very great amount of experimentation involving training procedures with reinforcement as to correctness of response, has done nothing to suggest that the notion of the child restructuring his own cognitive structures is without value. Recently, Beilin (1965) in such an experiment involving number, length, and area conservation, concluded that training is most likely to affect subjects at a transitional conservation level but is not sufficient to make for extensive conservation across all tasks. As recently as 1964, Piaget again stated (Ripple & Rockcastle, 1964) and in this country, that such a conclusion might be expected. It seems that on the Piagetian view we need a wider, longer-lasting, and more fundamental approach that involves far more of the pupils' activities than do such training procedures, before we can accelerate the growth of mathematical concepts (cf. Phemister, 1962).

REFERENCES

Ausubel, D. P. Some psychological and educational limitations of learning by discovery. *Arith. Teach.*, 1964, **11**, 290-302.

Beilin, H. Learning and operational convergence in logical thought development. *J. exp. child Psychol.*, 1965, **2**, 317-339.

Berlyne, D. E. *Structure and direction in thinking.* New York: Wiley, 1965.

Bourbaki, N. *Eléments du mathématique. Première partie: Les structures fundamentales de l'analyse.* Paris: Hermann, 1939-63. 8 vols.

Bruner, J. S. *The process of education.* Cambridge: Harvard Univer. Press, 1960.

Courant, R., & Robbins, H. *What is mathematics?* London & New York: Oxford Univer. Press, 1941.

Dienes, Z. P. *Concept formation and personality.* Leicester: Leicester Univer. Press, 1959.

Dienes, Z. P. *Building up mathematics.* London: Hutchinson, 1960.

Dienes, Z. P. *An experimental study of mathematics learning.* London: Hutchinson, 1963.

Dienes, Z. P. *Modern mathematics for young children.* Harlow, England: Educational Supply Association, 1965.

Dodwell, P. C. Children's understanding of number and related concepts. *Canad. J. Psychol.*, 1960, **14**, 191-205.

Dodwell, P. C. Children's understanding of number concepts: Characteristics of an individual and of a group test. *Canad. J. Psychol.*, 1961, **15**, 29-36.

Dodwell, P. C. Relations between the understanding of the logic of classes and of cardinal number in children. *Canad. J. Psychol.*, 1962, **16**, 152-160.

Dodwell, P. C. Children's understanding of spatial concepts. *Canad J. Psychol.*, 1963, **17**, 141-161.

Fisher, G. H. Developmental features of behaviour and perception. *Brit. J. educ. Psychol.*, 1965, **35**, 69-78.

Flavell, J. H. *The developmental psychology of Jean Piaget.* Princeton, N.J.: Van Nostrand, 1963.

Inhelder, B., & Piaget, J. *The growth of logical thinking from childhood to adolescence.* London: Routledge, 1958.

Kneebone, G. T. *Mathematical logic and the foundations of mathematics.* Princeton, N.J.: Van Nostrand, 1963.

Lovell, K. A follow-up study of some aspects of the work of Piaget and Inhelder on the child's conception of space. *Brit. J. educ. Psychol.*, 1959, **29**, 104-117.

Lovell, K., & Slater, A. The growth of the concept of time: A comparative study. *J. child Psychol. Psychiat.*, 1960, **1**, 179-190.

Lunzer, E. A. Some points of Piagetian theory in the light of experimental criticism. *J. child Psychol. Psychiat.*, 1960, **1**, 191-202.

Phemister, A. Providing for 'number readiness' in the reception class. *Nat. Froebel Found. Bull.*, 1962, April, 1-10.

Piaget, J. Les stades du développement intellectual de l'enfant et de l'adolescent. In P. Osterrieth *et al.* (Eds.), *Le problème des stades en psychologie de l'enfant.* Paris: Presses Univer. France, 1955. Pp. 33-113.

Piaget, J. Introduction. In P. Gréco *et al.* (Eds.), *Problèmes de la construction du nombre. Études d'épistémologie génétique.* Vol. 11, Paris. Presses Univer. France, 1960. Pp. 1-68.

Ripple, R. E., & Rockcastle, V. N. (Eds.) *Piaget rediscovered.* Ithaca: Cornell Univer., School of Education, 1964.

Smedslund, J. Concrete reasoning: A study of intellectual development. *Monogr. Soc. Res. Child Develpm.*, 1964, **29**, No. 2 (Whole No. 93).

Staats, A. W., & Staats, Carolyn K. *Complex human behavior.* New York: Holt, Rinehart & Winston, 1963.

Suppes, P. On the behavioral foundations of mathematical concepts. In L. N. Morrisett & J. Vinsonhaler (Eds.), *Mathematical learning. Monogr. Soc. Res. Child Develpm.*, 1965, **30**, No. 1 (Whole No. 99), 60-96.

Tough, J. A study of the contributions made by relevant experience and language to the formation of a number concept in five-year-old children. Unpublished master's thesis, Univer. of Leeds, 1963.

Wohlwill, J. F. A study of the development of the number concept by scalogram analysis. *J. genet. Psychol.*, 1960, **97**, 345-377.

CHAPTER 14

THE TEACHING OF MATHEMATICS
IN THE ELEMENTARY SCHOOL

HOWARD F. FEHR

TEACHERS COLLEGE, COLUMBIA UNIVERSITY
NEW YORK, NEW YORK

This chapter is concerned with concepts, those of significance in instruction in the elementary school. The approach is not a psychological one but rather one of a substantive and practical nature. The major investigation, then, is to uncover the manner in which a mathematician or a mathematics teacher considers a mathematical concept and the paths and obstacles to acquiring these concepts.

WHAT IS A MATHEMATICAL CONCEPT?

A study of the literature published during the last 35 years makes it quite evident that there is no one general definition or description of a concept. Furthermore, there is no general agreement on the nature of a concept, nor the manner in which the human mind acquires concepts. That this is so is no reason to disparage the many excellent investigations carried out and theories postulated by the psychologists, for they are dealing with one of the most complex and intricate fields of study—the human mind. Further, they have clarified many of the issues in the study of human learning that give us greater insight into our problem of learning mathematical concepts even though a solution is yet not apparent.

One of the obstacles to the solution of the problem is the lack on the part of the psychological investigators to understand the way the mathematician conceives of the elements in his subject. It is easy for a mathematician to see how Piaget confused set operations and arithmetical operations as being identical, when, in fact, they are disjoint. It is easy for a mathematician to see how ordinality and ordinal number are indistinguishable to a layman. It is easy to see how similar sets may be misinterpreted for equivalent sets, or at least the difference not recognized (Lovell, 1964, pp. 27-28). Now, these misinterpretations are not so serious for studying concept learning, but they are serious for developing methods for learning correct mathematical concepts. It is readily conceivable that in some similar way mathematicians may have misinterpreted the psychological point of view with regard to the nature of a concept.

In recent work, Skemp (1964, pp. 7-9) differentiated between a *fact* and a *concept*, although he admitted the difference is not easy to explain, and suggested it will be necessary to approach the matter in a roundabout way. To explain the difference he quite correctly described mathematical knowledge to be not a set of isolated (rote) facts used by induced habits, but to be a structure of related ideas and skills. For Skemp, the fundamental related ideas (concepts) are learned through intuitive methods through the use of well-chosen sensory activity situations, in proper sequence of presentation. In this way the fundamental concepts build up a schemata, which, acquired by the age when reflective activity of the mind has developed (age 12 years on), enable the child to appreciate and construct formal mathematical systems. Thus, Skemp rejected, so far as the elementary school is concerned, any formal reflective procedures for the formation of basic mathematical concepts. He did accept perceptory–intuitive generalizations from sensory activity situations as the means of building the basic mathematical concepts.

This is quite in agreement with Piaget's philosophy, developed through his study of children's thinking, namely, that "to know a concept is to act on it," but it does not tell us how the concept is acquired. Piaget also says a mathematical operation gets greater depth in the learning of its reversibility, that is, I assume, that adding a number gains greater meaning when we learn that subtracting the number from the sum restores the operand with which we began. Piaget, however, gives us no help in showing why or how the *greater meaning* comes—it is only assumed.

Piaget also assumes, quite correctly, for all subsequent experiments have verified it, that until the child acquires the concept of conservation of matter despite its shape or rearrangement, the child is not ready to develop a concept of number. In most of these psychological experiments, however, it is assumed that a child can *count*, that is, say the number names in correct order as he touches or looks at objects. Mathematically speaking, however, just the reverse is considered to be the case, that is it is the conservation of the "manyness" of a set—despite the arrangement of the elements that leads to the concept of cardinal number—and this subsequently through an order concept, to the operation of counting.

Another approach to concept formation has been given by Bruner and his associates. The definition states that a concept is ". . . a way of grouping an array of objects or events in terms of those characteristics that distinguish this array from other objects or events in the universe" (Bruner, Goodnow, & Austin, 1956, p. 275). This definition and its extension have been adequately explained by Rosskopf (1958). Its main tenet is that of *categorization* which is commonly used by most psychologists to identify concepts. It suffices to say that in all these theories there are general concepts and specific concepts, and the kind which are learned first depends on the situation in which the child finds a use for them. For example, a child learns such specific concepts as red, blue, orange, before he develops the more abstract concept, color, but, on the other hand, he learns a general idea of manyness, before he learns such specific concepts as two, four, three, which lead him to learn the abstract concept of cardinal number.

For the purposes of the following presentation, the general word concept is taken as undefined and is described as a form of mental construct. We shall try, however, to clarify some specific mathematical concepts as conceived by mathematicians.

A MATHEMATICAL CONCEPT IS NOT A MONAD

A mathematical concept, even the most elementary or so-called basic one, is not a simple thing but a very complex entity. Similar to the structure of an atom which in its nuclear description becomes a more and more complex structure, the apparently simple idea "cardinal number" becomes on investigation a multiplicity of ideas. Indeed a general concept of *number* is attained only by very few persons after many years of mathematical study.

What is the concept of a cardinal number? Let us examine it in extension first, assuming that a child has already learned the concept (such as 3) as the manyness of equivalent collections of objects. Very soon he intuitively learns another concept, that of *order*. This idea assigned to the numbers he has learned, gives him a collection of counting numbers, which enable him not only to find the number of a set of objects, but to construct a system of numeration so that the counting can be extended. The set of numbers $(1,2,3,4,\ldots,n,\ldots)$ is now quite a more general concept of cardinal number than that of twoness or threeness.

Starting with a segment, or tape, or rubber band, we use these numbers as operators, that is they operate on (or multiply, if you wish) the object. Thus 0 operation on the segment causes it to disappear, shrink to nothing; 1 operating on the segment leaves the segment identical to itself; the other cardinals operating on the segment cause it to stretch so that it takes 2, 3, etc. of the original segment to cover the stretched segment, where the word *cover* is used in a special sense. Thus the cardinals take on a new concept as transformers, that is, they tell us, if we know what a unit of something is, what 2, 3, . . . , 10, . . . , and so on units of the thing will be.

Having learned this, we can take the beginning point of a segment as 0, its terminal point as 1, and as the segment is transformed in cardinal order, label all the successive points 2, 3, 4, and so on. We now have assigned a point to a number. What heretofore denoted the manyness of a set, or a stretcher, now merely designates a point on a scaled line. We say the cardinal numbers are calibrations of a ray, or they form a number scale. This scale turns out to be a fine measuring device, as well as a coordinating device, and the cardinal numbers have taken on a broader concept.

As this concept of coordination and counting is extended, and applied to elements of infinite sets such as points on a line, the cardinal number becomes the chief agent for studying denumerability and leads to the study of transfinite cardinal numbers. In this final form, cardinal number becomes the base of the logical development of modern analysis which has been called the arithmetization of analysis. In fact, cardinal number is the base on which all extensions to other number systems—integers, rationals, reals, complex, quaternians, Cayley numbers, and so on—are made.

There is great difficulty in labelling or naming a mathematical concept so as to convey a simple idea. Yet, for purposes of instruction, for building suitable curricula for mathematical study in the elementary school, it is necessary to isolate some basic concepts, and limit the development of them to the intuitive, that is perceptual, first approximations of these concepts. In this context, it must be remembered that the use of names such as "cardinal number," may be misleading and frequently convey a sophistication that is not intended.

BASIC CONCEPTS OF ELEMENTARY SCHOOL MATHEMATICS

1. *Set.* There is no doubt today, that the concept of a *set* is basic to the understanding and study of all mathematics. This was always so, even in classical mathematics, but it is only in the last 100 years that the

clarification of sets, operations on sets, and the ensuing theory became basic and self-contained, not dependent on other branches of mathematics. (Why this has come about is another question, not to be discussed here.) The type of sets from which intuitive ideas of number come about are physical and finite. While the concepts of space and geometric figures involve in most cases an infinity of elements (points), this infinity is not recognized in the primary concepts of line, figure, and region that occur in the mind of a child.

The fact that a concept of number is abstracted from a physical set has led to the belief that a set of numbers is called an *abstract set* because of this abstraction. To be sure, we use the word abstract in this way in elementary school mathematics. A mathematician, however, uses the word in a completely different connotation, namely, devoid of all meaning. Mathematics, per se, is concerned with abstract sets, axioms, and logical derivation, and the elements of a set have no other meaning than that given by the axioms and logical derivation. The set exists at the start and it was not abstracted from anything. Of course, such use of abstract has no place in the elementary school.

It is in this difference of the use of *abstract* that much of the controversy about elementary school mathematics rests today. For the concrete application of number and space to the usual problems of most people in everyday life, these abstractions from the physical universe, built into some schemata, suffice. They even suffice for some extended study of algebra and geometry. A large group of educators conceive this approach to mathematics to be the proper purpose of elementary school mathematics. However, there is a fairly large group of mathematicians, a few of whom are taking a prominent role in advocating and trying to initiate change in elementary school teaching, who insist that elementary schools should deal with their concept of abstract. They feel that elementary instruction should develop correct language and formal procedures for the subsequent development of formal mathematical structures.

2. *Mapping.* The concept of a *mapping*, similar to that of set, is an idea that has been used nebulously for ages, but only in the past 200 years has it come to the fore as basic. Here the essential element is an *ordered pair;* where the first element is selected from one set, and then a second element which is assigned to the first, from another set. Once an element is selected from a first set, it is never selected again, that is, it has only one object of the second set assigned to it. There are three fundamental mappings, that children must intuitively grasp in order to develop a schemata of arithmetic, and they are called into or *injective,*

onto or *surjective,* and one-to-one or *bijective.* These are the only mappings and they are needed in the study of elementary mathematics.

3. *Relation (Equivalence, Order).* The concept of *relation* in mathematics is broader than that of mapping. All mappings are relations, but the converse is not true. Relations arise by pairing elements from one set with those of another or by pairing the elements of a set among themselves. For relations it is perfectly possible that the first element may have more than one element of the second set assigned to it. To understand cardinal number, for example, if a child uses collections of fingers as model sets, then he can assign to the set of fingers on one hand any other collection of objects into which the fingers can be bijected. The intuitive grasp that this relation (can be matched one-to-one) (a) relates on itself, that is, fingers may be matched with fingers; (b) relates both ways, that is, fingers to objects and objects to fingers; and (c) carries over, that is, fingers to objects and objects to other objects means fingers match with other objects also, leads to equivalence of sets. Thus many sets are assigned to the set of fingers in a bijective mapping. This type of relation just described is called an *equivalence.* It is doubtful that children can differentiate between same or equal, or having a common relation such as just described and therefore being equivalent. For everyday use the distinction is not important, but for pure mathematics it is very important. For example, equality is an equivalence relation, but so is "similar to," "congruent to," "parallel to," and so on.

Order was always accepted in elementary school mathematics, but hardly ever extracted as a unique concept. It is important for building a correct schemata of arithmetic. Order is a seriated relation which enables us to arrange objects or ideas in an acceptable succession. The concept of less than, or greater than (comes before or comes after) are essential in creating a useful set of cardinal numbers. However, ordering of sets of physical objects by an injective relation should precede any ordering of numbers.

4. *Cardinal Number.* This concept has already been discussed from an extensive point of view. We can now see the intension of this concept. Cardinal number is in a sense the property of the manyness of the elements of a set. But it is more than this. When a child learns that a certain manyness is two, he soon learns that all other sets that have "an element and another element" are two in manyness. But this is a specific concept. A little later a child may learn by specific usage that five is the manyness of the set of fingers on his hand, and of all other sets that biject to it. But cardinal number really comes into general concept when he

learns that equivalence classes formed by the relation "is bijected onto," have different numbers, and that these numbers can be ordered.

Thus, a child must learn what 2 is, what 4 is, what 3 is, and so on, then he must learn to order these numbers by an order relation, then he must have a mental construct of these numbers as $(0, 1, 2, 3, 4, \ldots)$ and now he has a fairly intensive concept of cardinal number.

5. *Counting.* This is in one sense an operation, but the way it is intuitively grasped at the elementary school, it is the result of a specific kind of mapping. Here it is desired to find the number of a set of objects. So a set of objects is injected into the set of ordered cardinals, beginning with 1. The objects may be taken in any order, but the cardinal number of the terminal matching yields the cardinal number of the set. Thus mapping is essential to counting. After the counting, the set of objects *may* be given the order in which they were selected and now the set of objects is also an ordered set. The two sets are then referred to as similar and there is a unique bijection, and only one, between two similar sets. An analogy is to count the basketball players when they are in a huddle (no order), equivalent sets, and then to count them as they are lined up to start the game, where they are ordered, and similar sets. An extension of counting leads to the concept of numeration.

6. *Numeration.* This is usually a systematizing of names of the first k cardinals or their symbols (digits) into a procedure of counting by ks. In the one universally used system, k is 10, and the system is called a *place–additive–multiplicative decimal system of numeration.* Every one of these words signifies a subconcept that enters into understanding numeration. What, indeed, makes the concept even more complex is that the multiplicative idea enters here usually before the operation of multiplication is taught. That the system of numeration can be learned for useful action in spite of this, indicates that the set idea of a collection for which the number is 10 and the operator or transformer concept of the cardinals from 0 to 9 operating on these sets is sufficient to give a workable concept of decimal numeration.

Numeration to bases other than 10, e.g., 2, 5, or 8, have been advocated for teaching in the elementary school. The hypothesis is that other bases than 10 will tend to develop the understanding of the decimal system, but this hypothesis has never been proved. It would appear that for the great mass of future citizens, the specific concept of numeration, base 10 is sufficient for all their needs. Specific concepts of base 2, base 5, base 12, and so on should be helpful in developing a general concept of place–additive–multiplicative system, but for a general concept of numeration, one would have to study other than place systems as indicated by those of the Babylonians, early Greeks, and so on. This generalization, although interesting, seems of little instructional value for general education in the elementary school.

7. *Operation*. The digital electronic computers do all their arithmetic by counting. It is thus evident that the calculations of sums, differences, products, and quotients are not primary; they can be related back to counting. However, these calculations are useful to all persons, and for some time in the future will continue to be, so they should be in the instructional program. As such they are related to what are termed *operations*. The intuitive idea of these operations is usually abstracted from corresponding *operations* on physical sets. From these intuitive concepts, the *facts* or basic tables of operations can be constructed. These suffice to construct understandable and efficient algorisms for computation. This appears to be sufficient for elementary school instruction. For mathematical study, however, the concept of an operation as a mapping (or function) of the product set $E \times E$ onto E (surjection) is essential.

The operation of addition, denoted by $a + b$ assigns a number c to the ordered pair (a,b) called the sum. The number c is the number of the union of two disjoint sets with numbers a and b, respectively. Thus, the operation of union of sets, denoted by $A \cup B$ becomes a requirement for building a concept of addition of numbers. Both of these operations are binary operations, because an ordered pair of elements is needed before the assignment of the *result* of the operation can be given. Fundamentally, all internal laws of composition of a binary nature can be represented as

$$a \times b \quad = \quad c$$
$$\text{operand} \times \text{operator} = \text{result} \quad \text{or} \quad \xi : (x,y) \varepsilon E \times E \to z \varepsilon E$$

The operations of addition and multiplication are such that the operand and operator, if interchanged, give the same result. This is called *commutativity* and deepens the concept of these two operations as contrasted with those of subtraction and division.

To further strengthen the binary aspect of the operation, an expression such as abc or $6 + 9 + 3$ is held to be meaningless until it is defined. One can define these operations to mean

$$(ab)c$$

which involves two binary operations. For addition and multiplication, it is apparent that $(ab)c$ always yields the same result as $a(bc)$, but this is not true of subtraction or division. This property is called *associa-*

tivity and further contrasts the operations $+$ and $\times$ with those of $-$ and $\div$. A further concept of *distributivity* of multiplication over addition or

$$a(b+c) = ab + ac$$

combined with the system and rules of decimal numeration permit the children to learn the concept of an algorism.

8. *Algorism.* This is purely a system of applying to a given ordered pair of numbers the operations on number given by the fundamental facts (or tables) and the properties of the decimal system of numeration, to obtain the result of the operation for the given ordered pair. There are many algorisms for each operation, and, although which is a more efficient one may be debated, a concept of an *algorism* should be acquired before the child can intelligently proceed to acquire one that he can use skillfully.

9. *Classification of Numbers.* If one wishes to continue in the study of mathematics, there are certain concepts which may expedite the learning. Among these are the classification of numbers. These classifications depend on knowing the operations, or fundamental characterizations of number. The following concepts are illustrative of the useful ones: *odd number, even number, factors of a number, prime number, composite number, greatest common factor of numbers,* and *least common multiple of numbers,* the latter two being binary operations on two numbers, or a sequence of numbers. In the study of these numbers the concept of numerical *exponent* is also useful.

OTHER BASIC CONCEPTS

The detailed account of basic concepts given above was intended for the nonmathematical specialist so as to give an appreciation of the complexity of concepts and uncertainty of a schemata in which they can correctly and efficiently be established. Any one of these basic concepts can be further critically analyzed and to continue to describe others in detail would serve no real purpose here. The following can be considered other basic concepts in elementary school mathematics.

10. *Fraction.* Quite generally in mathematics a numerical fraction is the quotient of any two numbers, and it can always be expressed as the indicated quotient $n_1 \div n_2$ *or* n_1/n_2; or the computation can be carried out so as to express it as a terminating or nonterminating decimal (either repeating or nonrepeating), or a complex number. In arithmetic a fraction is usually restricted to the number represented by the quotient of two cardinal numbers, in which the divisor is not zero. There are other inter-

pretations than that of a quotient, for example, an ordered pair of whole numbers (3, 4) or (multiplier, divider) or (stretcher, shrinker). In all cases, the fraction idea can be deepened by considering it as an operator or transformer and then a refined calibrator of a number line or ray. It must be noted in passing that some persons consider a fraction to be a symbol for a rational number, and hence do not consider a fraction to be, only to represent, a mathematical entity.

11. *Rational Number* (*Positive or Zero*). By an equivalence relation placed on the set of all fractions, we obtain equivalence classes of fractions, e.g., ($\frac{1}{2}$, $\frac{2}{4}$, $\frac{3}{6}$, $\frac{4}{8}$, . . .). As calibrators or transformers all these fractions become names for the same point and hence represent only one value which is referred to as a rational number. The concept of rational number then is an equivalence class of ordered pairs of cardinal numbers (x,y) $y \neq 0$. This is already an abstraction of the third order and perhaps not obtainable in the elementary school program.

12. *Measure*. This concept is built on the concepts of set, unit, transformer, or operator. To measure any magnitude we select a part (subset) of it as a unit. We then partition the magnitude in disjoint subsets, each of which is a unit. The number of units is the measure of the magnitude in that unit. This concept requires some usable meaning of the concept of magnitude (length, area, volume, time, weight, or mass, etc.). Closely allied to this concept are the next concepts.

13. *Ratio, Proportion, and Percent*. There is no general agreement among mathematicians on the concept to be ascribed to these words but the different concepts proposed in the literature generally lead to useful skills and interpretation.

14. *Space*. Geometry was really never taught in the elementary school of the United States until quite recently. While the measure of length, area, and volume of certain geometric objects was taught, it was not as a study of space. What is space? This is indeed a difficult concept, and this may be one of the reasons why geometry was not taught in the past.

Space, to a mathematician, is a set of points (finite or infinite) undefined, but having well-determined properties derived from a set of particularly chosen axioms. Thus, projective, affine, Euclidean, metric, topological, and other spaces are developed, as well as 0, 1, 2, 3, *n*, and infinite dimensional spaces. All this is very abstract and does not belong in elementary school. Here space is the world about the pupil. The intuitive idea of point, line, plane, and parts of line are physical and related to physical objects in the world. If the vertex of a cubical block is a point he can move the block and the point will move through points or locations in space. The question of how a child's concept of space is developed into an intuitive geometry of undefined objects (point, line, plane) and finally to a formal geometric structure is unanswered today.

No doubt there are other concepts which some persons will consider basic to elementary school mathematics, but in general, those presented above are sufficient for the construction of other, more complex, concepts that are developed in subsequent study of mathematics.

THE LEARNING OF CONCEPTS

Can we categorize all the concepts to be learned? Perhaps we can do this substantively, for today there are well-defined structures of mathematics, all based on sets and set operations, divided into algebraic structures and topological structures which soon merge in more complex structures. By starting with sets we could make a categorization of all the ideas as they enter the development. I doubt that this would be of much help, if any, to elementary school learning.

Can we categorize these concepts as to their psychological implications? I think not, for we know so little as to how the mind organizes and structures the knowledge it acquires, and we know too little about the psychological properties of any concept, with regard to its use in constructing further concepts. Again there are several psychological theories on approaches to concept formation or learning of which reinforcement (as emphasized on programmed instruction and rat training) and Gestalt (as emphasized in structural relationships and problem solving) are most prominent. In some points these theories show some agreement and at others they are almost contradictory. In teaching we must use those aspects in which the theories agree as to basic concepts and ways of learning them, and in research we must attempt to see if a hierarchy of concepts exists, or if several different hierarchies exist.

In recent conferences sponsored by UNESCO, Dienes (1965) indicated the following common features in experimental work on learning mathematical concepts.

(1) Emphasis on structured learning

(2) Emphasis on meaning, understanding, and discovery as primary as opposed to rote learning

(3) Creation of a positive attitude (motivation) toward learning

(4) The extension of concepts beyond those of the four fundamental operations

(5) Induction always precedes deductive approaches

When it comes to the substantive approach to learning, however, the methods differ widely. Among the approaches are:

(1) A basic set approach (sets, set operations, and logical relations)

(2) An intuitive physical set approach

(3) An arithmetically oriented approach—to develop proficiency in arithmetic before the study of the concepts

(4) A geometrically oriented approach (number and sets are related from the start to the spatial concepts)

(5) A symbol-game oriented approach as exemplified by Cuisenaire rods

(6) An object-game oriented approach which encourages the making of abstractions, but the simple is always imbedded in a more complex situation (this is Dienes' own approach)

Perhaps the real difference in theory of concept formation can be illustrated by comparing the structured materials game approach (using commercially produced apparatus) with that of abstracting from the environment that exists in and about the learner. In the game-oriented approach, the number names (at least 1 to 10) are assumed to be learned in order by rote and that they can be used to count. Then games are assigned to rods and/or colors and by manipulating the rods and colors, the learner discovers number relations, e.g., $2 + 3 = 5$, $3 \times 3 = 9$, etc. These operations are related to the activities the learner carries out with the rods. Further by an interchange of the position of the rods, or colors, the learner discovers (?) commutativity and associativity. Then, by practice, he builds his fundamental knowledge of arithmetic. What concepts has he learned? This is seldom asked by persons involved. It is only shown that the children can do arithmetic, they can act, and hence they must have some concept.

In the environmental approach, using scientific inquiry, that is observing, selecting, abstracting, generalizing, by intuitive process, the children learn first how to observe collections or sets of objects in the room, how to construct a set of objects, and how to describe a set. Next they match two sets of objects, by pairing elements, to discover which set has more, fewer, or the same manyness of objects. It is essential at the start that the learners recognize the conservation of a set regardless of the arrangement of the elements. This recognition is further strengthened by making numerous rearrangements of each set, and numerous mappings in which the more, fewer, or the same remains constant. For small sets, the manyness of all sets that match exactly (are the same) is called its number and given a name.

In all this work there is no symbolism except the numerals, such as 3, 5, 2, . . . which are the number names. In fact, such symbolism as

$$n\{\Delta, 0, [\ ]\} = 3$$

is a formalism, unnecessary and perhaps a hindrance to the intuitive grasp of number. For later work in problem solving, which involves the recognition of a concept in a real situation, and the building of a model of related mathematical concepts to interpret a physical situation, it may be that the intuitive-nonsymbolic-informal approach to first learnings is, indeed, the best.

The learners can construct a scrapbook (or collection) of pictorial and other representations of sets that match exactly (can be bijected into each other) and come to recognize the manyness named by a stated number as the common property or characteristic of all these sets. The symbol on the cover names this number. They also describe and construct equivalent sets in their environment. Thus they intuitively grasp the concept of special cardinal numbers. After they have learned the cardinal numbers from 1 to 5 (even 0 for the empty set may be included) or 0 to 10, they arrange sets and their number names in order. Now they learn how to use these ordered names to count the elements of a set. Having learned to count to 10, they can readily count groups of 10 and learn the decimal system of numeration. Now operations become internal laws of composition related to operations on sets. Furthermore, once a fundamental concept is acquired, it becomes another aid to learning a new concept and a structured schemata is built.

One may say the first is Leopold Kronecker's viewpoint that God created the whole numbers, the rest is the work of man, whereas in the set approach the learner creates his own whole numbers by the use of the mental and sensory abilities that God has given him.

OUTCOMES OF MATHEMATICAL LEARNING

The acquisition of basic concepts is a necessary and desired outcome of mathematical instruction. As "basic" implies, however, they are not the only desired outcomes of learning, nor are even more complex or more abstract concepts the only desired outcomes. In addition to the liberal education that is given by such concepts, it is the usefulness of mathematics in the affairs of man that dictates the more desirable outcomes of its study. In general there are three further desirable outcomes that should result from the learning of basic concepts.

One of these is skill in manipulation. This means both skill in numerical calculation, as well as skill in recognition of mathematical relations. Such skill is demanded in the routine application to ordinary situations in which the desired procedure is known for obtaining a required answer or solution. It frees the mind for further thinking about applications of the results.

The second large outcome is in the application of the concepts to problem solving. Whereas skill in calculations are obtained by a systematic practice of meaningful algorisms, there is no known system which the mind can practice for developing problem-solving ability. All we know is that it is accomplished by a complex of concepts which eventually fall into a related pattern or Gestalt that yields a solution. There are various hypotheses on the manner in which problems are solved but certainly without a host of well-developed concepts, it is very unlikely that a problem can be solved or new knowledge created.

Finally, another learning outcome, a noncognitive one, is the appreciation and esthetic satisfaction that derives from the knowledge and use of mathematical concepts. One of the main points in favor of the contemporary conceptualization and teaching of mathematics is in its stress of discovering meaningful concepts as opposed to memorizing rules and procedures. Perceptual-intuitive abstracting of concepts from physical situations, with unhurried calm, has motivated children to learn and enjoy the learning of mathematics. This will lead, on the part of many learners, to extended study of the subject.

RELATION OF CONCEPTS TO GOALS

The basic concepts outlined in this paper are of particular importance with regard to the whole of mathematics learning. Not so many years ago there was, and even today in many places there is, an elementary school study consisting principally of computational arithmetic. This is followed by a grammar school (seventh and eighth grades) study of applications of arithmetic and concrete geometry (measurement). Then there follows a high school study of algebra (2 years), geometry, and trigonometry. The university study begins with analytic geometry, more algebra, and the calculus. Thus there is a distinct different mathematics, with quite different and unrelated concepts, for each level of learning.

Today, this separation is no longer held a valid procedure. The concepts set, mapping, relation (including function), number, space, and structures based on them are basic to all levels of instruction. At the elementary school level the concepts must be of a highly intuitive and informal nature, but useful. At the secondary level they grow more complex, deeper, and more formal. At the university level the same concepts are basic and they are not only deeper but abstract, and so the learning of elementary school mathematics concepts is, indeed, basic for all subsequent learning.

At each level of learning the nature of the concepts involve, among others, psychological, substantive, and practical aspects for their acquisition. Although these several aspects may say contrary things about the manner in which concepts are acquired, without too much compromise the aspects must be unified into an acceptable procedure of learning that will ensure their acquisition. At the elementary school level, the concepts must be learned intuitively by all the pupils. At a higher level of abstraction, they must be acquired by a sufficient number of persons to meet the higher professional demands of our industrial–technological–scientific culture.

REFERENCES

Bruner, J. S., Goodnow, Jacqueline J., & Austin, G. A. *A study of thinking.* New York: Wiley, 1956.

Dienes, Z. P. (Ed.) *Current work on problems of mathematical learning.* Report of the 1964 Stanford Conference on Mathematical Learning. Palo Alto: International Study Group for Mathematics Learning, 1965.

Lovell, K. *The growth of basic mathematical and scientific concepts in children.* (3rd ed.) London: Univer. of London Press, 1964.

Rosskopf, M. F. The strategy of concept attainment. *Teach. Coll. Rec.,* 1958, **60,** 1-8.

Skemp, R. R. *Understanding mathematics: Teacher's notes for Book I.* London: Univer. of London Press, 1964.

CHAPTER 15

THE ROLE OF CONCEPTS
IN SCIENCE TEACHING

JOSEPH D. NOVAK

PURDUE UNIVERSITY
LAFAYETTE, INDIANA

Those of us who focus attention on science education struggle with two questions that face all educators: (1) what knowledge and skills should be taught and (2) what are optimal methods for transmitting them. We recognize the great importance of imparting appropriate attitudes, but since attitudes are learned concomitantly with knowledge and skills, though methods of learning grossly affect attitude development, this chapter will focus attention on the knowledge in science important to transmit and the methods that may be most appropriate for transmitting this knowledge.

The growth of new knowledge in the sciences has been very great in recent years and the rate of increase has also been accelerating. Science in the early nineteenth century contained a substantial body of knowledge, but this knowledge was only a small fraction of the total knowledge in all disciplines. Though new knowledge has been obtained in all disciplines, the rate of growth of new knowledge in science and mathematics has been so great that the total knowledge in these fields may equal the total knowledge in all other disciplines. A broadly trained scientist in 1820 could, and did, know the major principles in astronomy, biology, chemistry, and physics, but this became impossible by 1900. The very character of science, that is, the fact that each problem solved opens the way to solution of many new problems, results in an accelerating growth in new knowledge. The "endless frontier," as Vannevar Bush (1945) identified science, continues to expand. And with the increasing role science and associated technology has played in our society more men and resources have been attracted to the advance of knowledge, so that today it is estimated that over 90% of all scientists who have lived are alive and productive. These scientists will double our fund of knowledge in probably less than a decade; the present impossibility of an individual mastering knowledge in more than one restricted area of science will require that further increased specialization in science must occur. Today we face the problem that biologists or physicists in one area of specialization find it difficult to communicate with colleagues in another area of specialization. The "two cultures" that C. P. Snow (1959) has suggested for sciences and humanities have their analogs within a branch of science where, for example, a biologist interested in enzyme synthesis and action may find little to discuss with his colleague (perhaps next door to him) who is interested in migration patterns in a species of birds.

And yet, as Szent-Györgyi (1964) suggested, the nature of science is such that there is a reduction in the number of major generalizations in science, each one of which subsume an enormous body of information. Our understanding of the relationship between molecular motions and energy transfer provides for explanations in physics, but also applies in chemical reactions, weather perturbations, and the metabolism of cells.

Returning to our focus on education, the implications of new advances in science are not necessarily that transmitting an understanding of science to students will become increasingly difficult; the reverse may be true. New knowledge may provide the basis for new generalizations which organize and encompass larger quantities of information and make potentially simpler the process of education in the sciences. But here lies the crucial element; education in science focused on individual facts and principles will become increasingly ineffective, whereas education focused on development of understanding of the major generalizations of science may become progressively more successful. The task for science education becomes identification of major generalizations or concepts in science and methods of instruction most successful for imparting to students an understanding and appreciation of these concepts or intellectual achievements of science.

One of the problems that occasions great concern among some psychologists is appropriate referent terms for "concepts" of science. In the literature dealing with science teaching, one can find the terms (1) concept, (2) conceptual scheme, (3) theme, (4) organizational thread, (5) major generalization, (6) major concept, (7) fundamental idea, and (8) major principle used synonymously. Though this loose usage of terms by science educators may provoke anguish in other circles, most workers in this area prefer not to belabor the definition of terms but choose instead to provide an illustration for the term used, for example, evolution is a major concept in biology, and then proceed to use the term with reasonable consistency. In this chapter I have used various of the above terms in accordance with the group being discussed, though my preference is to use *major concept* to refer to the construction presented by the other seven terms.

It is apparent from the literature on concept formation that little agreement exists on the definition of the term "concept," although there is a general tendency to limit the use of this term to refer to relatively simple aggregation of experience. This usage is of little value to persons interested primarily in classroom instruction and it is not likely that these individuals will change their language patterns to fit definitions of psychologists. In my opinion it would be better to accept the widely diverse use of the term *concept* and construct, if possible, a "taxonomy of conceptual levels" analogous to Bloom's *Taxonomy of Educational Objectives* (1956). At the lowest levels (for instance, 1.01 level) we would have the concepts referred to by experimental psychologists working with groupings of nonsense syllables and at the highest levels (for instance, 6.60) we would have concepts of the type referred to by the economist when he speaks of the concept of the "market" or the biologist when he cites the concept of evolution. Such a taxonomy of concepts may even prove of substantial value for further research on concept formation. In any case, what I will call *major concept* would be at the highest levels on a hypothetical scale of concept levels.

The general education movement in high schools and colleges during the 1930's brought with it concern for the major themes or "big ideas" in various disciplines that the understanding of which was considered to be the central objective of the general education program. Serious teachers devoted considerable energy to the development of new courses and identification of the major ideas upon which these courses would focus attention. The books by the Progressive Education Association Commission on Secondary School Curriculum (1938) and McGrath (1948) summarized many of these innovations in high schools and colleges. Another effort by scholars to identify areas of major importance in the sciences and philosophy of science, but not focused directly on curriculum development was published as the *International Encyclopedia of Unified Science* (Neurath, Carnap, & Morris, 1938).

The attempts to identify a set of fundamental ideas in a discipline, what Bruner (1960) has termed the "structure" of a discipline, had impact on teaching in college general education courses. But somehow the majority of college courses remained immutable, especially courses in the sciences. The result, in many schools, was a creeping necrosis from upper division or "majors only" courses and decay of the general education courses. Many schools became disenchanted with courses which even conservative old professors regarded as "not bad."

By 1955, many colleges had abandoned general education courses in favor of "substantial" introductory courses required for both majors and general education students, with this movement accelerated by the heightened interest in education occasioned by Soviet atomic bombs and the Korean War. But almost as soon as the movement to "regular" courses for majors in sciences as well as for nonmajors began, a new movement was taking form that will lead within a decade to a major restructuring of the entire curriculum in science departments. Some of the impetus for the revision has and will continue to derive from the substantial improvement in secondary school science and mathematics. There are today active groups supported with funds from Federal and other agencies which are examining carefully the important ideas in chemistry, physics, biology, and other areas with the express purpose of total curriculum improvement. Unfortunately there remains too much concern with introductory or general education courses (cf. *Proceedings of the Boulder Conference on Physics for Nonscience Majors,* 1965), but in my opinion colleges are ready for a much broader examination of their science programs and several leading universities will probably restructure their total science offerings with the view of achieving better integration of concepts in all areas of science and mathematics. My concern now, however, is that almost no attention is being directed at careful examination of the learning process and appraisal of optimal instructional regimes for conceptual learning.

Only a few published reports present direct efforts at identification of major concepts in science. In 1955, the National Academy of Sciences–National Research Council ". . . convoked a priming conference of representatives from a wide variety of biological disciplines, not for the purpose of trying their hand at 'designing concepts' (which would have been not only presumptuous, but unrealistic), but rather to examine whether or not the purported deficiency [in emphasis on conceptual ordering] actually existed, and if so, to what to ascribe it and how to meet it" (Gerard, 1958, p. 93). A provocative paper by Gerard on "Concepts and Principles of Biology" served as a springboard for discussions, a condensed transcript of which was published in 1958. Although no concise statements of major ideas or concepts in biology were agreed upon, the conference report did place focus on the need to search for such concepts ". . . only dimly perceptible through the fog that still envelops 'biological concepts' " (p. 93). To my knowledge, no comparable effort has been published in other areas of science, with the possible exception of the suggested "themes" presented in the recent Boulder conference report (Correll & Strassenburg, 1965). With the exception of the Biological Sciences Curriculum Study (BSCS), secondary school curriculum projects, supported largely by the National Science Foundation, did not begin with identification of major concepts or themes in the discipline. The BSCS project identified nine "themes," seven dealing with the content of biology and two with the methods by which this content is presented. These themes are described at length by Schwab (1963). The themes were identified to guide the writing of three different "versions" of high school biology, each theme pervading throughout the materials and not isolated into separate chapters or units.

Brandwein in his paper, "Elements in a Strategy for Teaching Science in the Elementary School" (Schwab & Brandwein, 1962), emphasized the importance of identification of conceptual schemes for planning elementary science curriculum. The six conceptual schemes Brandwein proposed were intended to guide curriculum planning with elements of each conceptual scheme developed longitudinally throughout the elementary science program. Unlike so many earlier suggestions where concepts have been identified and "grade placement" for each concept suggested, Brandwein's conceptual schemes were each to be illustrated through appropriate instruction at every grade level.

The difficulty of identifying major concepts experienced by the participants of the 1955 conference on concepts in biology has led some individuals to maintain that any attempt to describe such concepts would not meet with success or wide acceptance. Sponsoring agencies have been wary to endorse new efforts on the premise that it is better not to support an attempt at identifying concepts in science, important as this appears to be, than to risk association with an attempt that failed. Moreover, there exists today in science curriculum projects an imbalance of opinion weighted heavily toward the pole that it is better to identify good science activities for pupils without confounding the work with any conscious effort to plan these activities with the intent that they may lead to understanding of specific major concepts. This point of view provides no restrictions on the curriculum workers except that the activities should be representative of science, a happy situation indeed! But the products of this approach to curriculum planning, good as many of them are, do not constitute a program in science that schools can employ from primary grades through the high school, nor it is likely in my opinion, that they will in the future. The task recognized by scientists as most difficult, namely, the organization of curriculum to lead to some understanding of basic ideas in science and the process by which these ideas are advanced, is left to the schools to tackle. The school systems that have tried found they need help.

THE NSTA EFFORT IN CONCEPT IDENTIFICATION

As a result of repeated requests for aid in planning from school super-intendents, science consultants, and curriculum groups in elementary and secondary schools, the National Science Teachers Association formed a Curriculum Committee to study the problem. Early statements by the committee emphasized the need for planning science curriculum on a kindergarten (K) to grade-12 basis, with careful integration of material at each grade level. The question constantly arose, integration around what? Clearly some major conceptual threads or themes were needed. In November, 1963, unable to obtain funds from other agencies, the National Science Teachers Association sponsored a Conference of Identification of Concepts in Science. The 2-day conference attracted outstanding participants (without honoraria) and succeeded in reaching some general agreements. The Conference transcript provided the basis for a follow-up conference with several of the original participants and a final report was published by the National Science Teachers Association in *Theory Into Action* (1964).

Throughout the NSTA Conference of scientists, one problem served to focus efforts of the group; if possible, some kind of statements which could serve as guidelines for planning science curriculum for grades K–12 was needed. This specific focus on statements that could be useful for K–12 science *curriculum planning* probably served to facilitate the work of the group, since many statements which could have been written summarizing an important idea or concept in science would have little utility for curriculum work though the statements may be perfectly valid for contemporary science. In the end, 12 statements were agreed upon, 7 dealing with the intellectual products or "conceptual schemes" of science and 5 with the process or methodology of science. Each statement was accompanied by an elaborating paragraph, but only the statements are given below.

Conceptual Schemes of Science:

    I. All matter is composed of units called fundamental particles; under certain conditions these particles can be transformed into energy and vice versa.

    II. Matter exists in the form of units which can be classified into hierarchies of organizational levels.

III. The behavior of matter in the universe can be described on a statistical basis.

IV. Units of matter interact. The bases of all ordinary interactions are electromagnetic, gravitational, and nuclear forces.

V. All interacting units of matter tend toward equilibrium states in which the energy content (enthalpy) is a minimum and the energy distribution (entropy) is most random. In the process of attaining equilibrium, energy transformations or matter transformations or matter-energy transformations occur. Nevertheless, the sum of energy and matter in the universe remains constant.

VI. One of the forms of energy is the motion of units of matter. Such motion is responsible for heat and temperature and for the states of matter: solid, liquid, and gaseous.

VII. All matter exists in time and space and, since interactions occur among its units, matter is subject in some degree to changes with time. Such changes may occur at various rates and in various patterns.

Major Items in the Process of Science:

I. Science proceeds on the assumption, based on centuries of experience, that the universe is not capricious.

II. Scientific knowledge is based on observations of samples of matter that are accessible to public investigation in contrast to purely private inspection.

III. Science proceeds in a piecemeal manner, even though it also aims at achieving a systematic and comprehensive understanding of various sectors or aspects of nature.

IV. Science is not, and will probably never be, a finished enterprise, and there remains very much more to be discovered about how things in the universe behave and how they are interrelated.

V. Measurement is an important feature of most branches of modern science because the formulation as well as the establishment of laws are facilitated through the development of quantitative distinctions (National Science Teachers Association, 1964, pp. 22-31).

The above statements, even with their elaborating paragraphs, were not intended to be used by the average classroom teacher. Clearly, the ideas contained within them require individuals with considerable knowledge of science to translate these statements into specific proposals for classroom activity. Our experience has been that many school curriculum groups have shown great interest in the conceptual schemes proposed and the potential they believe these would have in providing order and integration in their somewhat haphazard science offerings. But when they write NSTA for further explanatory materials and assistance, there has been little to offer. Teachers recognize that organizing a science program around an idea that all matter in the universe is made up of units which can be classified into hierarchies of organizational levels is a much more potent theme than "transportation" or "weather" or any similar themes that abound in published "scope and sequence" charts accompanying science books. The reason is simple: even a poorly trained teacher recognizes that "transportation" is *not* a major concept in science, although one might organize some interesting activities for students under this heading. A vertical ordering of experiences from K to 6 or K to 8 around "transportation" can provide no assurance that sequential growth of the children's understanding of the major ideas in science will occur. This organization is at best irrelevant to science; at worst it completely confounds science and technology into a grand mass of facts to be memorized—and soon forgotten.

To use the statements developed by the NSTA Conference as a basis for curriculum planning it is important to recognize that the methodology or *process* of science cannot be taught except as it is exemplified in the experience provided to children to teach the conceptual schemes. Students observing cell structure in various living things, as well as other "hierarchies of organization," can also recognize that observations made by one investigator (student) can be corroborated by a colleague—process statement II. The critical task is to select appropriate experiences at each grade level that contribute to understanding the conceptual schemes, and simultaneously, the nature of science. Experiences need to be planned horizontally through a grade level and vertically from kindergarten through grade 12 or higher. The curriculum matrix could be diagrammed as shown in Fig. 1. Local climate, resources, etc., would mean that the specific experiences planned would vary among school systems, but the underlying conceptual structure should be universally the same.

In Fig. 1 the relationship between conceptual schemes, process statements, and science curriculum is suggested. The x axis represents considerations in the process of science that would be involved in planning specific student activities; the z axis represents the products or conceptual schemes that would serve to suggest relevant activities; and the y axis represents time with early school experience at the origin and later experience vertically indicated. Each block would constitute some activity which could be presented to students to illustrate a given conceptual scheme and "process" idea. Of course, it is not possible to illustrate the interdependence of the various conceptual schemes, gains in each one of which would affect growth in understanding of others. Moreover, a given student activity might result in growth of understanding in two or more concepts and processes of science. The lines dividing the base of the curriculum at the origin of the graph are arbitrary divisions, for different organizations of conceptual schemes and process statements may vary in the number of units identified. The three-dimensional representation of curriculum would be one interrelated matrix of experience, analogous to the matrix of ideas and methodology that constitutes the matrix or corpus of science.

Can there be agreement among scientists on statements of conceptual schemes and methodology in science? I believe there can be. In general, the NSTA Conference participants were enthusiastic about the final draft of the statements as presented in *Theory Into Action.* Other scientists to whom these statements were submitted for comment also reacted

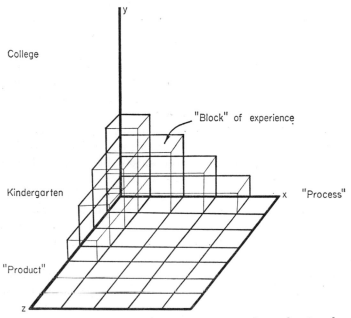

Fɪɢ. 1. Schematic representation of science curriculum planning based upon selected "blocks" of experience that may lead to understanding of the "process" of science together with major concepts of the "products" of science. See text for explanation.

with strong approval, although some reservations were indicated. One of the Conference participants rejected the report and prepared a reply which has been published by NSTA (Glass, 1965). The arguments Glass presented against publication of the conceptual schemes centered around the thesis that education based on a framework of conceptual schemes ". . . would do a great disservice to science as a whole, while proving disastrous for the development of the biological sciences in particular" (p. 29). This argument is reminiscent of those of botanists, who argued that to merge botany and zoology into a biology course would be disastrous to botany, a position against which Glass has provided leadership.

Biology courses taught by broadly trained professors often utilize plant materials more than animal materials, since plants are frequently more practical to use to illustrate important ideas in biology. In my view, biology would benefit, at least in the elementary grades, if science instruction were based on conceptual schemes similar to those proposed by the NSTA Conference primarily because responsible curriculum planners would find that many important concepts in science can be illustrated best with biological systems. Not only would concepts in biology be an integral part of elementary science but the dull "zoo parade" that passes as instruction in living things in many elementary classrooms might also be displaced.

It remains to be seen whether or not a curriculum designed specifically with guidelines provided by a set of conceptual schemes and process statements will advance or hinder the improvement of science education. Glass's observation that the BSCS themes were "found to be of very little use in detailed curriculum planning" (p. 83) may well have resulted from the fact that the writers were not trained in their college courses to focus on major ideas and a few briefing sessions on the "themes" were not likely to compensate for this.

For my own work I have found the statements in *Theory Into Action* very useful. A somewhat modified set of conceptual schemes, or major concepts as I prefer to call them, has proved useful to me in curriculum planning with teachers in which I have been engaged. These major concepts in science can be stated as follows.

(1) Matter in the universe is organized into units which vary in size and complexity; the larger units encompass the properties of the subunits and possess additional properties of their own.

This concept can easily be illustrated in kindergarten or first-grade activities such as observing that plants have stems and leaves and other "units" and in turn these units have veins, hairs, etc., or smaller units. Rock can be broken into chips or sand into powder; and mountains can be weathered to rock and sand. At higher-grade levels, more abstract illustrations are possible with students engaged in microscopic observation, or study of planetary and galactic systems of organization. Properly designed activities would illustrate concomitantly the process of science.

(2) Units of matter interact; the different kinds of forces involved in the interactions are few in number.

To illustrate this concept we can have children work with weights and springs, or magnets, or water poured over soils. A tremendous range of interactions can be shown, but we must link this concept closely to the next, for they are very much interrelated.

(3) When units of matter interact, energy may be exchanged, but the sum of energy always remains constant. Matter can be changed into energy and vice versa, but the sum of matter and energy involved does not change.

Atomic bombs, radioactivity, and solar energy are becoming so much a part of the television exposure of children that mass–energy transformations probably should not be distinguished from so-called "ordinary" changes; mass–energy transformations are *not* unnatural or extraordinary. Though we may need to wait until higher grade levels to explain more fully how mass–energy changes occur, we can begin to lay the foundations for this understanding early, just as we have in the past explained in kindergarten that plants need light to grow without pursuing the mechanisms of photon capture and utilization by chlorophyll.

(4) The behavior of matter can be described on a statistical basis only. The interaction of units of matter occurs in such a manner that the results must be described only in terms of what is likely to happen.

In primary grades we can observe that not all seeds may germinate; we do not know in advance which will fail to grow. Later we can discuss the diffusion of molecules or the mutation of genes. We also illustrate that though we may not be able to predict what will happen to a given unit of matter (who will die of cancer, for example), we can with appreciable certainty predict what will happen to a large population of these units under given circumstances (more smokers die of cancer than nonsmokers).

(5) Interaction among units of matter occur in time and space and result in changes which take place at different rates and in different patterns.

Children recognize that they grow, clouds appear and disappear, gasoline is consumed in an automobile, and a host of other changes occur. They need to be guided to observe more subtle changes and to recognize that these are the result of interaction between units of matter and involve exchanges of energy and changes in organization over time. A burning candle, an erupting volcano, a new strain of virus disease all illustrate this concept.

ROLE OF CONCEPTS IN PLANNING INSTRUCTION

I have tried to indicate that there is no single identifiable set of concepts which summarize knowledge in the sciences; equally valid alternative sets could be constructed. It is possible, however, to obtain agreement from scientists in a variety of fields on a set of statements representing the major intellectual achievements or the concepts of science. Collectively, these statements represent the "structure" of the discipline; these concepts exist in the minds of scientists (though, not as precise statements) and provide the basis by which they design and interpret new observations. These concepts exist in the population of scientists; our role as educators is to facilitate transmission of concepts from the cognitive structure in the collective minds of scientists to the modified cognitive structure of our pupils. Figure 2 shows a representation of this process.

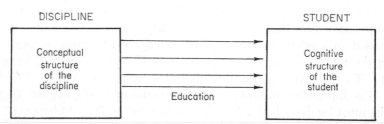

FIG. 2. A representation of the process of education when viewed as the transfer of conceptual structure as it exists in the discipline to the student's cognitive structure.

Knowledge in science constitutes a large matrix of interrelated principles and generalizations. It would be possible to identify almost any number of "major concepts," each of which would be valid in a particular frame of reference. As a basis for curriculum planning two or three concept statements would be only somewhat better guidelines than a single statement, for example, matter and energy undergo changes in space–time, but are conserved. On the other hand, as many as 20 to 30 statements begin to overwhelm a curriculum worker since he cannot consider all statements concomitantly as he plans activities. Glass reported during the NSTA Conference that BSCS writers found it difficult to keep in mind constantly the nine "themes" that were to course through the books and laboratory work. The fact is that the knowledge in science can be divided into any number of concept statements, but it is likely that there is an optimal number of statements that can serve for what Ausubel (1960; 1963) called *expository organizers*. The number of identified expository organizers may be different for curriculum workers and students, though I see no reason to expect this. On the basis of arguments by Miller (1956) our minds may be limited to retaining seven, plus or minus two, independent "chunks" and this may account for the difficulty the BSCS team found in using nine themes.

What implications for science teaching result from a theory that centers on building curriculum guided by statements of major concepts in science? One of the most important, I believe, is that although these statements of concepts may be only verbal descriptions of large bodies of knowledge to the curriculum planner, who for the most part has not been trained to relate new knowledge he has learned to major concepts in science, a K-6 or K-12 curriculum with activities overtly planned around these concepts can lead a child to form internalized associations of knowledge. These associations or concepts now become what Ausubel (1960) called *comparative* organizers which the student can use at successive grade levels to aid him in organizing and learning new information impinging upon him. Science study becomes not a repeated experience of memorization of more unrelated facts, soon to be forgotten, but rather a constant search for "fit" between new information and the continuously developing "anchorage" (Ausubel, 1963) concepts he has. A model for the interpretation and measurement of concept development along these lines has been presented elsewhere (Novak, 1965).

It is important, of course, that the "anchorage" concepts used not become invalid before the student finishes school or his younger productive years. Though we cannot predict what new discoveries will occur, it is not likely that the "anchorage" concepts suggested above will be poor representations of our scientific knowledge in a decade or even 3 decades. These concepts have a history extending back several decades and they may continue to be useful to scientists for a few more decades.

Another important consideration arises. In a typical elementary science class, each new topic is, in effect, a distinct body of information to be learned. Consideration of the life cycle of a fern plant or computation of current flow using Ohm's law, for example, constitutes in practice an almost isolated body of information to be memorized. This has one pedagogic advantage: individualization of instruction can be kept to a minimum since all students begin at virtually the same starting point for the particular learning task. Though the rates of gain in knowledge and relative achievement will vary substantially, the next new topic now finds all class members at almost the same conceptual level to begin the new learning task. In contrast, science instruction based vertically through the grades on major concepts means that each new presentation builds heavily on the quality of what Ausubel (1960) called "anchorage" concepts already formed. Typical class instruction where all students receive the same input of information and are held to the same criteria of success, e.g., scores on tests requiring recall of this information, becomes almost irrelevant to the individual's growth in understanding the concepts of science. Also, in a typical classroom (especially in college) we see too much of the medieval model of teaching–learning where the teacher is interposed between the knowledge and the student with information "filtered" by the teacher (and his conceptual limitations) and passed to the student for whatever organization he can make. Figure 3

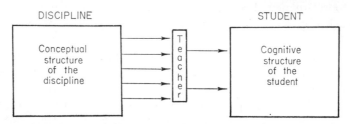

FIG. 3. The process of education where the teacher serves as the principal source of information for learning.

shows a schematic representation of this. We need to train teachers to become facilitators for learning, not filter systems, where they help to organize an array of information input sources. At Purdue University, Professor Postlethwait (Postlethwait, Novak, & Murray, 1964) has organized a botany course in this manner using audiotape to program the information input, with him and his assistants standing by to facilitate learning in the variety of ways a teacher and an individual student can interact. Figure 4 represents this approach to teaching–learning.

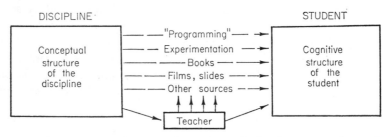

FIG. 4. The process of education where the teacher's role is primarily in planning for appropriate learning resource material.

IN CONCLUSION

The course of science education, like that of the history of man, has shown periods of rise and decline in the importance of identifiable factors. From Aristotle's and Lucretus' conceptions of natural phenomena through the decay of learning in the Dark Ages and a rebirth conceptual ordering with Copernicus and Newton, science and science teaching with emphasis on concepts has continued to ebb and flow. Each new cycle, however, has added new dimensions. The movement toward greater emphasis on themes or major concepts in science which I believe we see taking form again brings with it this time strong reinforcement from rapidly advancing learning theory.

Other factors also mediate in favor of science instruction centered around developing an understanding of basic concepts in science. New knowledge emerges at an increasing pace and with increasing impact on our society. New technological devices for transmitting knowledge, together with society's increasing ability and willingness to pay for these, render obsolete the student's dependence on the teacher for new knowledge so characteristic of our schools and colleges. We may experience an increase in the availability and acceptance of new knowledge exceeding that resulting from invention of the printing press. As Gerald Holton has suggested, we may be entering a new renaissance much greater than that of the arts and humanities in the seventeenth century.

REFERENCES

Ausubel, D. P. The use of advance organizers in the learning and retention of meaningful verbal material. *J. educ. Psychol.*, 1960, **51**, 267-272.

Ausubel, D. P. *The psychology of meaningful verbal learning.* New York: Grune & Stratton, 1963.

Bloom, B. S. (Ed.) *Taxonomy of educational objectives.* Handbook I. *Cognitive domain.* New York: McKay, 1956.

Bruner, J. S. *The process of education.* Cambridge: Harvard Univer. Press, 1960.

Bush, V. *Science, the endless frontier.* Washington, D.C.: U.S. Government Printing Office, 1945.

Correll, M., & Strassenburg, A. A. (Eds.) *The proceedings of the Boulder Conference on Physics for Nonscience Majors.* Ann Arbor: Commission on College Physics, 1965.

Gerard, R. W. (Ed.) Concepts of biology. *Behav. Sci.*, 1958, **3**, 89-215.

Glass, B. Theory into action—a critique. *Sci. Teach.*, 1965, **32**, (5), 29-30, 82-83.

McGrath, E. J. (Ed.) *Science in general education.* Dubuque, Iowa: W. C. Brown, 1948.

Miller, G. A. The magical number seven, plus or minus two: Some limits on our capacity for processing information. *Psychol. Rev.*, 1956, **63**, 81-97.

National Science Teachers Association. *Theory into action.* Washington, D.C.: Author, 1964.

Neurath, O., Carnap, R., & Morris, C. W. (Eds.) *International encyclopedia of unified science.* Chicago: Univer. of Chicago Press, 1938.

Novak, J. D. A model for the interpretation and analysis of concept formation. *J. Res. sci. Teach.*, 1965, **3**, 72-83.

Postlethwait, S. N., Novak, J., & Murray, H. *An integrated experience approach to learning, with emphasis on independent study.* Minneapolis: Burgess, 1964.

Progressive Education Association, Commission on Secondary School Curriculum. *Science in general education.* New York: Appleton-Century-Crofts, 1938.

Schwab, J. J. (Supervisor) *Biology teachers' handbook.* New York: Wiley, 1963.

Schwab, J. J., & Brandwein, P. F. *The teaching of science.* Cambridge: Harvard Univer. Press, 1962.

Snow, C. P. *The two cultures and the scientific revolution.* Cambridge: Cambridge Univer. Press, 1959.

Szent-Györgyi, A. Teaching and the expanding knowledge. *Science,* 1964, **146,** 1278-1279.

CHAPTER 16

TOWARD A DEFINITION OF "ENGLISH"

STANLEY KEGLER

UNIVERSITY OF MINNESOTA
MINNEAPOLIS, MINNESOTA

The subject I have been asked to discuss is indeed broad. I have been asked to deal with concepts of English; how those concepts are organized; what the implications of the system of organization of concepts are for learning in the field itself. All of these are issues—indeed hot issues—and very broad questions at that.*

It is almost a routine practice in current writing that an expositor enter a disclaimer before he begins to develop the ideas in a paper. Such a disclaimer enables the writer to wrap himself in the mantle of innocence if anything goes awry; at the same time it allows him to express himself freely, although without authority, on the subject. Such freedom of expression has been most characteristic of the field of English, and more often than not by authorities who have not had the integrity to enter a disclaimer.

I should like to enter a disclaimer, not as much for myself as for the field of the discipline of English. The reasons for the disclaimer are multiple: only lately have we in English begun looking for answers; indeed, only lately have we begun to ask questions. And the key question has been; "What is English?" To this question—the definition of the discipline and the structure of knowledge within that discipline—is what I should like to address myself in this paper.

It is common knowledge that there has been a great deal of ferment

---

* Let me say before I begin my discussion that many of the ideas I shall mention are not mine alone, but are derivative of the discussions held in the English Projects Center at the University of Minnesota with Professor Harold B. Allen of the English Department and Professor Donald K. Smith, a professor of rhetoric. The lack of facility or clarity with which I express those ideas is my own responsibility, however.

in the fields commonly taught in our lower schools. This ferment derives more, I think, from the need to define an already crowded school curriculum than it does from a genuine desire to examine the nature of the discipline itself. My observation is that the accretion of materials, procedures, and practices is such that "something's gotta give." I do not wish to demean the efforts of the fine scholars who have devoted many years to defining the limits of the discipline; it is only honest to recognize that the explosion of knowledge in recent years has tended to force the analysis of the discipline, however reluctant.

A number of individuals and groups have addressed themselves to the question, "What is English?" The results have not been uniformly successful. For example, William Riley Parker (1962) indicated:

As a teacher of English, I am fascinated by the fascination that the concept of *structure* currently has for educators. What lies behind this? Is it, by any chance, the notion, which I know is cherished by some foundation officials, that all knowledge can be neatly fragmented and codified and eventually programmed for use by some teaching machine of the future, thus bringing a dramatic breakthrough to the staggering problem of educating the restless masses of Africa and Asia? Have the experiments of Pressey and Skinner caused the ghost of Comenius to walk again? Are we going not only to structure knowledge but also to atomize it into particles of useful fact that can be fed into a machine? (p. 210).

Professor Parker went on:

Two things we have learned recently without help from others, though we shall need plenty of help in the implementation of our knowledge. The first thing we learned was that our subject badly needed redefining, and there is a growing conviction among us that English should consist of just three things and no more: English is language, literature, and composition—period (p. 212).
. . .—new recognition that language, literature, and composition are closely interrelated; that each has a natural, built-in, cumulative development; that this sequential, progressive development must hereafter be respected in curricula, along with the child's ability and normal interests; and, finally, that the future training of English teachers must have a direct relationship with what they will be expected to teach (p. 213).

Professor Parker stated that a concept of structure did not yet exist as a pedagogical feasibility; he was quite certain, on the other hand, what the basic elements of the discipline were. Professor Parker was not alone in these assertions; the Commission on English of the College Entrance Examination Board (CEEB) issued a *pronunciamento* along the same lines about the same time.

This assertion that the discipline was really three disciplines has, in my estimation, acted as a major deterrent to clear thinking and direct attention to problems of defining the structure of knowledge in the curriculum. Almost invariably the proponents of this kind of definition of the curriculum have refused to look beyond the traditional confines of the discipline to other relevant sources of information. Almost invariably they have settled for three vaguely defined, yet interrelated structures. And almost invariably they have given up the search for a central structure for the discipline.

All of the would-be analysts have not been so myopic. Graham C. Wilson (1964), for example, indicated that one of the major problems was to define the discipline itself. He said:

There is *language,* which may include grammar, philology, anthropology, semantics and general semantics, psychology, and English as a foreign language; *literature,* which may be English, American, European, world, and, when the time comes, interplanetary; *composition,* which may include grammar (again), rhetoric, semantics (again), and logic. Language artists speak of reading, writing, speaking, and listening. This is quite a mixture. In this age of increasing specialization, it is pleasant to feel that in at least one academic area, the totally qualified teacher will be a true Renaissance man or woman—communicative, comprehensive, contemplative—and nonexistent (pp. 71-72).

Even in this analysis the tendency is to fall back upon the tripod of language, literature, and composition. Professor Wilson then went on to describe research in the several fields indicated, and never did come to grips with the problems of the structure of knowledge in English *in toto.* He ended by saying:

I doubt that an over-all structure in the discipline called English can be satisfactorily demonstrated. It remains, as someone has said of history, "a sack of snakes." I have suggested here, though, that it might be useful to think of English as language and literature, and that if we do, we can discover a good deal of order. Twentieth-century study of language has given us new insights into the nature of languages and into their structures. Twentieth-century literary criticism has done the same things for literature. Twentieth-century common sense—and of course, insight—tells us much about how and when this knowledge may be best placed in the classroom. Somewhere there must be a little twentieth-century money to enable us to work out the details and to begin the job (pp. 85-86).

Here, at least, we have moved to two components of the discipline.

I should say at this juncture that the history of the field of English itself has contributed, at least in part, to some of the difficulties involved in defining our discipline. It is a history which must be read to be believed; a history of coincidence and accident. As a collegiate subject, we are "johnny-come-latelies" on the academic scene—about a century old, as a matter of fact. From the first, we have been saddled with the doctrine of immediate utility as a criterion for what we teach in our classrooms. No other discipline has been saddled in the same ways, or to nearly the same extent.

Then, too, and largely because of the doctrine of utility, we have gone through periods of reductionism in our discipline. As larger numbers of students, some of them less able than our previous clientele come to our schools, we have taken grammar—the structure of a language—and made it into usage, which is still the backbone of so many so-called "grammar" series. We have, in other words, taken grammar, things permissible in language, and substituted for it usage, things permissible in social situations. We have taken principles of rhetoric and reduced that study to the study of oral and written composition. We moved, after the turn of the century, from the study of principles of rhetoric to *application* of those principles; since then we have moved to reduce this field of study still further so that now we speak of composition, and usually only in the written form. We took the study of logic and reduced it, by a series of fragmentations, to the application level; we find elements of the study of logic in "critical thinking" in English and social studies and in the "scientific method" in mathematics, science, and other disciplines. In short, we have moved, in the last 50 years, from a study of the structure of the language and from the study of principles of rhetoric and logic to considerably less than that. And we have done it, I submit, with very little research or empirical support.

Not the least of our historical problems derives from the variety of diverse views which an historically diverse discipline gathers within it. It is quite possible for three professors, all of whom bear the title "Professor of English," to deal with three subject matters all quite different from one another. Linguists, for example, have less in common with colleagues in English departments and more in common with colleagues in foreign languages, classical studies, anthropology, psychology, philosophy, speech, and rhetoric. And the linguists' tendency to study the structure of the language often serves as a barrier to scholars and teachers who view language as verbal behavior, in the total context of the communication situations.

I should also point out in this regard that many scholars in the fields of English are not willing to submit to the search for a central focus for the discipline of English. Professor James Sledd (1963), for example, argued ably that such a search is nonsense. "Why," he asked, "should we assume that we can or should unify the group of quite miscellaneous and separately valuable studies that our history (there it is again) has brought together under the name of English?" One could counter, of course, with the rejoinder, "Why not?" Why accept the series of unhappy accidents which have made our discipline what it is?

What I have attempted to do thus far might appropriately be called "prefatory remarks." I have sketched out some of the early attempts at defining the structure of our discipline, and I have pointed to some of the problems attendant upon this effort. I should now like to move in the direction of the title of my paper, "Toward a Definition of English." I will assert at this point that I am not sure that I will be able to say clearly what the structure of concepts will be. I will point to what I consider to be the proper focus of the discipline called English, and will point to what I feel are kinds of concepts which relate to studies in that field.

There have been several attempts to answer the question, "What is English?" and "What should be the focus of the curriculum in English?" H. A. Gleason (1962), for example, said:

1. We should teach composition and literature so that people are helped through them to *understand language* and its operation. We understand this function thoroughly only as we try seriously to extract that meaning from passages, or to express fully and succinctly such meaning in language.
2. The second emphasis in the new *language curriculum* must be on the *manipulation of language*.
3. The third emphasis in the new curriculum must be on the *appreciation of language. I mean to include the appreciation of the language as structure.*

It is plain to see where Gleason would put the emphasis in the discipline called English—upon the study of language.

In that same year, speaking from within a pedagogical context, Kegler, Allen, and Smith (1962) argued:

To replace the disordered and fragmented instruction about language, instruction in the skills of speaking, reading, writing, and listening should proceed *within the context of instruction about language.* If this were effected, language instruction could well provide the core around which the communication skills were taught. Each classroom experience in reading, writing, speaking, and listening would be viewed as another experience with language—another significant opportunity for instruction about language. For example, instruction about the differences between spoken and written language could be accomplished in a variety of contexts—yet this has seldom been done. It has too long been assumed that students need "know" only those prescriptions immediately applicable to classroom exercises in the communication skills. The result has been that students have come to know little about language, and much of that allegedly "known" does not represent any real understanding of the nature of language. It is probable that lack of attention to systematic instruction in language has frustrated the development of communication skills. For example, the student who sees the development of new habits of usage as the search for control over a new "dialect" is quite likely to make better progress than one who is told that the dialect which serves his family and community is wrong, and that he must now learn to speak and write "correctly."

With the body of information and concepts about language now available, it seems quite clear that a team of dedicated scholars representing diverse academic disciplines and sound pedagogy can establish the relevant frames of reference within which the information and concepts of language can be categorized and from which informational and conceptual learning about language could proceed in an orderly way. Such frames of reference are: (a) nature of language (as viewed by the psychologist); (b) structure of language (as viewed by the linguist); (c) the history of language; (d) the problems of meaning, reference, and proof; (e) major forms within which utterance takes place (literature and its genres, persuasive and expository discourse and its genres); and (f) media influences on form and function (pp. 2-3).

And still more recently, the Commission on English (1965) of CEEB stated in the introduction to the monograph *Freedom and Discipline in English:*

The answer (to "What is English?") rests on the unstartling assumption that language, primarily the English language, constitutes the core of the subject; and on the further and equally unstartling assumption that the study and use of the English language is the proper content of the English curriculum (p. 2).

What I am suggesting should be quite clear by this time. I submit that the study of language *broadly conceived,* and with *examples from and application to* the English language is the proper content of the discipline called English. I submit further that the other two legs of the so-called tripod—literature and composition—are extensions of language study, which extensions and relationship I should like to examine later.

Before I go further into a discussion of a language-based approach, however, I should like to suggest *why* such a focus seems appropriate. Let me cite a few passages from Kegler and Kemp (1964) which, in essence, provide the philosophical framework for a language focus:

We believe that the proper concern of the English curriculum is the study of man himself and that the most vital information about man can be found through the study of the language he uses. We believe that the study of language, broadly conceived, will reveal how man views himself, by what and for what man lives, and how man orders his existence. We believe that one of the most clearly observable features of humanity is man's ability to manipulate verbal symbols in a complex way. As the Danish linguist Hjelmslev puts it, it is in language that we find, "the distinctive mark of personality, for good or ill, the distinctive mark of home and of nation, mankind's patent of nobility." We believe that understanding the operations and the nature of language is of central importance in an open society, which must, by the nature of its political and social structures, make decisions affecting group and individual actions. Again in the words of Hjelmslev, "Language is the instrument with which man forms thought and feeling, mood, aspiration, will and act, the instrument by whose means he influences and is influenced, the ultimate and deepest foundation of human society."

Our Goal is the education of linguistically sensitive persons. By this we mean persons aware of influencing and being influenced through language, conscious of the multiple ways in which language operates, appreciative of the artistic use of language, as in literature, and informed about the nature of the language they use. As speakers and writers, our students should be aware of their responsibilities to make and support assertions using appropriate language and patterns of thought. As listeners and readers, our students should be aware of their responsibilities to evaluate the assertions of others. Our students should be conscious of the variety of human functions performed through language. Our students should be appreciative of the artistic use of language in varieties of literature, the uses of language which offer special insight into human experience. Our students should be informed about the symbolic quality and structural characteristics of the language they use.

A common element in all of our concerns is language, its uses and its nature. This concern is proper, we believe, because we live, using the figure of Neils Bohr, "suspended in language." Very little which we do is not verbally mediated. With our major goals the understanding of language operations and the development of competence in language operations, we place great emphasis on the fundamentally human enterprise of language. Such an emphasis allows us to incorporate our conviction that a curriculum must look to the future as well as the present and the past. A curriculum in English must be so structured that it prepares students to meet the problems of the future within the context of today's problems and yesterday's solutions and failures. With the rapid rate of change characteristic of our society, it seems impossible to predict with any accuracy the problems our students will be called upon to solve. It seems, rather, that a curriculum must prepare students to deal with unknown problems in unknown ways. It seems certain that the manipulation of verbal symbols will play an important role in the solution of any human problem. We feel that a curriculum devoted to a broadly conceived study of language and the manipulation of verbal symbols will serve our students well (p. 3).

What, then, is the intellectual framework for the language focus of the discipline of English? Again, let me say at this point that much of what follows derives from the work of my colleagues in the Minnesota English Projects Center, more specifically Professors Allen and Smith, whom I mentioned earlier. Let us start with linguistic behavior, which I will define here as that part of audible, symbolic behavior manifesting the structured system of language. This structured system of language has certain basic, distinctive characteristics: (a) the system appears in the learned vocal behavior of human beings; (b) it is a code, generating symbols which carry meaning; and (c) the code permits communication.

Speech, within this context, would be defined as a behavior manifesting a code of learned, conventional audible symbols, and accompanying visible symbols used in communication. Grammar can be described as the set of finite rules describing the system found in language which enables the speaker to generate, and the listener to understand, a relatively infinite number of sentences.

The principle that language itself is a system, in which audible and visible units are operated according to established conventions of human behavior, calls for rather detailed attention. It requires attention to some features of the discipline of phonetics, for example. But along with this principle is a cognate one, that each language has its own unique system; this calls for attention to English as English. For a long time some reluctant half-awareness of this fact has appeared in linguistic writings; but it was not until anthropologists, working with American Indian languages about 70 years ago, decided that they must start from scratch in their studies and no longer rely upon the framework of Indo-European grammar; this has led to the bold insistence that each language must be viewed as a separate entity, from its sounds to its syntax.

Closely related to linguistic behavior, and clearly part of the communication act, are paralinguistic behavior and kinesic behavior, which I shall differentiate here, but which are not clearly discriminable in much discussion in this field. Paralinguistic behavior is that part of audible symbolic behavior not now describable as a structured system. That is, vocal aspects can be classified from what is said and heard to provide background and modifying information affecting interpretation. The degree to which these aspects can be named and described is difficult to suggest, but it is clear that some of the following paralinguistic events can be identified:

(a) Voice set: the general ways in which voice identifies or suggests age, mood, and the like.

(b) Voice modifications: pitch range and control, rhythm control, resonance, and the like.

(c) Vocal characterizers: laughing, crying, giggling, snickering, sobbing, yelling, whispering, moaning, and so forth.

(d) Vocal segregates: specific vocal gestures substituted for meaningful statements; *uh-huh, ssh,* and the like.

Kinesic behavior is here defined as the body set and movement exemplified by facial expressions, gesture, posture, movement, and the like.

From this we move to writing—defined here as a behavior manifesting a code of learned, conventional visible markings used primarily but not exclusively to represent speech. The written code represents primarily the linguistic behavior found in speech; it includes certain paralinguistic features such as orthography, the use of light and dark space on the page, punctuation conventions, and the like, which are based only in part in speech. Writing also generates abbreviations, symbols standing in place of the longer symbols based on speech.

From this basic set of statements about the nature of language, speech, and writing, let me move on to the study of discourse, which can be suggested as the larger units of speaking or writing used in the communication system of a given society. The functions of discourse suggest whole areas of study in the discipline; these functions of discourse are the communicative purposes found in discourse: exposition, persuasion, inquiry, and evocation. A study of these functions of discourse would in and of itself provide a kind of structure for the study of language, together with the related studies in literature and composition. Another kind of structure might be formulated about the forms of discourse, which are often called *types* or *genre* in some more narrow classifications. This kind of structural set could revolve around differing sets of criteria, not always mutually exclusive, such as (a) prose and poetry; (b) fiction and non-fiction; (c) drama, novel, short story, poem, public speech, essay, discussion, debate, interpretative reading, editorial, news story, and so forth.

Each category above suggests a list of subcategories, as is the case with poetry, for example, when questions arise as to whether a selection is lyric or narrative, or as is the case with drama when the discussion centers on whether a piece is comedy or tragedy.

Both the study of forms of discourse and the study of the functions of discourse are interrelated through the study of the total theory of discourse. This can best be described as a system or systems for describing the nature of, or the workings of, discourse revealing certain functions of forms. The major theoretical systems which reveal such functions are commonly suggested as logic, rhetoric, semantics, and literary theory.

Logic is the system we apply to units of discourse which purport to use evidence and reasoning in support of some claim or conclusion. It embodies the rules for judging whether the claim or conclusion is justified by the evidence and reasoning given in support.

Rhetoric is the theory of effective discourse. It embodies statements and concepts about speaking and writing which purport to explain how discourse gets results, or attains its end in the audience. In the main, this system is applied to expository or persuasive discourse, but it can be applied to any discourse if the effort is to explain the effect of that discourse on the reader or listener.

Semantics is here defined as the system which purports to explain the relationships between words or units of discourse and their referents.

Literary theory is designed to differentiate imaginative discourse serving an evocative function from practical discourse—that is, the discourse of inquiry, persuasion, or exposition. It is the theory of discourse as a fine art, in this case, literature. Quite clearly, the system tends to include aspects of rhetoric and semantics.

In the space remaining, let me suggest some of the concepts for study in a language-focused view of English; and some of the sources from which these concepts are derived.

The first, and probably most important concept to be analyzed carefully, is that language is constantly changing. This concept, often referred to as *new*, was first enunciated by Bopp and Rask and Grimm nearly 150 years ago. But this concept itself rests upon two others: analysis of speech must rest upon the assumption that speech is primary, and the language has system. The first concept was demonstrated largely through the errors in Grimm's work and the success of Rask. Subsequent work by these scholars provided the foundation for the investigation of unique language systems, including those done with the American Indian languages referred to earlier.

It is, therefore, important that students become aware of the fundamental shift of English from its status in 1000 A.D. as an inflected language, with bound morphemes as system signals, to the basically different structural classification today, with syntactic arrangements as the most important signals. And it is also important to follow the periods of lexical accretion to the multilevel vocabulary of the twentieth century.

The underlying premise that language exists for communication, and that its symbols are meaning-carrying symbols, correlates with the principle of language change to produce the need for the study of English lexicography. It is axiomatic that the modern dictionary can be fully adjudged only with some knowledge of its origins and precursors.

Another basic concept of language study, that language features correlate with the nonlinguistic context in a variety of ways, has led to the study of dialect differentiation. For centuries before Paul's *Prinzipien der Sprachgeschichte* in 1880, it had been assumed that in any given language there had once been an original pure form which later became corrupted through its being spoken by ignorant people. Paul observed the reverse to be true. Standard speech does not break down into dialects. On the contrary, standard speech is simply a dialect that has acquired prestige because of its use by people living in an important commercial, economic, political or educational center. Paul, too, is largely responsible for the establishment, in modern times, of the concept of usage. He was the first among the nineteenth century philologists to suggest what most modern linguists see as the differentiation between grammar as the linguistically permissible and usage as the socially permissible.

In a sense, then, the concept that language changes can be restated to suggest that language changes in time, space, by speaker, by situation, by audience, and the like.

I know that I have dwelled perhaps too long on language concepts without relating them to literature. I hope that my references to writing —the art of composing—have been sufficient in the short space allotted me. But let me suggest some of the ways by which language and literature are and can be interrelated, with language as the focal point. Most students of language would agree that language is the result of an attempt to order the universe, or at least an attempt to impose an order upon it. Most students of language would also agree that the functions of discourse—inquiry, exposition, persuasion, evocation—can be characterized by the ways in which they attempt to impose or utilize this order, although some would argue that the twentieth century is one in which much, if not all, language seems aimed at persuasion or survival.

Certainly much literature deals with precisely this topic, the attempt to bring order—or describe meaning—to natural, personal, and social phenomena. In literature this typically involves an attempt to view these phenomena through some *perspective;* by controlling the perspective, the artist tries to evoke new and more meaningful insights. The earliest myths and folk tales, for instance, were an attempt to explain the causes and significance of natural occurrences, generally by establishing a metaphorical perspective which enabled people to relate natural occurrences to some form of deity. In other literary discourse we might expect to see the artist's attempt, via perspectives, to explore or explain man's relationships to the universe, to his deities, to his fellow men, or to himself. To these considerations, literary studies aimed at examination of types or *genre,* to which I referred earlier as a possible kind of structure, are essentially tangential, as are elements of literature such as plot and character development. What is important in the study of literature—the basic aim of instruction in literature and learning about literature—the essence of the literary experience—is what Frye called the education of the imagination. And it is only through an approach that emphasizes the language of literature—the language of evocation—I submit, that the student grasps the essence of the literary experience. It is only through the avenue of language study that the opening of the doors to the imagination can take place.

REFERENCES

Commission on English. *Freedom and discipline in English.* New York: College Entrance Examination Board, 1965.

Gleason, H. A. What is English? *CCCC J.,* 1962, **13** (3), 1-10.

Kegler, S. B., & Kemp, R. L. A guide for the curriculum in English. Unpublished manuscript, Univer. of Minnesota, 1964.

Kegler, S. B., Allen, H. B., & Smith, D. K. Preparation and evaluation of curriculum materials and guides for English language study. Unpublished manuscript, Univer. of Minnesota, 1962.

Parker, W. R. The concept of structure in English. *Educ. Rec.,* 1962, **43**, 210-216.

Sledd, J. In defense of history. *Coll. English,* 1963, **24** (8), 608-612.

Wilson, G. C. The structure of English. In G. W. Ford & L. Pugno (Eds.), *The structure of knowledge and the curriculum.* Chicago: Rand McNally, 1964. Pp. 71-86.

AUTHOR INDEX

Numbers in italics refer to pages on which the complete references are listed.

A

Allen, H. N., 259, *265*
Archer, E. J., 37, 38, 39, 40, 42, 43, 44, *48, 49,* 74, 79
Austin, G. A., 38, 39, 45, 46, *48,* 89, *94,* 225, *237*
Austin, J. L., 10, 11, *17*
Ausubel, D. P., 92, *94,* 170, 174, *175,* 212, *221,* 250, 251, *253*

B

Baggaley, A. R., 151, *154*
Ball, Rachel S., 29, *33*
Bartlett, F. C., 81, *94*
Bayley, Nancy, 117, 118, 119, 127, 130, 131, 132, 134, 136, *137*
Beck, L. H. A., 199, *203*
Beier, E. G., 152, *154*
Beilin, H., 221, *221*
Belbin, Eunice, 136, *137*
Bergum, B. O., 60, *62*
Berlyne, D. E., 82, 86, 90, *94,* 213, *221*
Bernstein, B., 191, 194, *203*
Birren, J. E., 136, *137*
Blake, E., Jr., 170, *175*
Bloom, B. S., 180, *187,* 241, *253*
Blum, Lucille H., 145, *154*
Bourbaki, N., 208, *221*
Bourne, L. E., Jr., 38, 40, 41, 44, *48*
Bousfield, W. A., 43, *48*
Brandwein, P. F., 243, *254*
Bransome, E. D., Jr., 199, *203*
Bronson, G., 133, *137*
Brown, B. R., 191, *203, 204*
Brown, F. G., 38, 40, 44, *48*
Bruner, J. S., 38, 39, 45, 46, *48,* 89, *94,* 194, *203,* 210, *221,* 225, *237,* 241, *253*
Bulgarella, Rosaria G., 39, 40, *48*
Bunderson, C. V., 41, *48*
Burgmeister, Bessie B., 145, *154*
Bush, J. S., 239, *253*

C

Cameron, J., 127, *137*
Carnap, R., 241, *253*
Carroll, J. B., 83, *94*
Cherry, Estelle, 191, *203*
Christensen, P. R., 32, *33*
Cohen, B. H., 43, *48*
Conrad, H. S., 117, 119, *137*
Correll, M., 243, *253*
Courant, R., *221*

D

D'Amato, May F., 44, *49*
Dana, R. H., 121, *137*
Danick, J. J., 43, *48*
Deutsch, Cynthia P., 195, *203*
Deutsch, M., 191, 193, 199, *203, 204*
Dienes, Z. P., 211, 212, *221,* 233, *237*
Dodd, D. H., 40, *48*
Dodwell, P. C., 219, *221,* 222
Dominowski, R. L., 40, 41, *48,* 55, *62,* 148, 149, *154*
Downs, Sylvia, 136, *137*

E

Ebbinghaus, H., 70, *79*
Ekstrand, B. R., 57, *63*

F

Fantz, R. L., 195, *203*
Fields, P. E., 88, *94*
Fisher, G. H., 220, *222*
Fitzgerald, D., 170, *175*
Fitzgibbon, C., 47, *48*
Fivel, Myrna W., 151, *154*
Flavell, J. H., 221, *222*
Fodor, J. A., 12, *17*
Freedman, J. L., 44, *49*
Frick, J. W., 32, *33*

G

Gagné, R. M., 29, 32, 85, 87, 92, *94*
Geach, P. T., 7, *17*

267

SUBJECT INDEX

A

Anxiety
  and concept learning, 152
  in school situation, 100-102
Association
  backward, 54-56
  forward, 56
  verbal, 31
Attentional processes
  as prerequisite to learning, 197
  by stimulus field manipulation, 198
  channeling, 198
  measuring device, 199

C

Chaining, 31, 86
Cognition, 31, 98
Cognitive
  development, 102-113
  processes, 98
  structure, 160-174
  units, 98
Complexity
  (see Information, irrelevant)
  of classification, 89
Comprehension
  verbal, 19-22
Concepts
  acquisition of, 157-175
  and meaningfulness, 65-78
  assimilation vs. formation, 164-167
  classification of
    categorical, 15-16
    hierarchical, 15, 16-17
  conjunctive, 38-39, 53, 59, 89
  disjunctive, 39, 53, 59, 89
  formal analysis of, 3-17
  formation vs. attainment, 143
  in mathematics, 207-221
  probabilistic, 39
  psychological characteristics of, 40-48
  psychological nature of, 37-48
  relational, 53, 89
  role in science teaching, 239-253
  situational, 86, 90

  three kinds of, 68-69
  transformational, 86, 90
  utility of, 45, 51
Conceptual growth
  a developmental approach, 97-115
Conditioning
  classic, 29
Conformity
  pressure for in school, 101
Contiguity
  instance, 41, 54-55
  of concepts in complex learning, 91
  response, 54, 55, 56
Cultural relativism hypothesis, 201
Curriculum
  English, 255-265
  enrichment for the disadvantaged, 202-203
  mathematics, 223-237
  science, 239-253

D

Dimension
  abstract—concrete, 58
Discrimination
  auditory, 195-197
  multiple, 31
  of stimulus objects, 83
Dominance
  of attributes, 58

E

English
  toward a definition of, 255-265

F

Failure
  expectancy, 100
Feedback
  delay, 41
  information, 41-42
  post information, 42
Fluency
  associational, 20-22
  word, 19-22

270

G

Generality
   of inquiry model, 186
Generalization
   mediated, 44
   of concepts, 91-92
   primary stimulus, 69, 143-144
   secondary stimulus, 69
Gestalt, 25, 32, 233

H

Hypothesis
   evaluation, 98, 109
   testing, 151

I

Identification
   similarity to models, 99-100, 111
Impulsivity, 110, 112
Individual Differences
   in concept learning, 139-153
Information
   irrelevant, 38, 40 (see Complexity)
   relevant, 38-39, 40
Inhibition
   proactive and retroactive, 149
Inquiry
   analysis of, 177-187
   cycle, 182-183
   definition of, 178, 180
   model (see Motivation, Mediation,
      Storage, Organizers, Retrieval,
      Validity)
   process, 177-178
Instance
   positive and negative, 87, 89
   spacing, 55
Integrative reconciliation,
   in programming instructional material,
      170-174
Intelligence, 25
   age trends in, 122-124
   and concept learning, 150-152
   consistency, 124-127
   related to achievement, 133-135
   sex differences, 127-135
   the role of, 117-137

L

Language
   as core of intelligence, 132-133
   background of disadvantaged children,
      191-192
   in concept attainment, 165-167
   in learning, 212
Learning, 32
   adulthood, 117-137
   associative, 59-61
   conceptual, taxonomy of, 143-146
   conditions of, variations in, 147
   discrimination, 88, 144
   free, 51
   in adulthood, 117-137
   individual differences in, 139-153
   in the disadvantaged, 189-203
   meaningful, 159-160, 233
      in the classroom, 161-163
      vs. rote, 158-159
   meaningful reception, 157-175
      pedagogic implications of, 167-169
      role of discriminability in, 169-174
   overlearning, 170
   paired-associate, 51
   principle, 32, 81-94
   probability, 58
   reception vs. discovery, 92, 158
   relationships between concept and ver-
      bal, 51-62
   response, 59-61
   reversal and nonreversal shift, 153
   rote, 31, 53, 233
   stimulus—response, 29-31
   structured, 233
   verbal, 41, 51, 52, 58, 62, 217
Learning set, 44
   meaningful, 158, 159, 161
   (see Transfer, positive)

M

Mathematics
   basic elementary school concepts, 226-
      233
   behavioral approach, 210, 213-214
   concepts in, 207-221, 223-224
      nature of, 210
   developmental concept formation in,
      216-219